A LIFE UNFORESEEN

The author as he appeared on his travel certificate, 1959.

A Life
Unforeseen

A MEMOIR OF SERVICE TO TIBET

Rinchen Sadutshang

Foreword by His Holiness the Dalai Lama

Wisdom Publications, Inc.
199 Elm Street
Somerville, MA 02144 USA
wisdompubs.org

Library of Congress Cataloging-in-Publication Data
Names: Rinchen Sadhutshang, 1928 or 1929–2015.
Title: A life unforeseen : a memoir of service to Tibet / Rinchen Sadutshang
   ; foreword by His Holiness the Dalai Lama.
Other titles: Memoir of service to Tibet
Description: Somerville, MA : Wisdom Publications, Inc., [2016] | Includes
   index.
Identifiers: LCCN 2015031848 | ISBN 161429223X (pbk. : alk. paper)
Subjects: LCSH: Rinchen Sadhutshang, 1928 or 1929-2015. | Refugees,
   Tibetan—India—Biography. | Politicians—China—Tibet—Biography. |
   Central Tibetan Administration-in-Exile (India)—Officials and
   employees—Biography. | Tibet Autonomous Region (China)—Politics and
   government—1951– | Tibet Autonomous Region (China)—Biography. |
   Tibetans—India—Biography.
Classification: LCC DS432.T5 R485 2015 | DDC 951/.505092—dc23
LC record available at http://lccn.loc.gov/2015031848

ISBN 978-1-61429-223-4   Ebook ISBN 978-1-61429-241-8

20 19 18 17 16
5   4   3   2   1

Photos courtesy of Rinchen Sadutshang. Cover design by Gopa&Ted2. Interior design by Jordan
Wannemacher. Set in Adobe Garamond Pro 10.5/15.

Wisdom Publications' books are printed on acid-free paper and meet the guidelines for
permanence and durability of the Production Guidelines for Book Longevity of the Council on
Library Resources.

This book was produced with environmental mindfulness.
For more information, please visit wisdompubs.org/wisdom-environment.

Printed in the United States of America.

Please visit fscus.org.

CONTENTS

PART TWO: ENORMOUS, IMMINENT CHANGES IN TIBET

PART THREE: A REFUGEE AND STATELESS IN INDIA

THE DALAI LAMA

FOREWORD

R inchen Sadutshang is one of the few Tibetans of his generation to
have had the opportunity to learn English and receive a modern education during the late 1930s and 1940s, a time when Tibetans urgently needed
to understand the workings of the world beyond their borders.

Enrolled in Tibetan government service in 1948, he worked with dedi-
cation and was present on several occasions that proved crucial to Tibet's
eventual destiny. He accompanied the Tibetan delegation to Beijing in 1951,
when the Seventeen-Point Agreement was signed. Later, he was a member of the Tibetan delegations to the United Nations in 1959 and 1961. In
between, he was a member of the party that accompanied me when I visited
China in 1954 and India in 1956. All of these events he describes here with
characteristic candor and acute observation.

In exile, he worked assiduously for the Tibetan cause, serving the Central
Tibetan Administration in various capacities, becoming a Kalon minister
and ultimately our representative in New Delhi.

I have frequently encouraged Tibetans who have lived through the last
sixty years or so and have taken part in this most difficult period of Tibetan
history to write their memoirs so that Tibetans who have been born since

1959 and other interested people should have access to their recollections. I am pleased Rinchen Sadutshang has seen fit to record events as he saw them. Perhaps because he began his career at such a young age, his memories are particularly clear and closely observed. I commend this book, confident that it sheds light on critical events in recent Tibetan history.

Tenzin Gyatso, the Fourteenth Dalai Lama

PREFACE

In happier circumstances my father, Rinchen Sadutshang, would have written this preface himself. Unfortunately, he passed away on June 14, 2015, at the age of eighty-seven, before the final publication of his book. Since I had been assisting him with the process, the responsibility has fallen to me, his daughter.

My father bore firsthand witness to the defining moments of Tibet's modern history. As a government official, he saw up close the entire course of events that led to the takeover of Tibet by the Chinese Communist government—from the failed attempts of the Tibetan government to elicit the help of foreign powers to deter the Chinese incursion, to its desperate attempts later to safeguard Tibet's sovereignty during negotiations with the same aggressor when confronted with the threat of complete occupation, thinly veiled as "liberation" by the Chinese. This, as well as the Dalai Lama's exhortations to older Tibetans born in a free Tibet to record accounts of their lives both in Tibet and in exile thereafter for the sake of future generations, moved him to compose this autobiography.

In the typical self-effacing Tibetan way, Rinchen Sadutshang hardly admits to having made any valuable contribution, but his service to the

Tibetan government and to the Tibetan people should not be downplayed. One only needs to read this book to see why. In many instances he was the person most suited to fulfill a given assignment, for he had certain advantages over other officials of that period.

At a time when literally only a handful of Tibetans in Tibet spoke English or had a modern education, Rinchen Sadutshang was blessed with both. In Tibet he was able to use this asset to the benefit of his country by being employed at the foreign ministry and by serving as an interpreter for senior officials during talks with foreign governments. Later, when the Dalai Lama sought asylum in India, Rinchen Sadutshang's role became even more vital, for suddenly, virtually the entire government in exile was faced with the enormous problem of inability to communicate with Indian officials compounded by its unfamiliarity with India itself. Hence, he proved indispensable at the Dalai Lama's private secretariat when it first opened in India. He was also invaluable when the government in exile sought to embark on a most important mission in the early 1960s, that of sending a delegation to the United Nations, which it did three times. In much the same way, he was highly suited for his last appointment as representative of the Dalai Lama at His Holiness's bureau in New Delhi, as this required sensitive communication with embassies and foreign organizations. His predecessor, though well versed in Tibetan, did not have a modern education and could not speak English.

Having been raised in a family that earned its living through trade, Rinchen Sadutshang undoubtedly knew a thing or two about business, unlike most other Tibetan officials of the time, who were born aristocrats and lived on the proceeds of their estates. Therefore it was no surprise that the Tibetan government saw him as an obvious choice when it appointed him a trustee of the Dalai Lama's Charitable Trust, for the trust dealt with the management of money derived from the sale of the Tibetan government gold and silver brought over to India from Tibet in the 1950s. Likewise, he was persuaded to work for Gayday Iron and Steel Company, an ongoing business enterprise in which the Tibetan government had investments, though being astute, he could see from the start that this enterprise was ill fated. His years in the company were fraught and stressful because of the constant problems the company faced, which he details here. At the time, bureaucrats in Dharamsala, the seat of the exile government, simply had no idea of the hurdles he faced, since they knew very little about running a company. He acquired a great deal of experience on the job and, being intelligent, quickly became familiar with corporate law, the running of an industry, and the norms of banking.

He used this same experience to successfully negotiate the sale of G. S. Mandidip Paper Mills, another company the Dalai Lama's trust had invested in and which was also on the verge of collapse. Thanks to his contribution, the trust, as well as all the Tibetans who had invested what little money they were able to bring over from Tibet, not only got back their capital but interest as well, which far exceeded their expectations.

Rinchen Sadutshang the man was affable and pleasant, but this concealed a fierce courage and determination. He was highly articulate, but he preferred getting on with the work at hand to talking endlessly about it. He was a meticulous and capable official, never satisfied until the end result was achieved. At the same time he was a good human being, compassionate and kind and always ready to help those in need, officially or otherwise. This sometimes prompted my mother to complain that he was more interested in helping others than his own family! Perhaps best of all, he was upright and honest. He abhorred deviousness, deceit, and the sometimes medieval-like intrigue in the politics of pre-1959 Tibet. He had a deep sense of justice and fair play. When he returned to Tibet after schooling in India and saw the system of governance there, he was not happy about the stark inequality between classes of society. Strangely enough, this inequality was very soon leveled out, both in Tibet, when it came under Communist rule, and in India, when the old systems became obsolete.

Above all, he had an unshakeable sense of loyalty to the Dalai Lama and a profound sense of duty to his government. This resulted in him neglecting his own family somewhat during the early years of exile, when we children were young. He felt the Tibetan government in exile at the time needed his service more than did his own young family, and he was prepared to make that sacrifice, to the point of refusing two lucrative job offers. Even upon retirement his concern did not wane. He refused to accept both a pension and compensation for medical expenses to which he was entitled, not wanting to impose even the slightest financial burden on the Tibetan government in exile.

As a father he was both loving and caring. He wrote letters prolifically to his children and constantly kept in touch, as there was no email in those days, and long-distance phone calls were a luxury. Though loving, he was nevertheless a strict father, and he could be short tempered. He held high expectations of old-fashioned good behavior from his children, be it respect for elders, obedience to parents, polite speech, honesty, and moral integrity. He strongly disapproved of indolence and expected his children to study hard and not waste time in frivolousness.

Later, when his grandchildren came along, he was equally concerned about their well being. He learned to use the computer so he could keep in touch, and he also phoned them frequently. This strong bond that he created is evinced by the fact that eight out of his thirteen grandchildren came to see him before he passed away. Of them, four made the journey from North America. I might also add that four of his five surviving children were with him constantly, caring for him during his months of illness. His youngest daughter even left her job in Seattle so she could be with him indefinitely.

Having paid this tribute to my father, in conclusion and on his behalf, I would like to thank Wisdom Publications for agreeing to publish his autobiography, which I hope will be of interest to both Tibetans and non-Tibetans and enlightening to the Tibetan youth of today. In particular I would like to thank David Kittelstrom, our editor, for his guidance and his valuable advice over the course of getting this book into print.

Yangchen Dolkar Tsatultsang
Kathmandu, Nepal

PART ONE

The Hope and Optimism
of Youth

1. MY EARLY CHILDHOOD IN KHAM

W hen I look back into the past, I realize there were many times when I missed my mother a great deal. Many of these moments occurred even after I myself had become a father of six children. I never missed my father very much. He passed away when I was a tiny infant, so I don't recall his face, much less his closeness to me. On the other hand, I do recall how loving my mother was. I always slept in her arms until the day I left for Lhasa, little realizing that I would never ever see her again. I must have been a little over five years old that summer when I went on a long journey, a journey that would not only take three months but would also separate me forever from my mother and the land of my birth.

I come from Kham in eastern Tibet. I was born in the year of the earth serpent, which is 2056 according to the Tibetan calendar and 1928 according to the Western calendar. The village in which I was born lay in a lush, green valley surrounded by distant mountains. Just a kilometer to the north a beautiful river flowed west to east. Forests in the interior provided the main source of timber for construction in the valley. Close to the valley, hills verdant with grass in the summer provided plenty of good pasture for cattle, so there were many cattle farmers in our district. The mountains along the southern range were snowbound most of the year and provided a backdrop of incredible beauty.

My house was in a village called Lingtsang, about thirty kilometers from the town of Karzé, which lay east across the river. To the west, about three kilometers away, was Dargye Monastery, home to more than two thousand monks. Farther west, about two hundred kilometers away, was the notorious Dergé Tro Pass, one of the most hazardous and difficult to cross in Kham. Beyond that lay the kingdom of Dergé along the Yangtse River. The entire area, stretching from the foothills of Dergé Tro Pass across the vast valley right up to Tau, was known as Trehor, and the people living in this region were known as Trehor Khampa. My father, Abo Bhu Sadutshang, originally came from Gakhok, about six hundred kilometers northwest of our village. The people in that region were known as Gapa, and the entire region was under the rule of the king of Nangchen. There were twenty-five districts, or *bekhu*, in the region, and my forefathers came from the bekhu of Dera Sertsang. At one point in time, about four generations prior to my own, there was a disagreement between the head of the district and my forefathers, and this resulted in them moving away and settling in Trehor.

My grandfather, Sadutshang Aney or Sadu Aney, had three sons and two daughters. Both my aunts became nuns, and one of my uncles, Ngarak Tulku, was identified as a reincarnate lama. Ngarak Tulku lived at Ngarak Monastery, which lay perched on a hill about fifteen kilometers east of our house, on the way to Karzé. Later, he would end up playing a pivotal role in a dispute that would have far-reaching consequences for our family. My other uncle, Sadu Thomey, was married to Yakho, daughter of the Hosangtsang family of Karzé county. They had four sons and a daughter. My father Abo Bhu was also married to a daughter of Hosangtsang, but she was much younger than Yakho. Their marriage was not arranged in the usual fashion. Indeed, it took place under unusual circumstances, to say the least. My father wanted to marry my mother, but her family had already agreed to give her away to the Phari Drakdongtsang family. She was on her way to the groom's home to be married when my father ambushed the marriage party and forcefully took her away to be his bride! This must have created a difficult situation for my mother's family, but somehow my father got his way, and an amicable settlement was reached with the aggrieved party.

My mother, Gonpo Dolma, gave birth to eight children—four sons and four daughters—and I was the youngest of them all. Sadutshang was a "joint family," as were nearly all families in Kham, where polyandry was widely practiced. The family owned substantial land, most of which was leased out to others. Trade was the main source of our income. Uncle Thomey and his family lived mostly in Lhasa, where they had acquired a modest-sized house in Banakshol, in the eastern part of the city. My father and his family lived in Kham, but my two eldest brothers, Lobsang Gedun and Lobsang Nyendak, were sent to Lhasa when I was still a baby. They were later joined by my two eldest sisters, Yangchen Khando (later Chadzötsang) and Pema Chöden (later Goshampa). Eventually my brother Wangchuk Dorji and I followed them. My two eldest brothers attended school in Lhasa, and the family business was run by our two older cousins, Sonam Chöphel and Lobsang Gyurme. Sonam and Lobsang's brothers Chözé Talha and Chözé Yugyal were both monks fully occupied in serving their respective institutions.

Chözé Talha was involved in trade in order to offset his monastery's maintenance expenses. He was also the primary advocate in trying to get the assistance of the Tibetan government to rebuild Dargye Monastery, which the Chinese had burned to the ground. Chözé Yugyal lived in Sera Monastery, where he worked in the capacity of a steward. As my eldest brother, Lobsang Gedun, or Lo Gedun, as we used to call him, got older, he began to help out in the family business. He was joined later by my brother Lobsang Nyendak, or Lo Nyendak. Lo Nyendak didn't last very long, however, as he was fiercely independent and rebellious, chafing at authority. My wild elder brother notwithstanding, the custom was for younger ones to help in the family business. They started off accompanied by a senior manager, who would advise them up until they felt capable of taking on full responsibility.

I still have some vivid memories of my early childhood. I remember playing with my brother Wangchuk Dorji, or Wangdor, three years my senior, on the open porch just outside my mother's bedroom. I must have been about four. Back then there were no manufactured toys; we amused ourselves by making animals out of clay and found a great deal of enjoyment in playing with them. I also recall going nearly every evening to the inner courtyard with a wooden bowl to get my share of fresh milk from the maids who milked the cows there. I would drink the milk immediately, while it was slightly warm, and enjoyed it immensely. There were plenty of cows so we must have had abundant milk, cheese, and butter in the house. I don't remember ever having playmates come to the house to play. Nor do I remember going out to play with any of the neighbors' children. However, I do remember going out into the fields with the domestic help to pick stinging nettles, which were relished by all when made into a broth in the evenings.

One particular incident I recall clearly. Wangdor and I went to a park where there were a lot of trees and greenery. I had acquired a slingshot and was excited to use it. Wangdor knew how to handle a slingshot and began to show me how. He had just taken a successful shot or two when, on his next try, as he was swinging the slingshot above his head just before letting it fly, the stone slipped and hit me. I was knocked down, and the next thing I knew, I had a cut and a big lump just below the crown of my head! To this day I bear the scar.

A handful of incidents from that time I remember were causes of great excitement. The first was the arrival of an important visitor. One morning, there was a flurry of activity and everyone was running about. I was told Gyapon Bhu was arriving. He was husband to my eldest sister, Rinchen Yangzom, and the son of a well-known and prestigious family called Gyapontsang. My mother and all the rest of the family went down to receive him outside at the bottom of the steps that led to our house. He was a young man dressed in a shining dark-brown silk robe. He was asked to sit right at the head of the main room in which we received guests and was offered delicacies. After exchanging pleasantries and spending some time with us, he left with his retinue, who were seen off at the main outer gate as a mark of respect.

The second incident was far more grave. It happened around 1930, when Dargye Monastery, aided by troops of the Tibetan government, fought Chinese invaders in a battle, and the monastery quickly began to lose. My family talked of running away and seeking refuge elsewhere. One day we left our home and traveled west, away from the battle zone. I recall being put in an *ambak*, a large fold of a Tibetan robe. It was not my mother's ambak, so it must have been that of a senior retainer's—someone trustworthy. Wangdor was old enough to be put on a pony by himself, and he was strapped securely to it. Although I do not remember it, I was told later that we were given shelter at the home of a prominent family called Denkhok Aduk Lakartsang, friends of ours. We stayed there until the Chinese troops retreated after a peace settlement had been reached.

Here I think it necessary to relate the relevant background of this incident, as my family was deeply involved. In fact, it originated with certain differences that my uncle Ngarak Tulku, who was head of Ngarak Monastery, had with Beru Monastery with regard to his control over certain monastic affairs. Ngarak Monastery was situated about eight kilometers west of Karzé, and being within the jurisdiction of Beru district, and therefore of Beru Monastery, the latter exercised a certain amount of authority over it. The differences could not be resolved, as my uncle was adamant that he would not relinquish any control. He approached Dargye Monastery for support, claiming that as the Sadutshangs were patrons of that monastery, he was entitled to their help. Dargye Monastery readily came forward with full support and threatened dire consequences to Beru Monastery, but Beru Monastery would not relent. Thereupon Dargye Monastery attacked Beru Monastery and got the upper hand, but not for long. A patron of Beru Monastery by the name of Berutsang Abo Bhu went to the Chinese district commissioner. At that time the Chinese had occupied Karzé district and kept a large garrison of soldiers there. He asked for the district commissioner's help, which the commissioner gave immediately. The Chinese sent a garrison of soldiers, but Dargye Monastery and their followers were not beaten; they even managed to chase the Chinese away. However, the Chinese then brought in a large contingent of reinforcements from interior China and began a renewed attack. Knowing it would be difficult to keep them at bay for long, as there were even more Chinese troops on the way, Dargye Monastery sent messengers to Lhasa and requested military help from the central Tibetan government. The Tibetan government sent six regiments, and initially they were able to drive the Chinese back some distance. But not long afterward the Chinese advanced again with an even larger contingent. Unable to withstand the onslaught, the Tibetan army gradually began to withdraw westward. Soon the Chinese were at the very doorsteps of Dargye Monastery, and after occupying it they burned it to the ground.

During the fighting, not long after the Tibetan army arrived, the Chinese took four Dargye Monastery monks hostage in Dartsedo, a trading town about 350 kilometers east of Karzé. Among the hostages was my cousin, Chözé Talha. He and the other monks had gone to Dartsedo to buy tea, an essential beverage in all Tibetan monasteries. In the meantime, the Tibetan regiments, which were under the command of Dapon Khemé, or Commander Khemé, managed to trap and take prisoner three Chinese army officers. This enabled a hostage exchange to be struck, and the monks were soon freed and returned safely to Dargye Monastery. Eventually a peace settlement was reached, and an agreement was signed in 1933.

The third incident I remember is when Wangdor and I were taken to Karzé for treatment to prevent smallpox. We stayed at my older sister Yangchen Khando Chadzötsang's house, as they lived in the middle of town. I remember being taken to a large room where there were many people. I was lifted up and put on the lap of a Chinese man, who administered a drop into my nose, and that was all there was to it. We must have stayed in Karzé for several days, because I remember going to the market and seeing many wonderful food items for sale. My favorites were walnuts and molasses, and there were plenty of these available. But there was one sight that left a strong and most unpleasant impression on my young mind. I saw a huge slaughtered pig hung upside down in a Chinese shop. A man was pouring boiling water over the carcass, probably to remove the bristles. I hated the sight and walked quickly away from it. Apparently I then got lost. Whoever was sent for me said he found me talking to a stranger, asking him, "Do you know where my house is?"!

2. THE JOURNEY FROM KHAM TO LHASA

In the spring of 1934 my brother Wangdor and I left for Lhasa. All sorts of preparations had been made for the long journey, and I was thrilled at the prospect of a great adventure. However, at just five years old, I could hardly imagine how hard it would be to be completely cut off from the tender care and love of my mother. To this day I miss her. I have never understood why my elder brothers never arranged for my mother to join us in Lhasa, leaving her instead in Kham all by herself. I suspect all of them were too caught up in running their thriving business to give much thought to comforting her.

The time for departure came early one morning. With my brother and I all dressed up in new clothes, the horses saddled and ready in the court-yard, we were too excited to worry about parting from our mother. Samten Chadzötsang, my brother-in-law, was the one in charge of taking us to Lhasa. My sister Yangchen Khando was by then already settled in Lhasa, and now Samten, who had come on a trade journey, was traveling back to join her. My mother had prepared long cotton bags with pouches at the two ends for my brother and I. The bags, flung across the saddle, were filled with all sorts of goodies like walnuts, molasses, dried cheese, and sweets. We boys had special saddles with wooden crossbars at the front and rear to prevent our falling forward or backward. A long raw silk shawl, called a *buré lemthang*, was wrapped across the saddle bars so as to prevent us from falling sideways. I'm sure my mother must have wept a great deal watching her youngest children depart, but I can't remember seeing her do so; I was preoccupied with my riding gear and pony.

We traveled in a caravan of about twelve to fourteen persons and eight pack animals. We had to carry clothes, bedding, and enough food to last us at least a month, which is how long it would be before replenishment in the next town. We usually started out early in the morning, and by two in the afternoon we pitched our tents and called it a day. I don't recall if we ever actually stayed in towns along the way, but we must have camped near them in order to stock up on some items. There was plenty of butter, cheese, and meat available, as there were many nomad camps close to the route we traveled.

I think I must have slept a lot on my horse, as I remember my attendant often shouting, "Look! A rabbit!" or "Look! A fox!" in obvious attempts to wake me up. It must have been difficult for him, as he had to constantly watch over me and see that I didn't fall asleep or lose balance and fall off, despite being secured to the saddle. This was an especial concern when riding down slopes. My attendant was Bongé Thupten, a distant relative and a kind and attentive person. My horse used to follow his while he held a long rope tied to my horse's reins. When awake I was typically preoccupied with my bag of goodies, either eating some or counting them to see how much was left. Somehow the bag never seemed to run out of goodies! I suspect my mother had taken care to pack enough for a long journey and that my bag was replenished time and again by my attendant without my knowledge.

One fine day we camped early. It was a beautiful day; the sky was a clear blue, there was a cool breeze blowing, and there was lush, green pasture all around for miles. Freed of their loads, the animals thoroughly enjoyed the vast grazing grounds. I think we must have stayed there for a couple of days so that we could relax and also give the animals a rest and a chance to enjoy the abundant, fresh grass. We used to take such breaks after a couple of weeks' travel, whenever we came across a suitable place, which was usually near a stream or a small river or else near a nomad camp. I used to love these stops, as we could play to our hearts' content. Sometimes we tried to catch rabbits, but more often we used to try and catch pikas, a Tibetan mammal that we called *abra* that is a small, cute relative of the rabbit, as there were plenty of them living on the vast grassland plateau.

Once when we camped near a stream, my brother and I first played in the water, and then, when we spotted a lot of these little rodent-like creatures in the surrounding area, we tried to catch one. A servant helped us, and on his suggestion we first tried to locate the two holes at opposite ends of a burrow. Then we patiently waited till we spotted an abra at the mouth of one of the holes; this assured us that the burrow was occupied. Then we frightened the creature back into the hole and waited for it to surface at the other end, which we had covered with our servant's *telham*: a long woolen boot coming up to the knees, with soles made of thick leather and held up with a long ribbon wound around the top of the boot. When that didn't work, we brought water from the stream and poured it down the hole, forcing the poor creature to emerge at the other end, straight into the waiting boot! Then we got a cord and tied it to the abra's neck. We took it to the stream to let it swim, and it was great fun to see it swim so effortlessly, right to the other side of the stream. After amusing ourselves with it for some time, we finally let it go free. Being Buddhists, we were always taught not to harm living creatures. So whenever we caught one, we always let it go free in the end.

It was around this time that my brother and I were permitted to fire a gun for the first time. I don't know who persuaded our brother-in-law Samten, but he allowed us both to fire two rounds each of his Mauser pistol. The pistol had a wooden case, and at the tip of the case was a steel lever that could be fitted to the end of the pistol, converting it into a stand. This makeshift stand could then be held against your shoulder, turning the pistol into a small rifle. Although I was very young, I was not at all afraid of handling a gun, whereas my brother showed some fear and had to be encouraged by Samten. Because my brother was afraid, I was especially proud of my courage that day!

One day, during one of the many rest camps, I encountered a gruesome sight. It was about midday and I was wandering around when I came across a yak being slaughtered. A couple of people from our own camp were busy skinning the poor animal. They must have run out of meat and bought the animal from one of the many nomads living in that area. I quickly ran off as I hated the sight before me.

We must have traveled for over three months before we finally reached our destination. For what was probably the lion's share of the journey, I had been asking often and with impatience when we would finally reach Lhasa. I would always get the same reply: "Soon!" When the actual day finally arrived, we set out on the last leg of our journey in the early morning, as we expected family members already living in Lhasa to come and receive us on the outskirts of the city. It must have been around noon when we met the welcoming party some seven kilometers east of Lhasa. They were a group of about eight people led by Chözé Talha, a dignified and impressive figure who was over six feet tall. Thanks to his stature, coupled with his strong personality, he stood out in any crowd. A monk of Dargye Monastery, he was in Lhasa organizing its reconstruction following the destruction at the hands of Chinese forces mentioned above. He commanded great respect not only in his monastery but throughout our region of Kham. Even within the family, though he was not the eldest but the third-eldest son, his word carried more weight than that of anyone else's. As I especially came to appreciate later, he was a man of great vision, intelligence, and conscientiousness. He was also amazingly affectionate and fatherly to his younger kin unlike my elder cousins, Sochö and Gyurme. They, along with my eldest brother Lo Gedun, should have taken more interest in looking after my brother Wangdor and me, since they were the men of the family. Instead it was Chözé Talha, the monk, who took more care with us and interest in us. Even as we got older, it was Chözé Talha who would often call us to his home and inquire about our schooling. It was he who would give us pocket money or buy us sweets. When we were lucky, he would also occasionally keep us at his home for a few days.

On the day of our arrival in Lhasa, Chözé Talha and the welcoming party had brought with them a great deal of food and butter tea. We stopped a bit farther down the road and had a grand lunch before setting off for Lhasa.

As we got closer to the big city, I saw for the first time in my life the great

Potala Palace of His Holiness the Dalai Lama, standing majestically on a hill west of the city. However, the excitement and the tremendous joy I felt was more about being allowed to ride by myself on a lovely horse brought along by Chözé Talha than about seeing this great wonder of the world!

3. LIFE IN LHASA

After nearly three months, we had finally come to the end of our long journey. We rode straight to the house where my brother and I were to live. The Sadutshangs had bought this house some time back, and it was situated in the eastern neighborhood of Banakshol. Out of the male members of our family, I remember that my eldest cousin, Sonam Chöphel, usually known as Sochö, was there; the other brothers and cousins must have been out of Lhasa on business. My third eldest sister Khando Chökyi, a nun, was there, and we were placed under her care. The youngest of my sisters, Pema Chöden, was also there. She must have been about fifteen or sixteen.

The house was a fairly big two-story stone building with a large inner courtyard. The main gate was on the east and let out onto a lane that joined the main road, which ran north. My brother and I were kept in the west wing on the top floor, where there were two rooms, one for us and one for our sisters. The main room of the house was a large one on the same floor, and it was used for receiving people and for conducting business. On either side were bedrooms and behind it a large shrine room. The kitchen was also on the upper floor. The ground floor was occupied mainly by our business managers and servants along with a couple of large storerooms. Below the east and west wings and the kitchen were the stables. We had a number of good horses. In those days horses were the only means of conveyance and had to be used often. When our traders arrived from various places, the courtyard would be full of horses. The commodities we traded in, mostly wool and tea and sometimes consumer items (and even construction material from India), came in large quantities on mule packs that often numbered over a hundred at a time. The mules were unloaded in the courtyard, and the animals were then kept in the suburbs of the city, where there was plenty of hay and grain to feed them.

It was not long after we arrived in Lhasa that we were admitted into a day school called Darpoling. As a matter of fact, all schools in Lhasa were day schools; boarding schools were practically unheard of. The schools were also all privately run except for one government school called Tse Lapta, which means "the school at the Potala." This school was meant exclusively for students who were to be drafted into the ecclesiastical branch of government service. The training provided at this school was of a very high standard, and a variety of scripts were taught. Some of the students were even sent to study Nepali at a school called Goryik Lapta, or the Nepali Language School, run by the authorities representing the Nepalese government in Lhasa.

The procedure for entry into schools in Lhasa was very simple. After selecting a school, one approached the principal with gifts and requested admission. Usually there was no difficulty in gaining admission unless the school was too crowded. Once admission was granted, a suitably auspicious day would be selected to begin attendance. On that day the new student and his or her family would come early and offer *droma dresil*, a sweet food always served on auspicious occasions that is made of cooked rice mixed with butter, sugar, raisins, and small sweet roots. This would be accompanied by Tibetan tea offered first to the principal and then to the teachers; only afterward would it be given to the students. Then *khatak*, white greeting scarves, would be offered to the principal. Afterward the new student would be shown his seat in class and introduced to his teacher, who was usually a senior student in the school. No school fees had to be paid. Instead the student's family could offer gifts of appreciation now and again, though this was not compulsory.

There were no textbooks for the students. Beginners learned the Tibetan alphabet by writing on wooden boards with a smooth surface. Paper was permitted only for those who had reached a higher standard. These boards, called *jangshing*, were about thirty inches long and ten inches wide. They had a small handle protruding at the end with a hole in it so that the board could be hung on a nail or hook when not in use. A chalk bag, about three inches square and one inch thick and filled with white chalk dust, was also needed. This bag had a long, thick string running through its center, and the string had a button fastened at each end so that it couldn't be pulled completely out of the bag. First the board had to be dusted lightly with the powdery chalk so that it evenly covered the surface. Then the string in the bag was pulled back and forth so that it was completely coated with chalk. The board was held horizontally, parallel to the floor. The left end of the string was held against the left side of the board while the length of the string was stretched across the face of the board, with the weight of the bag dangling over the right side to keep the string taut. The string was then pulled and snapped, making a crisp, white line. A series of lines were made in this way as guides for drawing the letters. The pens beginners used to write on this board were made of bamboo, with nibs about a quarter inch thick. Nibs got progressively thinner as a student advanced, and ink was introduced, with the beginner's brown ink, made of burnt cheese dissolved in water, later exchanged for black. Sometimes the senior students who used the black ink would put sugar in it to give their writing a stylish, glossy shine! The teacher who oversaw beginners would first write the entire alphabet, without ink, on the dusted board. The student had to then write over it with ink and show it to the teacher for corrections and more instructions. This process was repeated until a student was capable of writing on his or her own. After each use the board had to be washed in a large bucket kept at the far end of the classroom. In winter, when the water in the bucket would freeze, washing the slate every hour or so was a hard punishment.

My school principal, Gen Ugyen, was a clerical officer in the government and was required to be in the office six days a week, with Saturday as a holiday. The senior-most student in our school was left in charge of the school and acted as headmaster. We had only two holidays a month, which fell on the fifteenth and the thirtieth days. Sometimes there were special holidays for religious functions, and during the Tibetan New Year, an occasion for much merriment and celebration, there would be an extended holiday for several days. Occasionally the principal would grant an arbitrary holiday for reasons of his own. The principal himself only checked our progress from time to time, typically during exams, which were conducted every three or four months. During such occasions he would check each student's hand-writing carefully.

Although the whole school was divided into five classes, we didn't have individual classrooms but shared one big room, which faced an open court-yard opposite the principal's quarters. When he was home we could see him through his window across the courtyard, and the entire school would be very quiet! School started at dawn and finished at dusk, with half an hour's break for lunch. The timing was actually not set by the principal but by the headmaster. I remember that during lunch break, the headmaster would light an incense stick about ten inches long and tell us to come back before it had burned out. If we were late we were caned.

Corporal punishment in the form of caning or slapping was a common practice in schools. The worst time when it came to such punishment was after the exams, when the ranks were announced and we had to line up in order of performance. The student who came first had the privilege of can-ing each of the students of the entire class with a slim bamboo cane. He held the cane in his left hand, flipped it back, and let it go, hitting the boys on the left cheek and the girls on the palm of the hand. The student who came second hit all those ranking below him or her, and so it went, with the one who came last receiving the most punishment. Not only did the last-place student suffer the most, but he or she also had to bear the laughter and deri-sion of the whole student body because the student was then made to cane an empty yak-skin butter container, which made a loud noise. Sometimes students who were particularly mean would take this opportunity to inflict as much pain as possible on those they disliked. I myself was an average student, perhaps a bit on the lazy side, and I got my share of beating. Nev-ertheless, I emerged from it without much harm.

At times, when a very serious offense was committed, a student could receive a harsh punishment in the form of up to fifty lashes on the bottom with a leather whip. The power to impose such a stern punishment rested solely with the principal. The offending student had to lie face down in the middle of the stone courtyard and pull his pants down; girls were not whipped. A senior student or one of the student teachers would be appointed to whip the poor offender. The extent of the pain inflicted depended entirely on the person handling the whip. If the whipper were merciless, then the victim's skin would be cut and bleeding on nearing fifty lashes. Students who received such a whipping would hardly be able to get up and were certain to be bedridden for the next few weeks. Some students who were whipped in this manner would wriggle, cry, and plead for forgiveness. But some of the tougher boys would bite down on their clothes and would never shout or plead for mercy. Instead, they would wait for a chance to get their revenge on the one who whipped them!

I myself suffered ten lashes once. I remember that it was when the rest of the students were given a holiday, as it was a beautiful summer day. It must have been about two years after I joined Darpoling School, near the dreaded time of examinations. My brother Wangdor and I got the bright idea of running away to escape school! We were influenced by a former servant-boy of ours who had become a novice monk at Ganden, a highly regarded monastery about thirty kilometers east of Lhasa. This boy, who was about fifteen, had recently come to Lhasa on an errand, and we chanced to meet him. He told us about how nice it was up at Ganden, free of all the stress and hardship of going to school. Being very impressed, the two of us decided to trek to Ganden and become novice monks! That morning we persuaded the family business cashier to give us more than our usual pocket money of one and a half *sho*, citing the need to buy ink, chalk, pens, and other such supplies for the upcoming exams. We received twice our usual amount, so between us we had three *sho*. We left the house early, as we usually did on school days, but after a while my brother told me that he had to go somewhere briefly. He told me that I should go ahead and he would catch up with me. Since we had earlier found out which direction to follow, I carried on and reached a small bridge called Mondon, not far from our house.

Before crossing the bridge I stopped at a bread shop I knew. The shop was below the house of my older sister Pema Chöden, who had married into a noble family called Goshampa. I thought I might need to eat along the way, so I bought a dozen small pieces of bread and used up half the money I had. I then kept walking east along a road frequented by travelers. That day there weren't many people on the road, but a little ahead of me I saw a herdsman with a pack of loaded yaks. I soon caught up with him and asked him if he were going to Ganden. He said he was going in that general direction, and I asked him if I might tag along, as I wasn't sure of the direction. He agreed and we traveled together for some time. I didn't find it difficult to keep up, as the animals made very slow progress. Once or twice I looked back to see if my brother was coming, but there was no sign of him. Undaunted, I carried on by myself.

About six or seven kilometers from Lhasa, I neared some houses all painted yellow. Being thirsty, I thought I should try and get something to drink. All of a sudden I felt someone catch me from behind by the scruff of my neck. I heard someone say, "There you are! Running away from school, eh?" Turning around, I saw it was my cousin Serga, one of the older students at my school. Another student had also come along. Serga told me that he'd been sent by the school to catch me and bring me back. I knew I was headed for a lot of trouble, but there was nothing I could do against two big boys. I told them I was thirsty and wanted something to drink, so Serga took the remainder of my money and went to a nearby house where he bought a pot of *chang*: Tibetan barley beer! I also told the boys that I had some bread and that we could eat it together, so we sat down on some grass and had a meal before embarking on the unwelcome journey back.

It was around noon when we reached the Mondon bridge I had crossed earlier. There I was surprised to see all the students from my school swimming in the river and having a picnic! I asked Serga about this, and he told me that since it was a beautiful day, the students had been granted an impromptu holiday. They had all been permitted to go swimming. I, however, was marched straight to school.

On the way, close to my house, I met my sister Pema Chöden and my cousin Nyima Yudron. They were chatting at the gate of the Gyanatsang residence, the family into which Nyima Yudron had married. Naturally, they asked us where we were going, and then Serga told them the whole story. The girls were rather shocked and said, "Poor Rinchen! Why on earth did you do such a thing?" To console me they gave me a handful of peaches that they had just bought.

I reached the school and the dreaded confrontation with the principal. He gave me a sharp scolding and ordered that I be given ten lashes. I was then kept in school, practicing Tibetan script till dusk while the rest of my schoolmates were enjoying themselves outdoors. I was very cross with my brother, for not only did he go back on his word of coming along with me, but he also betrayed me and told the principal that I had run away to Ganden! I am not sure the rest of my immediate family knew anything of this incident. No one else scolded or punished me at home, not even my nun sister who was in charge of us and who could be very harsh, sometimes even ruthless, in punishing us young boys. If she had known, she would surely have given me a sound thrashing.

Life returned to normal. School life in Lhasa was tedious and quite joyless. I hated having to get up so early on cold winter days. There were even times when we were required to reach school before dawn. On those occasions, we'd also have to risk being bitten by the numerous stray dogs in the dark lanes. Often when we reached school the door would not yet be open, and we'd have to wait out in the freezing cold. I am told that I frequently ended up with my thick winter pants, which I wore under my thick winter robe, down around my knees. Evidently I would go walking around like that until someone helped me untie the sash around my waist, pull my pants up, and retie my sash to hold the pants in place. You see, Tibetan pants had no elastic, and I suspect that, since I was small, I couldn't manage to deal with all that thick clothing. I couldn't pull my pants up myself if they got loose and couldn't tie the sash. As if malfunctioning pants weren't enough, my nose also dripped all the time because of the winter cold. Since I had no handkerchief, I used to wipe it off on my sleeve. With my pants around my knees and my snot-encrusted sleeve, I must have looked a sight!

These miserable winter mornings nevertheless held one delight—hot milk sold outside the school gates. During the ten-minute break we got after sunrise, I used to rush over to buy hot milk along with bread from the same shop. My brother and I never got any tea or breakfast before we left for school, so this served as our breakfast. I was later told that I had racked up a sizeable bill at that shop, a bill that my family eventually paid. It was kind of the shopkeeper to extend credit to my brother and me. I suppose they must have known that we belonged to the well-off Sadutshang family.

Though my brother and I never had much pocket money, we managed to save a bit from the money given to us by our cousin Chöze Talha and our sisters. As a child I used to love sweets, perhaps because they were a rare treat for us. My favorite was a kind that came in the shape of a fish of different colors and different sizes. There was also a kind of sweet that was shaped and colored like an orange wedge. But my especial favorite was an Indian sweet called *jalebi*, which we called *bulu*, since the shape resembled a Tibetan pastry by that name. They were sold by Tibetan Muslims whose forefathers originated from Kashmir and who had come to Lhasa to do business, ultimately settling down there. Jalebis were made of flour and sugar and came in the shape of concentric circles. They were more expensive than the fish and orange sweets, but they were fresh and hot, so whenever I could afford it, I would run to buy one or two pieces. I also loved yogurt, which was available in small earthen pots. I used to buy a pot and quietly eat it by myself, sitting on a pile of hay in the corner of our stables. Somehow I don't remember doing these things with my brother Wangdor. He was three years older, so I suppose he went around with friends his own age.

One day I was privileged to get a very rare treat: a few biscuits that came from a tin and that were no doubt British in origin. I remember it was a late summer afternoon during a holiday. I was sitting at home when my nun sister called me. She said I was to take my eldest cousin's only son, Tsetop, who was about two at the time, and play with him in a nearby park. She sent a maid along with us and gave the maid a tin of biscuits, which she said were for Tsetop. However, she let the servant know that I could have a few pieces too. I enjoyed my outing, playing with a rag ball and eating these delicious biscuits. My nun sister had clearly exposed the bias in her preferential treatment of Tsetop compared to my brother and me. She did this both in terms of clothes and food, even though she was my own sister. She was always trying to please the cousins, who were the oldest members of the family and therefore had the most authority.

Life was much better in the summer. We wore lighter clothes and kept cleaner. Best of all, we went on picnics, which lasted for days. Everybody did this. People would pitch their tents in a park close to the river or in an open space where the grass was good. The fifteenth day of the fifth month, known as Dzamling Kyisang, or World Incense Burning Day, marked the beginning of the summer picnics and was celebrated by everyone. The whole family would go with all the gear for cooking, sometimes staying on for more than a week. Friends would join in and large groups would gather, all staying in the same area. On one of these picnics I remember my brother Wangdor and I were given a beautiful pair of short boots made of leather, which had been bought in India by one of our older relatives during a business trip. They were British made, as were most such things in India in those days. I was particularly impressed with the boots' rubber soles, which had six circular designs embossed within an oval frame. I had never seen anything like it.

During this same picnic an incident occurred that left an indelible imprint on my young mind. Early one morning I was walking between the tents when I heard shouting and the sound of a woman crying. I looked toward where the sound was coming from and saw my cousin Gyurme hitting his wife, Rinchen Lhamo. She ran out of the tent, but my cousin chased her and finally kicked her from behind, sending her sprawling to the ground. I became rather frightened and went back quickly to my tent. Later, I queried a servant and learnt that Rinchen Lhamo had been caught smoking a cigarette, which was something not done by Khampa women in those days. The irony of it is that years later, my cousin not only indulged in smoking but began to smoke opium as well. I remember Rinchen Lhamo to be a beautiful lady and a kind person. She came from a prominent family of the court of the king of Dergé in Kham. I feel neither my cousin Gyurme nor his older brother Sochö treated her justly. Perhaps this was because they were influenced by their mother's constant complaints about their wife. Regardless, it eventually came to pass that, after she had borne them a son, the brothers divorced her. Her son, Tsetop, was only three at that time.

One figure of my school days in Lhasa that I can never forget is that of our principal's wife. She was a short, fat lady with a sharp tongue. She often beat us with a thick cane, under the flimsiest of pretexts. She disliked Khampas and called us *khamtuk*, or "Khampa brat." If anything went wrong, she would blame the Khampa boys first. Fortunately she only interfered when her husband was not present.

I must relate an amusing incident concerning her and my second eldest brother, Lo Nyendak. He had also attended the same school but had already left by the time I joined. He told me about this incident himself, relating how he had been sent by the principal's wife to fetch water and fill her tub; she wanted to have a bath. He disliked her arrogant attitude, especially toward the Khampa students. To take revenge, he filled the tub with water and then quietly peed in it. Later when he saw the lady emerge from her so-called bath, he had a good laugh! My brother Lo Nyendak was never a very good student. He was already quite big when he joined school, and being fiercely independent by nature, he would never obey the orders of his teachers. Therefore the school principal and his wife would often make him do chores like cleaning or bringing tea from the kitchen. I believe he would always drink a cup himself before serving the principal his tea. I also heard that he once beat up the headmaster outside the school!

My brother and I got hardly any affectionate care at home when we were young. Our elder brothers, who were a great deal older than us, were too busy with their business activities. Our nun sister merely saw that we were fed and that we left for school each morning. The only relatives who gave us love and affection were Chözé Talha and our elder sister Yangchen Khando, who always treated us with much love when we went to see her. At those times she was like a mother to us. She must have understood how much I missed my mother's love and care. Because of her loving kindness I would try and get to her house whenever I could find an excuse. At times I would go without permission, risking a beating from my nun sister, who loved to rebuke and beat us for any minor offense. There was one occasion when I developed an infection in my mouth, which became quite severe, as no one took care of it. Fortunately my sister Yangchen Khando saw it and made arrangements for me to be kept at her house so that it could be treated. She looked after me with great affection. It must have been more than a month before I could rejoin school. In spite of the discomfort of the infection, this period was one of the most enjoyable during my childhood in Lhasa. Our favorite male cousin, Chözé Talha, called us to his home from time to time and gave us treats. Occasionally he would even keep us overnight. I used to love the novelty of sleeping on one of the folding beds that he had, no doubt imported from India, which he used to set up in his room at these times. He was also very generous, giving us not only sweets but also pocket money, especially during the kite-flying season so we could buy kites.

Kite flying was the most enjoyable outdoor sport we had. We had heard about football but had never touched one. I remember playing among ourselves with a ball made of rags and hanging our shirts up to mark the goal posts. We also used to go ice skating. We had no ice skates but devised a method of skating on ice by having a cobbler nail a large number of studs into the heels and toes of our boot soles! This enabled us to slide very effectively across large frozen ponds and rivers. The only indoor game we knew of was called *apchu*. The apchu pieces were handmade by rubbing the one-inch to one-and-a-half-inch kneecap bones of sheep or goats against a rough surface, making them flat so that they would slide smoothly across the floor. The pieces were then dyed different colors. The game was played by placing a few apchu pieces about ten feet away from the players, who would then spin their favorite apchu strikers across the floor in attempts to hit the apchu targets. It was a popular game with both boys and girls, and we spent quite a bit of our pocket money on buying apchu pieces.

I was about eight when I was withdrawn from Darpoling School, and to my delight I found out that I was to go to school in India within the month! However, it was only years later that I found out how the decision to send me to school in India came about. My elder brothers and cousins, since they were doing good business between Tibet and India, decided that either Wangdor or I should be educated in India. This way we could be made useful in the family's future business. They also decided that the other boy should be made a monk. It was customary in those days for a family having two or more sons to compel one son to take up spiritual activities. My elders consulted the family spiritual teacher, an incarnate lama, who performed a divination. This favored me to go to school in India and Wangdor to be made a monk, and that is how our futures were decided.

My progress in my two and a half years at Darpoling School had not been all that good. I had reached what was known as standard 3, which we called the *tsukthung* standard. That meant that I could now write one level above the large basic script. I knew how to read a little and could recite my times tables up to nine. Since every morning we had to recite prayers in praise of Manjushri, the bodhisattva of wisdom, I knew some recitations of prayers too. However, the majority of my time at school was spent at forming good handwriting. It was considered essential to have perfect handwriting, and a great deal of emphasis was placed on this in every school.

All that I remember of the days leading up to my departure for India is one particularly pleasurable moment of just sitting and enjoying myself on a huge pile of raw wool in the big courtyard. Many of our business's field managers, who had gone to various parts of northern Tibet to buy wool from the nomads, had returned with their purchases. They, along with many of our hands, were repacking the wool to be sent to India, and I was to be part of the caravan that would transport it all.

4. FROM LHASA TO KALIMPONG

We left on a bright morning in late autumn. My second eldest cousin, Gyurme, was leading a large caravan of over a hundred mules. These pack animals were carrying mostly raw wool and a large quantity of silver coins of Chinese origin. Since I was now almost eight, I did not need a servant to pull my horse. This time I was put on a brown mule that had been trained for riding. She was a gentle animal.

The journey to India took nineteen days, and I remember certain significant parts of it. The first of these came on the third day, when we reached the banks of the Kyichu River at the point where the Tsangpo River converges with it. This river is extremely large, and at this time it was in spate. The only means of crossing it was a large wooden barge that accommodated about twenty mules, their loads, and a few muleteers. I traveled in the first batch and waited for the rest to come across. This was the first time in my life that I'd seen a barge, let alone ridden one across a big river. It was a little scary in the beginning but also thrilling and exciting as I watched the swirling waters below me! I noticed the animals had some difficulty getting on and off the barge, as it was not level with the ground, so they had to jump.

In the evening we stopped in a village called Gampa Batsi, about seven or eight kilometers from the river. The next day we immediately began an ascent to cross Gampa Pass. It must have taken us over two hours to reach the summit. There we got a beautiful view of the famous Yamdrok Turquoise Lake. True to its name, the lake was a deep clear aqua blue. It was also very large and semicircular in shape. We had to descend to the lake's shore and then travel along its banks until we reached a village called Pedé Dzong, which was one of the district headquarters of the government. The following morning we continued to ride along the lakeshore until we reached Nangangtse Dzong, another district headquarters. From this point we entered a valley and finally left the lakefront.

Our next major stop was the town of Phari, which too was a district headquarters and also a post for the *dzongpon*, or district commissioner, as well as customs collectors to whom we had to pay taxes on wool and tea. I believe we stayed here an extra day to give everyone a rest. The Sadutshang trading company had a manager permanently stationed in the town, since it was an important center for trade and in close proximity to India and Bhutan, which were just a few hours' journey away. Phari was a collection point for wool for many traders, who brought it from northwestern Tibet. Wool arrived in Phari on the backs of yaks, but from here the bales were transferred to mules as yaks were unsuited to travel to the low altitudes of India. Phari, however, stands out in my mind for an altogether different reason.

The morning we were to leave Phari, well-wishers gathered at the gate of the house in which we had been staying. We were mounted and ready but had not yet departed when suddenly someone slapped the handsome horse I had been given to ride in lieu of my mule. It started galloping swiftly across the open field that lay ahead, giving me the fright of my life! I hung on desperately to the reins and tried to sit up straight while being tossed helplessly right and left. One of the servants on horseback was finally able to catch up with me and rein in my horse and calm it. My cousin soon rode up to me and was relieved to see I hadn't fallen off. He patted me on the shoulder and, obviously pleased, said, "You did well to stay in the saddle!" I also felt rather proud and pleased with myself. Certainly the person responsible for slapping my horse must have been immensely relieved. As it turned out, he was the manager of our Phari office, a man named Lo Tenzin, a distant relative of my mother.

From Phari we traveled west to Yatung, which lay in a valley. The Tibetan government had a commissioner posted there along with a small contingent of soldiers as guard. Yatung was only twenty kilometers from Nathula Pass, on Tibet's border with Sikkim. Also close to Nathula Pass was Dzelep Pass, which led to India. This is the pass we were to cross. In those days the British had a trade agent posted at Yatung, as they had established a postal system that passed through the town, running between Gangtok, the capital of Sikkim, and Gyantse in central Tibet. Our journey from Phari to Yatung took about two days, during which we descended from 14,000 feet to 9,000 feet in altitude by following a winding path that led deep into the valley. The weather became much warmer as we approached Yatung. On entering the small town, my attention was immediately drawn to the pitched roofs made of corrugated tin and painted red that topped the houses inside the compound of the British trade agent. To me these roofs looked much more attractive than the flat roofs of my own country. There was a big river flowing nearby, and we camped on the riverfront for the night.

The next morning we started early, as we had to now cross Dzelep Pass, which lay at 17,000 feet. After riding for about an hour, we began climbing and reached the summit a little after noon. The top of the pass was marked by a large cairn and by many fluttering prayer flags put up by travelers to ensure their safety and protection. The first man of our group to reach the summit gave a shrill cry praising the gods of the mountains, the gods of the local region, and the guardian deities. Each person then dismounted and threw some stones on the cairn as a sign of respect and prayed for blessings and for good fortune in the days ahead. I was told Dzelep Pass functioned as the demarcation between Tibet and India, and so we had now set foot on Indian soil.

In the late afternoon we reached a small village called Nathang, where we were to spend the night, and there I saw more red-roofed houses. At our lodging my cousin gave me an orange, the first I'd seen in my life. It looked so round and vivid in color and tasted simply wonderful! I longed to eat more of this delicious fruit. From Nathang it took us two days of continuous descent to reach our final destination, Kalimpong. On the final day of our journey, as we went along, more and more red-roofed houses appeared, and the roads improved tremendously. About five or six kilometers from Kalimpong, we reached roads that were tarred. I had never seen tarred roads before, and to me they looked so clean and so smooth!

As we approached even closer I saw an Indian carrying a big tin box on his head. I was amazed at how he balanced the chest with such ease as his hands hung by his sides. I was very curious and asked someone what the man was carrying in his tin box and was told that the box contained bread and cakes, which the man sold. The weather was now much warmer, and we began to shed the upper parts of our robes in order to be more comfortable. I saw Indian children dressed in just shirts and shorts, and to me they seemed barely dressed at all compared to all the thick clothing we wore in Tibet.

The Sadutshangs occupied a two-story wooden house about a kilometer and a half from the main town. It had a very nice veranda on the east, facing a range of the Himalayas and a valley through which flowed the Rangeet River. We occupied the upper floor, which had four rooms including a kitchen. The lower floor was partly occupied by two of our managers, and the rest was used as a storeroom. Just a short distance away, on much higher ground, we also had a huge *godown*, or warehouse, for our wool. All the wool we had brought with us was unloaded there. The warehouse had a large compound in the front, and all the pack mules were kept there to rest for a few days before returning back to Tibet with loads of various consumer items purchased in Kalimpong. My family was doing very good business in exporting wool from Tibet to India, and during their last trip to Kalimpong, my cousin Gyurme and my eldest brother Lo Gedun had bought this large warehouse with a view to expanding business, ultimately exporting wool directly to England and the U.S.A.

While my cousin and his field managers busied themselves with business affairs, I just waited to be sent to school. I think it was early November when we reached Kalimpong, and with the weather being so warm for us Tibetans, I was allowed to remain in just shirts and pants, which felt very comfortable. I was always eager to go to town whenever any of our workers had to make some purchase or the other. Everything was new to me, and I liked looking inside the shops, even though I was unable to make myself understood. It was during this period that I saw my first cinema showing moving pictures. I was taken by Chögyal, our senior manager. I remember sitting on long wooden benches in the front rows, which I later found out were the cheapest seats! I was extremely excited as I had heard about films and was most eager to see one. My first film was one featuring Tarzan, and I was absolutely captivated by his heroism. I would sometimes try to imitate the jungle call Tarzan made in the movies. And when I had nothing to do or anywhere to go, I used to sit on the veranda and look across to the forested hills opposite. I would imagine how Tarzan might be jumping from tree to tree and how I too could be roaming in the jungle, so that one day Tarzan might see me and take me to live with him!

5. SCHOOLING AT ST. JOSEPH'S CONVENT

One day, as I awaited the time when I would finally start school, an Indian-looking gentleman came to our house. I was told he was a teacher for my cousin, Gyurme, who wanted to learn Hindi. The teacher came every day for an hour. Before long my cousin told me that I had to go and live with this teacher and his family until I got proper admission into a school. This way, I too could learn to speak Hindi.

The teacher had a pretty little cottage built on the ridge above the town. He lived there with his wife and three sons, and now I had been added to the family. I couldn't speak a word of their language so it was difficult in the beginning, but soon I began to pick up a few words of Nepali; as it turned out, the family was Nepalese in origin and not Indian! The eldest son was about five years my senior and the second eldest about two years older than me. The youngest one was two years my junior. The two bigger boys went to the government high school, about a kilometer away and above the government hospital, in the center of Kalimpong. Many times the youngest son and I were taken along when the older boys went to school, and we were allowed to attend the kindergarten class. I enjoyed this thoroughly, as it gave me a chance to see new things and to play with children my age in the school playground. There were one or two footballs to play with, and so I got to play with a real football for the very first time. I got on pretty well with the three boys, though the two older ones sometimes tried to bully me, albeit without much success.

As to life with this family, I really enjoyed Nepalese food, especially the curries. Sometimes we were served chicken curry with rice, but I was oblivious to where the meat came from till one day I saw the mother take a live chicken and cut its head off! The poor bird struggled desperately and slipped from her grasp. The headless body fluttered around the ground for a while and finally collapsed. I hated what I saw, but as is the way of young boys, I soon forgot all about it. Occasionally we were given a thin round piece of bread called *shel roti*, which was almost always served with a cup of tea and which I enjoyed tremendously. I stayed with this family for about four months, and in that time I managed to pick up a good deal of Nepali. I could now communicate fully with the local people of Kalimpong, who were nearly all of Nepalese origin. Toward the end of my stay, I had even acquired a steel hoop to roll down the road with a stick like any local boy in the town. In the meanwhile my cousin and his staff had shifted to a better house called Raja Koti, close to the main bazaar in Kalimpong. It had a few orange trees and a nice big lawn in front. When I returned home from my Nepalese family, it was to this house that I came.

It was early 1937 when I gained admission to St. Joseph's Convent, a Roman Catholic boarding school three kilometers down the road from the new house, toward the Teesta River. My clothes and other needs were all prepared according to the requirements of a boarding student, very much along the lines of a student going to boarding school in England. My cousin had already left for Tibet by that time, so a family friend called Kunphel-la took me to school. Kunphel-la was a famous personality in Lhasa during the time of the Thirteenth Dalai Lama. He had become powerful due to being a favorite of His Holiness. However, after the Dalai Lama passed away at the young age of fifty-eight, Kunphel-la was accused by the government of holding back information about the seriousness of the Dalai Lama's health. He was banished and forced into exile to the east, in the Kongpo Valley of Tibet. After a couple of years he managed to escape and enter India through the northeast frontier. Since he didn't have any means of support, business-men like those of my family helped him out.

When I reached St. Joseph's Convent, the nun in charge welcomed me and immediately had me and my box taken to the boys' dormitory, where she introduced me to the supervisor. I barely knew a word of English but could communicate with the supervisor in Nepali, as she was a Nepalese Christian. Besides the Nepalese, I could also communicate with some of the boys in my dorm who were Sikkimese and Bhutanese, as they could all understand and speak Nepali. I did, however, find class difficult in the beginning but soon managed to adjust. The school was really meant for girls, but small boys were accepted into the kindergarten class for a maxi-mum of two years. I found most of the girls were British, but there were a few Anglo-Indian (Eurasian), Sikkimese, Bhutanese, and Nepalese girls as well. I was the only Tibetan among the boys. As I had arrived from Tibet only a few months earlier, I still had very rosy cheeks. This the older girls loved! They used to often come to see me, pinch my cheeks, and give me lots of sweets and chocolates, which I very much relished. They also talked to me a lot, but alas, I could only pick out a word here and there. Many of them had picture books, and I loved going through these. They wouldn't allow me to take these with me but would let me look at them during breaks in the school day.

In the beginning I was happy with my new and wonderful school and even made one or two friends. I was also picking up a few words of English. But after a couple of weeks the initial excitement wore off, and I wanted very much to go back home. One evening, after we were in bed as usual by 7:30 P.M. and the dorm lights were out, I decided to sneak out. The boys' dorm was on the first floor and close to the staircase at the foot of which was the parlor, where the nuns received visitors. I crept down to the front door of the parlor and then proceeded out into the open, toward the main gate, looking right and left to see if anybody was around. Thankfully there was no one. I continued walking a short distance down a path until I reached the main road, and then I headed toward town.

After a few minutes I heard a car behind me, and I put out my hand to stop it. It was an old British-made Austin and one of the few taxis in the area. The driver kindly gave me a lift to the taxi stand in town. From there I walked toward my house. But before descending down the path from the main road to my home, I suddenly felt a little frightened and I hesitated. I stood on the small ridge and looked down to my house. I could see our cook and another servant walking to and fro. After giving it some thought I decided it wouldn't be right to enter my house in this furtive manner, and I made up my mind to go back to school. I walked quickly for the entirety of the three kilometers back to school and, on reaching the school gate, looked cautiously about once more to make sure no one was about. The parlor door was unlocked, exactly as I had left it, so I crept back to my dorm, where all the boys were sound asleep, and slipped into my bed. The next morning I was a little apprehensive in case anyone had noticed that I was absent from my bed for over two hours the previous night. But nobody said anything, and I got away with this little adventure!

After a couple of months I made good progress with my English and was soon able to communicate well with the rest of my class as well as with the other students. I used to love cutting out pictures from newspapers and listening to stories that our teachers told us in class. One class period was devoted to scripture, and an old Irish nun called Mother Joseph used to teach it. She usually took the class out to a pavilion at the sports ground and told us Bible stories from a large book full of color pictures. I used to love looking at these beautiful pictures, but I'm afraid I didn't pay much attention to the stories.

After some time in school I found I didn't like the food. We were fed mostly rice and dal and seasonal vegetables. Of these I developed a strong aversion to okra, what we called "ladies' fingers." But since we had to eat whatever was served on our plate and were not permitted to waste anything, I had to swallow this slimy vegetable to the best of my ability. The other thing I had to swallow that I detested singularly was castor oil. Every Sunday morning we were given a tablespoon's worth of it to cleanse our bowel system, or so they said. I often threw up after getting a dose and felt sick even looking at it, but I was not spared.

Occasionally we were treated to a film screening. These films used to be shown by a monsignor who lived above the convent with a group of priests, who were engaged in social work in a village called Aragara about ten kilometers east of Kalimpong. I used to be very impressed with the monsignor's long black cassock, his dark pink sash, and his cap of the same color. I don't recall the films clearly, but in all likelihood they must have been on Christian themes. After all, it was the aim of Christian missionaries to try and convert all non-Christians to Christianity. On Sundays it was compulsory for all students to attend church. Sometimes the service seemed to go on forever for a young boy like me, and I found it painful to kneel for a long time on hard wood.

My first year in school passed quickly, and by now I was fully absorbed in my class activities as well as in various outdoor games such as football and marbles. The girls played field hockey and netball instead. In the evenings we often went on walks along the main road for about half an hour. We small boys wore shirts and shorts, which we called half-pants, and the girls wore navy blue tunics, white blouses, blue striped ties, and navy blue berets. We boys had to wear our uniform tie only when going to church, going to town for a function, or when we went home for the holidays. The school closed in November for the winter break, and I was happy to go home.

Once home there was no routine nor any checks and controls, and I enjoyed my freedom. My elders were busy with their business affairs, and I was left to amuse myself. Sometimes it was boring just sitting around with nothing to do and no one to play with, so I went to town frequently, either on my own or with anyone who happened to be going there on an errand. I tried to get to the cinema hall as often as possible but rarely had enough money. However, I soon found out how to get around this problem. When our muleteers came with a caravan of wool, they stayed for two to three days in order to rest. I knew most of the old hands and used to go along with them when they went to town to the cinema. Sometimes they'd be unable to get tickets, and then they would pierce a hole in the wall of the cinema hall with their swords, which every self-respecting Khampa carried. As the entire cinema hall was made of corrugated iron sheets, making a hole was not difficult to do with a sharp knife. Once they'd made a peephole, they could take a good long peep! Of course if the watchman found out, there'd be trouble, but more often than not the watchman would be loathe to confront knife-wielding Khampas. We children used to make full use of these holes.

During my first winter holiday home from school, my brother Lo Gedun came to Kalimpong to take care of business. But toward the end of my holiday, he had to leave for Phari in Tibet on urgent business, and he left Kunphel-la in charge. Kunphel-la had a senior accountant and two young clerks to help him look after things, and it was during this period that our cook and other servants talked of there being ghosts in the house. I decided to take advantage of this to play a joke on Kunphel-la's servant. I surreptitiously tied a long black string to his pigtail, and when he was climbing the stairs and had reached halfway, I tugged at the string. The poor man immediately turned around to find out who was pulling his hair and, on finding no one, was scared out of his wits!

However, there were times when I myself got goosebumps. One evening about eight o'clock Kunphel-la and I were waiting for dinner to be served when we heard someone in the next room, which was an office. From where I was sitting I could see through the curtains that hung in front of the glass mounted above the partition between the two rooms. The office was dark. But we clearly heard the intruder begin moving ledgers from one place to another. He also started playing with our abacus, the clicking sound of which is unmistakable. Kunphel-la called out, "Who is there?" There was no reply. He called out again, but there was only silence. After a minute or two we again heard the noise of the abacus being used. Kunphel-la got quite annoyed, so he took a shoe in his right hand with which to hit the intruder and went quickly to the office and turned on the light. There was absolutely no one there! I know, because I followed Kunphel-la to the door.

More so than the office, our storeroom on the ground floor was the center of much ghostly activity. At times you could clearly hear heavy sacks of rice or sugar being thrown to the floor with a loud thud. You could even feel the vibrations of the impact. Such commotion could go on for long periods. During one such particularly noisy occasion, our storekeeper and another servant picked up courage and went to see what mess and damage had been caused. I followed along because I was curious. We turned on the light, but everything was in perfect order; nothing had been touched! After that nobody bothered to investigate or fuss, as there was nothing one could do about it.

There was a time when I actually encountered a person who may have been a ghost. I was returning home after dark after watching a film in town. It wasn't very late. As I came down the slope leading to our house from the ridge, I clearly saw someone standing near the garage about thirty feet away from the house. He or she appeared to be wearing a long outfit of some sort, but the face was hidden. I came quite close, perhaps five feet away, and asked, "Who are you?" The person didn't reply and instead turned his or her back to me. I repeated the question, but still no response came. I went to the kitchen and alerted the cook and another servant of what I had seen. One of them went outside to investigate but could find nobody there. They said it must have been a ghost and that it was fortunate I hadn't seen the face; anybody who encountered a ghost face to face would be the victim of certain disaster!

Ghosts were soon forgotten, as it was time for me to go back to school. My eldest brother returned from Phari and had my school requirements checked and readied. Then I was back in school for my second year. In my first year I had made some friends, but none were very close. The closest was Nirmal Pradhan, a local Nepalese boy whose parents ran a nursery for plants just a kilometer away from school. In my second year I made two new friends, Ugyen Dorji and Jigdal Densapa. Ugyen Dorji was Bhutanese, and his family was known as the Raja Dorji family, the title of raja being given to his father by the British. Their residence in Kalimpong was known as the *durbar* in Hindi and *phodrang* in Tibetan, both of which mean "palace." This title came about after the Thirteenth Dalai Lama came and lived in this house for some time when he took refuge in India during the 1910 Chinese invasion of Tibet. Later my family became very close friends of the Dorji family. Jigdal was from the Barmiok Kazi family, a well-known Sikkimese noble family. Later I came to learn that three princesses from the Sikkimese royal family and two sisters of Ugyen Dorji also went to St. Joseph's Convent.

When I returned to school I was promoted to kindergarten A, and all my friends were also in the same class. I was now well adjusted and didn't feel homesick at all. Our mother superior was a kindly Irish nun called Mother John Mary. But the most popular of all nuns was Mother Cecelia with her bright, cheerful personality. Very energetic, she was always ready to help any student with any problem. In the evenings she conducted various sports and games. I was doing well in my studies. I had a talent for drawing, so my favorite class was naturally the drawing period. Once I drew the head of a lion, using a picture book to guide me. My teacher took me, along with my drawing, to the senior classes and told the big girls, "See how well this little boy has drawn this picture? There isn't one of you who can equal him!" Of course I felt very proud of myself! My second year of school passed very quickly, and soon I was once again home for the winter holidays.

Quite a few events took place during these long vacations, which lasted about three months. First, the youngest of my sisters, Pema Chöden, and her husband arrived from Lhasa en route to various Buddhist pilgrimage sites in India. I was very happy to see my sister after two years. While they stayed in Kalimpong I helped her with her shopping, as I was now able to speak fluent English and Nepali. In return I got plenty of *tuck* (English boarding-school slang for sweets, cookies, and the like), so I had a great time while she and her husband were around. During their visit a devastating fire broke out in the middle of the town. It was about three in the morning when we came to know of it, and from our veranda we saw flames towering in the sky. My cousin Gyurme was alerted by telephone, and he rushed to town. He returned about two hours later and told us that many shops had been gutted. He had gone especially to help a shopkeeper called Kayang Katuk, who was from the Indian province of Rajasthan. He was one of our regular suppliers and well known to my cousin. The poor man's shop had burned to the ground, and he had been crying and pleading for help on the phone. It was about eight hours before the fire could finally be extinguished. Kalimpong in those days didn't possess a fire brigade, and a fire engine had to be summoned from Darjeeling, the district headquarters. It took about three hours to arrive. During this time nearly all possible damage had already been done.

About a month after my sister's visit, we had the privilege of hosting a very distinguished spiritual teacher by the name of Jamyang Sharpa Rinpoche of Labrang Tashikyil Monastery. This monastery was the largest in Amdo and very famous in eastern Tibet. Rinpoche was also on his way to India on pilgrimage. We accommodated him and his entourage in our new house in the bazaar area. My cousin took advantage of Rinpoche's visit to request him to exorcise the ghosts that so obviously haunted our house. I remember the night before Rinpoche's visit, there was an unusual amount of commotion in our storeroom. Perhaps these beings were sensing that their time in Raja Koti was nearing its end. We received Rinpoche into our house with due honor, and then he proceeded to go into each and every room and consecrate it. The result was truly remarkable! From then on everything was quiet at night, and all of us slept peacefully at last.

6. ST. JOSEPH'S COLLEGE, PRIMARY DIVISION

It was about early February 1939 when I was told that I would no longer be returning to St. Joseph's Convent but would be joining a new school in Darjeeling called St. Joseph's College. It was one of the best boys' schools in the area and was run by Jesuit priests. A young Nepalese Christian who was fluent in English and who could type had been engaged to work for the family business. My relatives were entering the market for exporting Tibetan wool to America and needed to communicate in English, so they hired this young man on as secretary. It was he who was given responsibility to shop for all the clothing and other supplies that I needed for my new school. The young secretary was known by the simple name of Kancha, which in Nepali means "youngest boy." Perhaps he was the youngest among his brothers. Nobody seemed to know what his real name was. I always accompanied Kancha on his shopping trips and took a keen interest in everything that had to be bought.

My entire uniform and even my sheets and pillowcases had to be tailored. Back then there were no uniforms to be bought off the shelf. My ankle-length boots and shoes also had to be custom made. The only items that we could get already manufactured were handkerchiefs, vests, socks, and toiletry. I remember everything was very cheap then. First-class English wool serge cost only 5 rupees a yard. Finally, we bought a large steel trunk for my clothes and a canvas bedroll for my blankets and quilt. I was now all set to go and very excited at the prospect of going to an exclusive all-boys school.

The long-awaited day arrived sometime in early March, and Kancha accompanied me to my new school. There was no point in my cousin coming, as he couldn't speak English. We traveled in a taxi, and the journey took what seemed to me an interminable two and a half hours because I was stricken with motion sickness. This was my first long journey by car, and I never imagined it could be this arduous. However, by the time I reached school, I was feeling better, and with the novelty of everything I soon forgot about my sickness.

We were immediately taken to the dormitory supervisor, who led us to the dormitory with a school employee carrying my belongings. I was given a cupboard, helped to unpack, and taught how to put my clothing on different shelves. Then I was shown my bed and taught how to make it. After that I went down to the playground to play with some of the boys already there while Kancha returned to Kalimpong.

I found myself with completely new companions. None of my Kalimpong school friends were there, nor were there any Tibetan boys my age. I was put in the Primary Division, which consisted of children from kindergarten to class 3. Mr. Fitzgerald was our Primary Division supervisor. He was a most devoted teacher and a strict old man but was nevertheless popular. He was particularly conscious of training us in Western table manners. One time I got a slap for eating with my mouth open. I soon made friends and adjusted to the new surroundings. I felt very happy at possessing an abundance of new clothing, shoes, ties, and such. I loved my school uniform, particularly the cap. These were exact copies of uniforms from schools in England. I was especially impressed with the huge school buildings made of stone in neo-Gothic style, the large student faculty, the three big playgrounds, and the many classrooms and halls.

I was given a double promotion and put in class 2 instead of class 1, which would normally follow kindergarten. I presume I must have done well the previous year at St. Joseph's Convent to warrant this jump. I didn't have any difficulty in class and managed to get fairly good marks, though I was not among the top students.

I soon found out that there were a couple of other Tibetan boys in school, but they were significantly older than me. One was George (so named by his teachers) Taring. George Taring came from the Sikkimese royal family, but his family had chosen to settle in Tibet and had been given estates and titles by the Tibetan government. The other boy was Dondrup Kapshopa, also of Tibetan nobility. They were in the Middle Division, which consisted of boys from class 4 to class 6. The Upper Division consisted of boys from class 7 to class 9. On graduating from class 9, which was known as the senior Cambridge class, you could join the Special Department, which was the Cambridge "A"-level class.

Apart from my studies, I loved the sports we played. From March to May it was cricket, June to August football, and September to November was field hockey. My favorite was football. Our school, also known as North Point School since it was in an area called North Point, was the best in sports among all of the numerous schools from Darjeeling to the neighboring town of Kurseong. There were many trophies to be taken for each of these three sports. In addition to the schools, the Tea Planters Association, the Army, the Police, and other organizations also competed for these trophies. The main field of our school was one of the best in Darjeeling, so most of the final games were played on it. We cheered loudly for our school, which was often in the finals. The trophy cases in our school parlor were full of the cups and shields of previous victories.

The school had a total of about four hundred students, which included thirty to forty day students from town. Most of the students were European, primarily British, but there were also a handful of Indians, Nepalese, Sikkimese, Bhutanese, and Tibetans. My school year passed quickly, and the end of November brought "going-home day." For travel purposes the boys were divided into various batches: the Calcutta batch, the up-country batch, and the home batch, to which I belonged. The home batch, which consisted of students who lived closest to school, were allowed to leave first, and soon I was in a taxi heading for Kalimpong. I dreaded being sick again, which I promptly was, but I got over it by the time I reached Teesta, a half hour away from Kalimpong.

My brother Lo Gedun was home, and he greeted me affectionately, being happy that I had kept in good health and had grown taller. About a month into the holidays, our business manager in Shigatse, the second largest town of Tibet, arrived on pilgrimage to visit various Buddhist centers in India. His name was Dorje Namgyal, and he was a stout and cheerful personality. One day I was catching butterflies and had pinned one or two on some cardboard as I had seen children do in school. Dorje Namgyal saw this and was horrified, being a devout Buddhist. He told me it was a great sin to take the life of any living being, no matter how small, and I should never do such a thing in the future. He also asked me suspiciously, "Have you been converted to Christianity?" I answered that I had not. From that day on I heeded his advice and stopped catching butterflies.

During the long winter holidays I was again mostly by myself, and apart from mealtimes, I had no fixed routine. I used to often go to town by myself, and sometimes I'd accompany our office messenger to the post office. We had a couple of orange trees in the garden, and since I loved this fruit, I ate as many as possible when they ripened, which conveniently for me was in winter. Oranges grew well in that area, and nearby Sikkim was famous for its oranges, which were exported in large quantities to Calcutta and even to Tibet.

One fine day my brother told me I should check my school clothes to see that I had everything I needed, and I realized it was time to go back to school. Since I had no constant family member there to take care of me, I had learned to become quite independent. Though only eleven I was quite capable of looking after myself. I got all my school requirements ready and even marked my name on some new clothes I had had tailor-made. I left for school at the beginning of March, looking forward not so much to my studies but to my friends and the athletic games I would play.

Upon returning to school I unpacked and went down to the playground, where I found that two new Tibetans had joined the school. They were Rigzin Yuthok, who was about my age, and Jigme Yuthok, a year younger. The Yuthoks came from Tibetan nobility and belonged to the family of the Tenth Dalai Lama, who had been born in Lithang in Kham. There also arrived yet another new Tibetan boy named Shalo Tashi Norbu, who was put in the Middle Division because of his age, though class-wise he should have been in the Primary Division. The Yuthoks and I became friends. I was closer to Rigzin, with whom I often played. Jigme was more of a loner.

Early school days in St. Joseph's College, Darjeeling. Front row: Jigme Yuthok, Mr. Yuthok, Sochö Yuthok, Sursur Jigme. Second row: Rigzin Yuthok, author, and unknown. Back row: Dondrup Kapshopa, Shalo Tashi Norbu, and George Taring.

I was now in class 3, and most of my classmates were those who'd been with me the previous year, though a few new ones had joined us. The top student in my class was a German boy named Ronald. He was also very good at all the sports and captained the Primary Division teams when we played interdivision games. I used to admire him and envy his talents. I was rather good at football but never quite got the hang of cricket, which I found a boring game. I didn't mind hockey, but I wasn't much good at it.

While most of us boys enjoyed playing the competitive games, what we most looked forward to in school was watching the films we were shown twice a month. Since we were all in a good mood during a film, we shared our "tuck" more freely then! We were given four *anna*, which was a quarter of a rupee, as pocket money each Sunday. When the school "tuck" shop opened, all of us would rush to it, eager to spend our money. In those days, four annas could buy you a lot of tuck. Sometimes we left a little money aside to buy ice cream from the vendor who came to the school gates. I remember a cup of vanilla or chocolate ice cream cost only two annas. Rigzin loved ice cream and spent all his money on it. Once he ate so much he got such a bad sore throat he ended up in the school infirmary!

In early October each year we got a week's holiday known as the Puja holidays. It was the time of an important Indian festival celebrating the Hindu goddess Durga. Many students from nearby, or even some from Calcutta, went home. I always stayed at school during this time since I knew there was no one at home. My relatives came to Kalimpong on their business trips only in winter. However, that year the Yuthoks' father came with their youngest brother and sister and took the two boys out to spend the holidays in town. The Yuthok family probably knew my family, so one weekend Mr. Yuthok was kind enough to take me out as well, and I enjoyed this outing with Rigzin and Jigme.

The winter holidays came. Since the Yuthok boys spent part of their holidays in Kalimpong, I had company and the holidays were more enjoyable for me this time. That winter it was my cousin Gyurme's turn to take care of business in Kalimpong, and around January he granted me a holiday in Calcutta. I was thrilled, as I had heard that Calcutta was a big metropolis and that there were so many wonderful things to see there!

I went with our secretary, Kancha, who was being sent on business concerning our wool exports. We went by bus to Siliguri and then took a train to Calcutta. It was my first time seeing a train, and it was a memorable sight indeed! There were a great number of people on the railway station, all walking hurriedly up and down. Coming from a country with vast expanses of land and a scarce population, it was a little frightening for me, and I feared getting lost in this melee, so I stuck close to Kancha. We soon found our compartment and sleeping berths, and while we waited for the train to start, Kancha went and got us a cup of tea each from the many vendors on the platform shouting *chai garam!* meaning "hot tea!" The tea came in little disposable earthenware cups.

The train pulled into Sealdah station early the next morning. After a twelve-hour journey we had arrived in Calcutta. This station was far larger than the station in Siliguri and even more crowded. I had never seen so many people in my entire life! Outside there were many cars, rickshaws, and even horse carriages, all making a terrific din. Kancha hired a rickshaw to take us to our lodgings. Seeing one man pulling the two of us made me feel very uncomfortable. However, soon I was too absorbed to dwell on this as I was filled with awe at the sight of so many houses and tall buildings. We lodged not in a hotel but in the private home of a Muslim gentleman who had been introduced to us by a business contact in Kalimpong. He lived on Zakaria Street in a predominantly Muslim area that was one of the busiest and most crowded in Calcutta.

In Calcutta, English was the dominant language among the educated, but the locals spoke Hindi and Bengali. Since I was a stranger to this huge city and knew no Hindi, I couldn't move around by myself. I had to wait until Kancha finished his work before I could be taken around the city. Kancha was a devout Christian and didn't engage in any bad habits, and films seemed to fall within this category for him. However, since I loved films I managed to pester him into taking me to a couple. But what I truly enjoyed during that holiday was seeing a circus for the first time in my life! I was lucky in that there were several circuses performing at different parks around town at that time. The day I was to go to the circus, I waited restlessly for Kancha to finish his work, fretting that we might not get tickets for the evening show if we were too late getting there. We hired a rickshaw to take us to the circus, and the journey seemed to be interminable, owing to my anxiety. But all was well and we got tickets, though they were for the back row as we did indeed reach the venue a bit late.

The circular tent was nearly packed full, and as the show began I was utterly mesmerized by each and every item. The show that impressed me most was the trapeze, and I greatly admired the athletic skills of the trapeze artists. I also thoroughly enjoyed all the animal acts. I thought the ringmaster very brave for being able to control such dangerous animals as lions and tigers and such huge animals as elephants. I also paid special attention to the cycling act, as I was about to acquire a bicycle for myself. When the show came to an end, I was sad and thought how wonderful it would be if I could watch the circus over and over. In fact, after considerable nagging, I was able to "convince" poor Kancha to take me to see two more circuses, and I enjoyed these just as much.

When Kancha finished all the work for which he had come, I got him to take me to buy my bicycle. A few days before we had left on this trip, I had built up a lot of courage and asked my cousin if I could buy a bicycle in Calcutta. He kindly consented and instructed Kancha accordingly. The thought of getting my own bicycle was foremost on my mind throughout my stay in Calcutta, and I kept pestering Kancha, asking him when he would finish his work. All the cycle shops were on Bentick Street, and after shopping around I finally decided on the one I liked the best. I still remember clearly that Kancha paid thirty rupees for the bicycle. It was arranged that the shopkeeper would pack it and dispatch it by train. A regular goods train would take it to the railhead in Siliguri. Afterward it would be transferred to a smaller narrow gauge train that went up into the hills and ended at a point called Gelkhola, about thirty kilometers from Kalimpong. From there it would be sent by ropeway to Kalimpong. Luckily for me, the ropeway station was just below our wool warehouse. I was now most anxious to get back to Kalimpong as my cycle would arrive a few days afterward!

After we got back to Kalimpong I had no other interest beyond the imminent arrival of my bicycle. Every day I went to see if it had arrived, and every day I came back disappointed. The waiting seemed endless until about a week later, when my cycle finally arrived in a large crate. We took it home in a bullock cart, there being no motor vehicles available to transport large packages. Fearing my cycle might have been damaged on its journey, I unpacked it quickly. Apart from some minor dents, everything was fine, and I was quite satisfied. I tried it out at once and then ran and called my cousin and everyone else in the house to look at it. I was so happy that my cousin was also pleased for me. I was able to ride my lovely bicycle for about four weeks before going back to school.

7. ST. JOSEPH'S COLLEGE, MIDDLE DIVISION

I returned to school in March as usual, and since I was now in class 4, I was put in the Middle Division. My friend Rigzin Yuthok, being a class junior, was still in the Primary Division. I had to make new friends since I didn't have any close friends among my classmates. Shalo Tashi Norbu was in the Middle Division, and we got on well together, though he was a little older. That year I was good friends with a Bengali boy named Nath. He was a neat person in his habits and very agreeable, always consenting to my bidding. He was also good at his studies, and I got him to help me in subjects at which I was weak.

Our class teacher was one Mr. Johns, a man who was well dressed and always looked very smart. He was a good teacher but strict. It was toward the end of the year when we heard that Mr. Johns' wife had run away with a British soldier. All of us felt very sorry for him and wondered how he must be feeling. Mr. Johns was also our school film-projector operator. His father owned a taxi service with two German Opel cars, which we often saw as we passed the taxi stand on our way to town for an outing. In those days all the cars were imported from the West, mainly from Britain.

In class I was doing fairly well. There were two new subjects now: Hindi and Latin. I didn't find Hindi too difficult, as it held some resemblance to Tibetan, especially the alphabet and the vowels. You see, the Tibetan script was based on that which is used for Sanskrit, which is the language Hindi is derived from. Latin was difficult. Nearly everyone disliked learning it, but it was a compulsory subject. Perhaps this was because our school was a Jesuit school.

Our field games were the same as in the Primary Division. However, there was one game that was exclusively a Middle Division game: the "shield game." I loved it and always looked forward to participating in it. In this game there were twenty boys to each side, armed with tin shields in the left hand and a number of tennis balls. The aim was to pick up any number of balls lying on the ground and then try and hit someone from the opposing team. If a boy got hit, he was out of the game. One had to be sharp and alert in order to avoid being hit while at the same time trying to hit as many of the opposing boys as possible. As you can imagine it was a very active game. We also played indoor games in the big pavilion at the end of our main sports field, where we had two billiard tables and a couple of carom boards. I began to learn how to play billiards, and soon it was my favorite indoor game. A Jesuit priest by the name of Father Rosney was in charge of our Middle Division. I remember other priests too, like Brother Peter, bearded and dark, who was the storekeeper. He was assisted by Brother Udoff, who was an excellent gardener. He looked after the school garden, which was full of beautiful flowers and much admired by everybody.

One day toward the end of summer, there was a great tragedy in the Middle Division. We had just finished our breakfast and were coming out of the dining hall when someone shouted, "Crosby is hanging in the bathroom!" There was some confusion, and soon Father Rosney was at the scene. He checked the bathrooms and after a while emerged from out of the fourth bathroom with Crosby in his arms. The boy was taken to the infirmary, and sometime later in the afternoon it was announced that he had died. We were told that it was not a case of suicide but an unfortunate accident, a practical joke that had gone bad. Crosby, it seems, had excused himself early from the dining hall and gone to the bathroom. Standing on the pot he had tied one end of a rope to a beam in the bathroom and made a noose with the other end, which he put around his neck so that it would appear that he had hung himself. He had left the bathroom door unlocked, meaning to scare the pants off whoever entered first. Tragically he slipped on the pot and really hung himself.

That summer at school I had a rare visit from one of my family members. My second-eldest brother, Lo Nyendak, came to Darjeeling for a holiday and took me out for the weekend. He had rented a room in the house of a gentleman called Wang Babu, who was of mixed Chinese and Tibetan descent. When my brother came to get me he was wearing a short-sleeved shirt and khaki shorts, in the manner of a British tea planter. I thought the outfit looked odd on him since I'd only ever seen him in Tibetan clothes in Lhasa. He carried a long Chinese bamboo pipe with a tobacco pouch attached to it. He couldn't speak English, but he knew a few words of Nepali. I later came to know that quite a few years earlier our eldest brother had put him in an English boarding school in Kalimpong called Dr. Graham's Homes. After a year he refused to go back, which is unsurprising as he hated to conform to rules and regulations. To my knowledge he was the very first Khampa boy to be sent to an English boarding school. I myself was the first Khampa boy to have been sent to and regularly attend an English boarding school. Though there were other Tibetan boys in boarding school before me, they all came from the elite families of nobility in Lhasa.

My school year soon ended, and once more I was back in Kalimpong. I found my brother Lo Nyendak still in Kalimpong when I got there, but he left for Lhasa after a couple of weeks. My cousin Gyurme was also in Kalimpong, and I was told my eldest brother, Lo Gedun, would be arriving in a month or so. I think business was going well because I noticed we had bought a new car, a beautiful blue Vauxhall of English make. However, I was more interested in my bicycle, which I rode everywhere since I had now become a capable rider. I even knew a bicycle trick or two, in imitation of the circus performers I'd seen. I also came to know that we would soon be shifting to a new house we had bought. The new house was farther down the main road, toward the market.

A month later my brother Lo Gedun arrived. He was not alone. He had brought with him a new bride for the Sadutshangs named Tseyang. Kunphel-la had gone to receive them in Gangtok. By this time travelers from Tibet, except for muleteers, came to India mostly via the Nathula Pass in Sikkim, as it was more convenient and closer to Kalimpong. Tseyang was very young, not more than sixteen. On arriving she had to go to bed at once; she had been badly affected by motion sickness.

That winter holiday was one of the very best for me, thanks to my bicycle. I enjoyed myself immensely, riding my bicycle all over Kalimpong. I often went as far as Ringkingpong, a small hilltop south of the town. I would also go out to the seventh mile, below St. Joseph's Convent and west of town, as well as the eleventh mile east of the town. Gradually I became more skilled and could ride without holding on to the handlebars. In the evening I often had cycling competitions on the lawn with Wangyal, our young assistant accountant, and sometimes with an acquaintance from outside. I loved showing off my skills to the rest of the household!

My brother and Tseyang, along with a few assistants and friends from Tibet, left for Bodh Gaya, Sarnath, and Benares on pilgrimage. Since none of them were fluent in English or Hindi, they had to engage a guide and an interpreter to help them. Not long after they left, my holidays came to an end. I handled all of the preparations for going to school without any problem, as I was now an old hand at it.

It was good to be back in school once again and to see my friends. In course of time I also made a few new friends. There were two Chinese boys, Tit Mun-chun from Calcutta and Leong, a day scholar whose family ran a hair salon in Darjeeling. Later Paul O'Sullivan, an Irish boy, and Ashley Moss, a Eurasian, were also added to the gang. My old Bengali friend Nath was still around, but he was a shy fellow and didn't mix with us very much. My Tibetan friend Shalo Tashi Norbu was also there, and now the two Yuthok boys had joined the Middle Division.

I got on fairly well in class, though I must admit I rather disliked Latin and English literature. My best subjects were mathematics, history, and geography, and I was all right at Hindi too. The top students in my class were two Bengalis, both with the surname Pal. They came first or second in nearly all subjects. The younger one was slightly brighter, and I would be amazed at how he could memorize virtually everything that was taught in class. I envied his brilliance. There was also a Parsi boy called Tata in my class who I think was a relative of the now-famous industrialists in Bombay. Overall, I stood about eighth or ninth in a class of forty, so I suppose I wasn't too bad. Reports in progress and general conduct were sent weekly to parents. These came in different colors with pink standing for good, green for satisfactory, yellow for unsatisfactory, and gray for bad. Three gray cards meant expulsion.

We boys knew World War II was going on in Europe and often heard about Hitler and his atrocities. That year the war became more intense, and with the Japanese moving into eastern India, India became affected. In school, we had to prepare for any eventuality. Many sandbags were piled up in the school quadrangle, and windowpanes were plastered with strips of paper to prevent flying or falling shards in case of bombardment. All the windows had to have dark blinds, which were drawn before the lights were turned off in order to create a blackout. There was a real danger of Japanese war planes dropping bombs on us. One afternoon we heard sirens sound far away in town, and all of us boys were rushed into the valley below the school to hide in the forest there. After about an hour the situation was judged clear, and we came back to class.

Early on in every school year we had a short Easter break, which I used to enjoy. That year our Middle Division organized a couple of treasure hunts. The treasure contained plenty of Easter eggs with lots of chocolates and sweets in them, so everyone liked these hunts. My group of friends, our "gang" as we liked to call it, agreed that whoever found a treasure would share it with the rest. That way everyone had a much better chance of getting something.

In general it was a custom for all schoolboys to share whatever goodies they had with the rest of the members of any special gang they belonged to. This applied even to things like condiments that one could bring into the dining room. I didn't have much to contribute, as there was no one at home to take the trouble of sending parcels of edibles to me every now and again. Some students would arrange to have extra milk and eggs for breakfast. Every morning a waiter, or "bearer" as we called them, would bring a large container full of eggs and put it on one side of a platform in the middle of the dining hall. The father-in-charge, who sat on this platform, would call out the names of the boys who'd ordered extra eggs so that they could come and get them. Some of my friends and I sat on a table near this platform. When a good opportunity arose, one of us would distract the good father's attention using some pretext, and then a boy nearest the egg container would quickly swipe one or two! We'd share it later among ourselves. The result of course was that the last boy coming for his egg would miss his share. But they hardly made a fuss, and we got away with our mischief.

I continued to enjoy playing various sports in school, including the shield game. When football season came I took part eagerly, and I was picked to play for the Middle Division team in the interdivision games against the Upper Division. I played left back, as I was capable of kicking with both left and right legs. I was proud of being on the team and of being able to wear a sports uniform for the first time. The school year passed quickly, and once more we were packing to go home. That winter I looked forward to spending the holidays in the new house.

When I reached Kalimpong the car took me to a yellow three-story building with a staircase in the middle. I was taken to the top floor and put in a room facing south, in front of the kitchen and to the right of the staircase. On the opposite side there was a large dining room. My room had no attached bathroom, and I had to use one of the two bathrooms attached to the two bedrooms on the middle floor. Each of the middle-floor bedrooms also had a room in front of them used as a sitting room. The ground floor had two large rooms, one each on either side of the staircase. The left was used an office, and the other was a storeroom.

It was not long into the holidays when I was told that I had to go and stay at the Himalayan Hotel with the Yuthok boys. Since the Yuthok parents could not come to India to spend the winter with their sons, they had requested my relatives to let me spend time with them. The three of us boys were accommodated in a room in a long, single-story thatched house made of bamboo that was near the main hotel building. The hotel was owned by Mr. Macdonald, a stout Scotsman in his late seventies with thick eyebrows. He had married a local Lepcha woman and had three sons, one of whom was in the army while the other two were tea planters.

He also had three daughters, who managed the hotel. Their names were Annie, Vicky, and Vera, but we called each of them Auntie. The house we lived in had three rooms with a small attached bathroom each and a nice veranda in the front. We occupied the middle room, Mr. Macdonald had a room on one side, and Auntie Vicky had a room on the other side. Aunties Annie and Vera lived on the hotel premises. Auntie Vicky's husband was in the army, Auntie Annie was a widow, and Auntie Vera never married.

Mr. Macdonald was a former civil servant of the British government and had served mainly under the political officer in Sikkim. The political officer in Sikkim was also in charge of dealing with all matters relating to Tibet and Bhutan. I believe in his later years Mr. Macdonald was posted in Yatung, Tibet, as the British trade agent. He was therefore familiar with Tibet and spoke some Tibetan. He often took us for walks and showed us his knowledge of Tibetan lama dances by performing right there in the middle of the road, much to our embarrassment! He was a very nice and gentle person, and all three of us liked him. Occasionally we even teased him. He in turn often liked to tease us and ask, "Which was born first, the chicken or the egg?" Whichever way we answered we were always wrong!

The Yuthok boys and I enjoyed our stay at the Himalayan Hotel. We were there for over two months. The town was only a kilometer away, so we often walked there. We managed to get hold of a bicycle each and rode everywhere. We even organized a couple of bicycle-ride picnics. We'd ask Auntie Annie, who had the main responsibility of running the hotel, to have the kitchen prepare us some sandwiches, and we'd ride off to Ringkingpong or up the hill, east of Dr. Graham's Homes.

It was now getting close to Christmas, and the hotel was making preparations with enthusiasm. We boys had never celebrated Christmas, but we knew that it was celebrated with an exchange of gifts. We had noticed that old Mr. Macdonald was wearing torn socks and decided to buy him a few pairs of socks as a Christmas present. We collected some money between us and bought three pairs. We gave them to him on Christmas Eve, making sure that his daughters didn't see us, as we thought they might think we were insinuating that they weren't providing their father with proper care and thus be offended. A week later it was New Year's Eve, and the hotel had a big party. The hotel was the only good one in town and was frequented by local bigwigs and British government officers such as the subdivisional officer, retired British government officials, British businessmen like Mr. Odling, and local grandees like Raja Dorji and his family members. In fact, nearly every British visitor to Kalimpong stayed there. At midnight the lights went off, everybody shouted "Happy New Year!" and there was a lot of hugging and kissing. We watched this scene quite enthralled, particularly at all the women kissing the men, and we made a lot of fun of them!

It was toward the end of January 1942 when one day we saw Aunties Annie, Vicky, and Vera all crying. We asked Mr. Macdonald what had happened, and he told us there was bad news about the war. Sometime ago the British had boasted about the biggest battleship they had ever built. They called it the Prince of Wales and said it was invincible to the Japanese bombing. No sooner had the Prince of Wales arrived in Singapore, we were told, than a Japanese suicide bomber dove into its funnel, and the battleship was sunk right there and then, much to the horror of the world and particularly the British. As it turned out, the ship was actually sunk by torpedoes dropped from Japanese bombers. Regardless, this was the saddest of news for British India, and it made everyone cry. World War II was raging on and spreading, but we children were unable to comprehend the misery and suffering it was causing to millions. Coming from Tibet, which was still quite isolated from the rest of the world, the great war did not affect me much.

The hotel had a couple of Nepalese gardeners. One of them was an amiable chap, and we often talked to him and admired his *khukri*, his curved Nepali dagger. We asked him to get us a small khukri each and told him that we'd pay him the cost. He indulged us and got a blacksmith to actually craft us three small khukris! This took a few weeks, but we were delighted with the result and took to tying the daggers around our waists whenever we went on a picnic. We also got the gardener to show us how to use these knives to cut bamboo and trees like he did. Our vacation soon came to an end, and I went home to make preparations for returning to school. The Yuthok boys stayed on at the hotel, as someone their father had appointed in Kalimpong was to come over and help them with their own preparations. When the day came, we traveled together back to school.

8. ST. JOSEPH'S COLLEGE, UPPER DIVISION

Before classes for the year began, we had the proclamation of ranks for the entire school in the gym, which also doubled as our cinema hall. I was promoted to class 4, and though I should have remained in the Middle Division in terms of class, I was sent to the Upper Division because of my age. It was a welcome change. Most of my friends except for the two Yuthoks were also put in the same division, so we were all happy. The three older Tibetans, George Taring, Dondrup Kapshopa, and Shalo Tashi Norbu, had all left school.

I made reasonable progress in classes, and in sports I continued to take interest in football. The Upper Division field was big and well laid out. Since it conformed to the size of a professional football or hockey field, it was borrowed many times for major matches played between teams other than those of our school. We had a beautiful, big pavilion at one end of the field, and from there we could watch all the cup matches. There were also billiard and ping-pong tables in the pavilion and a tennis court just outside it.

My friend Ashley Moss shared my love of football, but Paul O'Sullivan and Chun preferred hockey. My old friend Nath was nowhere to be seen that year. Perhaps he had joined a school in Calcutta; I never knew. That year we had a new Bengali friend called Ray, who was a class senior to me

At the wedding of Bhutan's Prime Minister Jigme Dorji at Bhutan House,
Kalimpong, 1942. Left to right: author, Rigzin Yuthok, George Taring, Lhundup
Dorji (in front of Taring), Charlie Dunn, Jigme Yuthok, Jigdal Densapa.

and very fat. Hence our nickname for him, Fatty Ray. I had by this time
learned to smoke. I suppose it started with trying to copy bigger boys smoking on the sly during the previous year. We boys thought smoking gave us a
manly air and indulged in it despite it being against the school rules. Ashley
and Paul weren't too keen on smoking, whereas Chun and I liked it. As for
Ray, he loved it! Whenever there was a break he would rush to the toilet to
have a few puffs.

It was toward the end of the cricket season when those of us who smoked
ended up facing a serious dilemma: we had run out of cigarettes. It was very
difficult to buy any without going to town, which we didn't get a chance to
do all that often. One Sunday we were permitted to go for a walk toward
Lebong Tea Estate, two or three kilometers from school. Besides having to
go in a group, there were no special rules beyond returning at a stipulated

time. Having no doubt grown desperate, Fatty Ray said he knew of a house along the way to Lebong where the owners were away. This was pertinent information, he told us, because he knew there were cigarettes in the cupboard. He suggested we break in and steal some. At first we hesitated, but eventually we gave in and went to the house. Ray, being familiar with the place, managed to open a window, and he, Chun, and I climbed in. Ashley and Paul stayed outside to keep watch.

We opened a couple of cupboards and soon Ray had found the cigarettes. There were tins of Phillip Morris cigarettes, fifty in each tin, lying in a neat row on the top shelf of a cupboard. We decided to take only two tins, though Ray complained that we should take more. Then we quickly got out of the house, a little apprehensive but excited. For the next hour or so we enjoyed our smoke, though we found these cigarettes stronger than the brand we bought in the market.

That summer our gang got into trouble. It happened on a holiday. Since it was a lovely day, and no particular program of games had been organized, we decided to sneak out of school and go to town for a horse ride. We quietly slipped out and first went to see our friend Leong at the beauty salon. We stayed there a short while and then went to an area called the Mall, where all the horses for hire were kept. We hired a horse each and rode around the hill leading to our school. On our way back to the mall, we met some boys who tipped us off that Father Barry was looking for the boys who'd sneaked away from school! Someone had snitched on us. We got off of our horses immediately and told Leong, who was with us, to take the horses back; we took off at a run to school. Having failed to catch us red-handed, Father Barry eventually returned to school in a bad mood. In the evening, at study time, he announced that he knew some boys had sneaked off to town. Unless they owned up, he said he'd punish the entire division by not showing the film we were supposed to see the next day. Not wanting everyone to suffer on our account, we were persuaded to own up, and so we went and apologized. We were duly punished by being barred from watching the film and were given schoolwork to do instead. No doubt a yellow card would follow in the coming weekly report.

That year the Puja holidays, lasting for about ten days, were very enjoyable. The priests would try to make it an enjoyable time for those of us who stayed back at school. We went on several picnics, one of which was for three days at Kurseong. We stayed in a house in the nearby forest that the Jesuits maintained as a retreat house. A river flowed down in the valley not far from us, and we took sandwiches and fresh lime juice and went swimming. The evenings were equally enjoyable, as there was a billiard table and music too.

After the Puja holidays we were kept busy preparing for our final exams, and by the end of November it was time to pack for going home. When I got home I found my brother Lo Gedun was there attending to business. His wife, Tseyang, had also come back from Lhasa and was learning English from a tutor. Our family had by now become close friends of the Raja Dorji family. Raja Dorji and his son were of very high social standing in that region and were extremely nice people too. Jigme Dorji, the eldest son, who would later become Prime Minister of Bhutan, was then a young and very active person, full of good humor. He had become a close friend of my brother Lo Gedun. Raja and Jigme Dorji thought that since Tseyang was so young, she should go to school to receive a more formal English education. Following their advice, it was decided that Tseyang would join St. Joseph's Convent the following March, when school reopened.

9. A VISIT TO LHASA

It was now six years since I'd left Tibet for India, and I was very eager to go back for a visit, though I knew the journey would be long and arduous. Having made up my mind, I asked my brother for permission. Luckily one of our managers was soon returning to Tibet with a large pack of mules, so it was arranged that I should go with him. I was thrilled, and for the next few days I was busy preparing plenty of warm clothing for the long journey, which would be very cold at that time of the year.

A week later I was on my way. I traveled to Gangtok by car and spent the first night there. Bapa Thupten, our business manager, had gone ahead two days prior and was already there. From Gangtok it took us two days to cross the 17,500-foot snowbound Nathula Pass into Tibet. I always walked at the start of the journey in order to get warm. Sitting on a horse for long periods could make your feet almost frozen. Bapa Thupten was an extremely good walker and used to walk for miles to spare his horse the burden of having to carry him. On the other side of the pass we were now in Tibet, and halfway down we stopped at a village called Chumbithang for the night.

The next morning we started early and reached Yatung, also called Chumbi Valley, a few hours later. While the rest of the caravan proceeded to our next stop, I went with an assistant to the office of the British trade agent as instructed by my eldest brother. There I met Rimshi Sonam Topden of the Libing family in Sikkim, who was a senior officer of the British political office in that region. I requested his help in obtaining permission to use the dak bungalows located at various stops along the route up to the town of Gyantse. Apparently my family knew this officer, and he readily arranged a permit for us to present at each of the rest houses I wanted to use. The British had built these bungalows as mail stops, for postal purposes, but they were also used as rest houses for their personnel traveling to and fro. These houses were well built, clean, and fitted with wood-stove heaters and toilets. Such facilities were not available at the Tibetan rest stops.

After spending a night at Gao, a ten-kilometer climb from Chumbi Valley, we arrived at Phari. As I mentioned previously, Phari, which is situated at an altitude of twelve thousand feet, is an important trade post through which every trader traveling to India or Bhutan had to pass. We now owned a house in Phari, so there was no need to look for lodgings. Our manager there, having been notified of our impending arrival, came to receive us a few kilometers outside of town, bringing plenty of food and tea for a picnic. We rested an extra day in Phari and then continued on our journey. Every day we traveled about eighteen to twenty kilometers, starting early around sunrise and stopping by early afternoon. We could have traveled more but had to give consideration to the animals, as they were carrying loads.

From Phari we took a shorter route leading to Khangmar, instead of going to Gyantse. We had to make four stops before reaching Khangmar, our last stopover at a dak bungalow. On leaving Khangmar we traveled eastward up to the shores of the beautiful Yamdrok Turquoise Lake, and there we spent the next three days circling this huge semicircular lake, much as I had done on my first journey to India over six years ago. Finally we climbed up to Gampa Pass and then descended to the foot of the mountain, stopping at Gampa Batsi for the night. The next day we crossed the big Tsangpo River and two days later we reached Lhasa at last.

My brother Wangdor and some other relatives were waiting to receive us at a place called Keltsen Luting, about four kilometers outside of Lhasa.

They had arranged tea and snacks for us in the courtyard of a house there. Everyone expressed their pleasure at seeing me after such a long time and now grown into a young man! On my part I was very happy to see my brother after such a long time. When we first met I hardly recognized him, and seeing him in monk's robes really took me by surprise. No one had informed me that he had become a monk. He had also grown into a healthy and sturdy young man.

When I reached Lhasa, another surprise awaited me. En route my brother told me that we had acquired another large house close to the old one, and that it was very nice. But I was not prepared for the huge mansion that I saw. It formerly belonged to a well-known Lhasa noble family called Khyungram, but it had been confiscated and put up for sale by the government; that's when we bought it. My cousin Sochö was at home, looking after business. His younger brother Gyurme was also in Lhasa but had gone on a brief business trip. I spent the first day taking a good rest, as the journey had been long and tiring.

The next morning, as was customary, the first thing I did was to visit the Tsuklakhang, the central temple built by King Songtsen Gampo that is the spiritual heart of Lhasa. I offered *khatak* greeting scarves and lit butter lamps to the beautiful image of the Buddha Shakyamuni enshrined there. Afterward I made similar offerings to other sacred images in the temple. My brother Wangdor returned to his monastery, as he had to attend to his studies. He was at the Je College of Sera Monastery, the second largest monastery in Tibet. He was studying under the tutelage of Sadu Geshe, our great uncle, who had obtained his advanced degree in Buddhist philosophy many years ago and who was now tutoring many students, mostly from Kham.

I began my holiday on the second day, touring our new house, which was built in the middle of a large compound surrounded by a boundary wall. The main entrance, set in this wall, had a big gate to the south of the house. Inside it, to the right, were living quarters for the gatekeeper and the groom. Also to the right, along the length of a stone-paved floor, were the stables. Farther down was a long row of rooms that included the kitchen, storeroom, and quarters for the servants. In the northeast corner of the

The Sadutshang house in Lhasa, 1950.

compound was an independent unit with four rooms built around a central courtyard. There was another similar independent unit in the northwest corner of the compound.

The gate to the main house faced east and opened out into a large courtyard paved with stone. Inside, there was a large storeroom and a few rooms for assistants on the right-hand side. Across from these, on the left-hand side, were two rooms occupied by our storekeeper, each with windows looking out to the front garden. Beyond the courtyard, facing the entrance, lay a large hall used for different purposes. This large hall was particularly useful for my great uncle, Sadu Geshe, as during Monlam, the Great Prayer Festival, the monks of all of the three largest monasteries in and around Lhasa congregated in the capital for about a month. Sadu Geshe, who had over a hundred students, could accommodate them here with ease.

The first floor of the house led to four bedrooms, one in each corner of the house. Two had attached bathrooms. All along the south wall was an open veranda, which was accessible from the two bedrooms. The bedroom on the northeast corner of the house was a special one, reserved only for visiting spiritual teachers of high standing. A connecting room with a skylight and a mosaic floor led to this special room. Mosaic flooring was unheard of in Tibet, and craftsmen from India had to be brought over to have one installed. The walls of the special room were painted with beautiful murals by Tibetan artists. Between this room and the northwest bedroom was a large shrine room; this was also an important room, as this was where all the religious activities of the household were carried out. Directly opposite this, facing the south side of the house, there was a corresponding large room used for receiving guests or else as a dining room for parties. Apart from these major rooms there were also smaller rooms that served as storerooms, a servant's sitting room, and a toilet.

The house was not only structurally sound but one of the very best in Lhasa in terms of planning, design, and wall paintings. All the larger rooms had no pillars but were supported instead by steel beams. Very few houses used steel beams because they had to be imported all the way from India across mountain passes and rugged terrain on the backs of pack animals. This made steel beams a very difficult and costly affair. These steel beams were cut into pieces six feet in length and then joined together in Lhasa with fishplates secured by at least a dozen nuts and bolts. In terms of safety standards, no more than five joints were advised. Undoubtedly the people who built this house had spared neither expense nor effort to make it one of the very best in Lhasa.

I didn't know many people my age in Lhasa. However, I did have two friends there from school, George Taring and Dondrup Kapshopa. They were both now in government service. I also knew George's wife, Betty Taring, whose Tibetan name was Tsering Yangzom. She had been in school with me in Lhasa. Both these young men came from noble families, as I mentioned earlier, and all lay officials in the government came exclusively from noble families. You could say it was their birthright. I managed to make some new friends that winter. Among them was Ragasha Sé, born of an ancient and noble family, who also happened to be the nephew of George Taring. We often went out together, visiting nearby temples and family friends.

One of my favorite pastimes in Lhasa that winter was going horse racing at a place called Choragya, close to Taring House and east of the city. Choragya was not especially created for horse racing. It happened to be a wide road about two hundred yards long that ran alongside the long wall of a big park called Surkhang Lingkha, which belonged to the noble family of Surkhang. Every morning about seven men, riding good horses, would come and participate in a race. We had about five horses at home, so I used to take the best one and go and join the race.

In Lhasa only cantering was popular, and new horses were often sent to be trained in it. The competition was usually for solo rides, and people watched to see how fast a rider could canter, how consistent he was, and how high the horse could raise its legs. Horses that could go fast all the way without breaking out of canter and that could raise their forelegs nice and high were considered the best. Many people tended to begin with a fast canter, which would often break into a gallop, an undesirable outcome. Occasionally two, three, or even four horses would race together. Sometimes some horses that were famous for their canter would make an appearance. Everybody especially enjoyed watching them perform. These races were gatherings where one talked of nothing but horses but where one also made new friends.

George Taring and Dondrup Kapshopa didn't have much interest in horses, but Ragasha Sé did, and he used to join me at the races sometimes. I normally did not race my horse more than three times in a day to avoid overtaxing the animal. As was the common practice, I used to send my horse early in the morning to the river and have it wade until its belly was submerged. I would let it remain there for about ten minutes. This was said to help reduce the size of the belly and give it a better shape. Sometimes I fed the horse tea leaves with the fodder the evening before a race because it was said to stimulate the horse and make it high-spirited for a few hours.

I visited my brother Wangdor at Sera Monastery a few times. Of course, before seeing him, I first went to pay my respects to my great uncle, Sadu Geshe. Sadu Geshe lived at Sera Chöting, which though being a part of Sera Monastery, was located away from the main monastery and perched high up on a huge rock. It had the most magnificent view of Lhasa, the Potala Palace, and all the surrounding mountains. Geshe-la asked me all sorts of questions about India and my studies in Darjeeling. He also offered me a delicious lunch of steaming hot meat dumplings, which he had his students prepare for me.

A couple of times I also visited my two great aunts who were nuns. They were both over seventy and had devoted a great number of years to religious practice. They lived in a small house they had rented, set in a quiet hermitage area called Chösang Ritö, where there were about four other similar houses. It was located high up in the mountains, about two kilometers away from Sera Monastery and an hour's ride from Lhasa. They were two very sweet old ladies who always talked about Buddhism and gave me spiritual advice. They also had an assistant living with them. She was also a nun, and they had her prepare vast amounts of food on my visits. They loved to press me to eat, and though I tried my best to please them, they were never satisfied, always complaining that I ate far too little!

My six-week holiday in Lhasa soon came to an end, and although my visit was not long, I enjoyed it tremendously. Once more I prepared for the long journey to India. I traveled the same route I took earlier, and this time it took me seventeen days to reach Kalimpong, since I skipped the day of rest in Phari. My journey was uneventful except that I got a chance to shoot a rifle that one of our business managers had. Once I took a shot at a fox we saw climbing a hill near Khangmar, but otherwise I just had some target practice at boulders on the hillsides. As we arrived in Gangtok it was good to feel the warmer weather, and I was able to enjoy a leisurely bath after several days. Shedding all the thick, heavy clothing, I felt physically light and refreshed.

10. BACK TO SCHOOL
IN DARJEELING

After making preparations in Kalimpong I returned to school in Darjeeling by myself in a taxi. All my friends were back, and it felt good to be with them once more. I was now in class 7, or Junior Cambridge, a crucial year. I studied hard that year and hoped that, with the help of some private tuition in the winter holidays, I could get a double promotion so that I could do my Senior Cambridge the following year. My aim was not only to save a year but to get into the Special Department, the boys of which had many facilities and liberties that were not available even to senior students of the Upper Division. They had their own private rooms and also shared a common room, which had a radio, magazines, and newspapers. They could go to town any time they wanted and without permission. Their classes were called lectures, and they could do their own private study anywhere they liked: in their own rooms, in the hall, or even out in the open. They ate with the teachers and the Jesuit fathers in a separate dining room. Though they wore the school uniform, their caps were of a different design and had a gold tassel on the top. They commanded respect from not only the school but from the teachers and the fathers as well.

World War II continued and became more intense. In school the senior boys were formed into cadets, and British army personnel came to train us in various military activities. We were given a rifle each, and twice a week for half an hour, we learned to march with a rifle on our shoulder. This became a routine affair but not a very popular one! Later we were also given bayonets fixed to our rifles and taught how to charge at an enemy. We were trained in throwing hand grenades, crawling under barbed wire, and shooting rifles, all of which we liked much better than marching. For target practice we were taken down to the forest below the school, where we used .22 caliber rifles. Toward the end of our training in late September, we were given a khaki military sweater each and were required to put on a display of what we had learned in front of the rector, teachers, and students.

The Puja holidays started in early October, and those of us staying back in school looked forward to enjoying picnics and films. During one of the picnics we were taken down to a large reservoir at Lebong tea plantation. Since it was a beautiful day, we were permitted to swim in the reservoir, which was about nine feet deep with water that didn't look all that clean. I knew how to swim and swam once or twice across the pool. Seeing my friend Chun standing at the edge of the pool, I went over to him and asked him to join me but he refused. So I gave him a shove and he fell in. To my horror I saw him going up and down in the water, struggling desperately and flailing his arms wildly about. I realized at once that he was drowning, and fortunately so did another boy already in the water, who swam to help him.

Meanwhile the others and I rushed to call the father on duty, who wasn't far away. The father arrived on the scene and immediately jumped in the water. Together with the boy already in the water, he managed to save my poor friend Chun. Needless to say I was immensely relieved and realized how foolish I had been in playing a potentially deadly prank. I at once apologized to Chun and the father, explaining that I didn't know Chun couldn't swim. Afterward we joked about it, but it wasn't funny at that time. Later, since I had a fair amount of money saved up, as a gesture of apology I invited all my gang members to lunch and then tea at the rooftop of Keventer's restaurant, a favorite haunt for tea and ice cream.

During those Puja holidays my friends Fatty Ray, Chun, and I had the misfortune to be caught smoking. We had just been given a special dinner called Bara Khana, or "big feast," and afterward we recklessly went for a smoke in the quadrangle. That's when one of the fathers happened to come by. He immediately handed us over to the father prefect, who gave us a good scolding and three canes each. In those days corporal punishment was an accepted thing in boys' boarding schools. It was nothing compared to what we had to endure in school in Tibet. Caning wasn't the end of our punishment. We were also each given a gray card that week. Fortunately for me no one at home understood the implications of a gray card, since they couldn't read English, so I escaped a rebuking at home!

I was doing satisfactorily in my studies, studying harder than usual for the double promotion. We no longer had to do Latin or Hindi, and I was permitted to take Tibetan as a second language. The school had arranged

St. Joseph's College football team, 1945. Author is fourth from left in the back row.

for a Tibetan teacher to come twice a week to give lessons. He was not a full-fledged Tibetan and couldn't speak Tibetan fluently. It seemed he had studied Tibetan in a monastery or with a monk because he could only write in the U-chen script, which is normally only used in printing. Back in Lhasa we were taught U-mé, the sort of cursive script used for writing, so it took me a little while to get used to writing U-chen. In the end I found the lessons useful and educative.

In sports I still continued to take great interest in football and was chosen to play on the B team. We played many matches, including interschool matches, of which the highlight was a match we won against Gothol's, another Jesuit school. I was proud to represent my school and wear the jersey of light and dark blue stripes. At the end of November I returned home quite confident that I would get good marks at the proclamation of ranks that was to take place at the beginning of the next school year. This time I went home with my cousin's son, Tsetop, who had joined St. Joseph's College that year. After only a year at school he was already nearly fluent in English.

When I arrived home in Kalimpong I found my brother Lo Gedun and his wife Tseyang already there. After a few days of rest I decided to go and see a Catholic priest I knew. I was hoping to get some additional tutelage. Father Stalkey lived in the parish above St. Joseph's Convent and agreed to tutor me on a few subjects. My brother had that very year bought a two-bedroom bungalow just a kilometer away from the parish, so it was convenient for me to go for my tuition everyday. I began to study diligently, as I was determined to achieve my goal.

11. TO DELHI WITH THE TIBETAN DELEGATION

Around mid-January of the following year, a delegation of Tibetan offcials arrived in Kalimpong, led by Dzasak Khemé Sonam Wangdi, who was a close friend of the family. He, his wife, and his brother-in-law stayed with us. The delegation was on its way to Delhi to meet Lord Waverly, the British viceroy, before proceeding to China to meet General Chiang Kai-shek, the head of the Chinese Nationalist government. It was primarily a goodwill delegation sent by the Tibetan government to extend greetings and to congratulate these two governments on their World War II victories. After discussing it with Dzasak Khemé, my brother made arrangements for me to accompany the delegation in a private capacity as an English interpreter. Although an English interpreter would not really be needed for China, Dzasak Khemé agreed to take me along on both legs of the journey. Despite the interruption of my study plans, I was excited at the prospect of this long journey to places I had never seen, and I was also grateful to my brother for creating this opening. He was farsighted enough to recognize this great opportunity for me in terms of both education and experience.

The delegation consisted of five members and was led by both Dzasak Tarkhang, a monk official, and Dzasak Khemé. They were accompanied by

Rimshi Khemé, brother-in-law of Dzasak Khemé. Dzasak and Rimshi are titles for the third and fourth levels in the government service. They were also accompanied by two junior officials named Yeshe Dargye and Dorje Changnöpa. There were also three other monk officials traveling with the delegation; they were on their way to China to replace the three representatives of His Holiness the Dalai Lama who were already there. My friend Phala Wangchuk was also among the party.

The entire group left Kalimpong by car for Siliguri and then proceeded by train to Calcutta, where we transferred to another train for Delhi. When we reached Delhi, the political officer of Sikkim, who was acting liaison officer for the delegation, had come to the station to receive us. Arrangements were made for our stay at a large official house in New Delhi, not far from the government secretariat and the viceroy's palatial residence. About three days after we arrived, the delegation had its official meeting with the viceroy. The delegation had brought a large number of gifts, and these gifts took quite some time to prepare for presentation on the final day. On arriving at the viceroy's residence, the delegation was received by the chief of protocol, and each member was led to prearranged seats. Phala Wangchuk and I, not being official members of the delegation, were stopped at the main gate. However, as I possessed a movie camera and was carrying it at that time, I bluffed my way in by telling the security officer that I was the official cameraman for the delegation and that Phala Wangchuk was my assistant! Since we were both wearing long, dark brown silk Tibetan robes, the officer was convinced and let us in without too much trouble.

As we entered we found ourselves in a huge hall with big pillars and a very high ceiling. On either side were many rows of chairs facing a long passage about twenty feet wide and forty feet long. The passage cut through the center of the hall and ended at the steps of an elevated platform on which stood two large and very grand chairs. To my inexperienced eyes it was as if I had arrived at the set of a majestic palace in some movie! I noticed our delegation was seated in the front row on the right side of the hall. There were many Indian government officials, some seated behind our delegation and some standing around at the back and talking. Phala Wangchuk and I moved near a pillar to the right of the hall.

After about ten minutes an announcement came from the left, the resonant voice declaring, "His Excellency, the Viceroy of India!" Everybody got up and looked toward the entrance on the left from where the viceroy made a resplendent entrance, with Lady Waverly on his left. They were accompanied by two smartly dressed aide-de-camps behind them and a host of other officials as well. As they passed by, everybody bowed. The viceroy and Lady Waverly went up the steps of the platform and took their seats on the large throne-like chairs. Almost immediately, the viceroy made a small gesture indicating that everyone could be seated. Then, if I'm not mistaken, it was the chief of protocol who came forward to the viceroy. Standing below the steps, he took a bow and introduced the Tibetan delegation.

The actual meeting took place at eleven o'clock that morning, and it was on this occassion that, for the first time, I witnessed the formal dress of the Tibetan officials, which was indeed grand! The two heads of the delegation wore colorful hats and long, golden silk Tibetan robes, over which they wore rich brocade sleeveless jackets. The junior officials were dressed similarly, but their clothes were plainer and of a more somber color. The monk officials all wore their simple, dark red monastic robes. Our delegation had previously been briefed about protocol and rose for the introduction. The viceroy then gave a short welcome address, which Raisahib Sonam Topden, the official interpreter of the political officer in Sikkim, translated into Tibetan. The head of the Tibetan delegation then thanked the viceroy for the welcome. Afterward he officially extended greetings and, more importantly, heartiest congratulations on behalf of both Regent Takdrak Rinpoche and the government of Tibet to His Majesty's government, with respect to the victory in World War II. The delegation then presented the gifts, which were brought in by a long line of bearers and paraded in front of the viceroy and the guests. The viceroy then expressed his appreciation and asked the delegation to convey his thanks to the regent and the government of Tibet for the generous gifts. He ended by inviting the delegation to tea at the Moghul Gardens. I might add that there was also already an official invitation to lunch for later in the day. I noted that during the entire ceremony the Tibetan delegation had to stand below the steps, facing the viceroy and Lady Waverley, who were seated about nine feet above them.

When the ceremony was over, the two dignitaries got up and left while the entire hall respectfully remained on their feet.

The Tibetan delegation was led to the Moghul Gardens, where tea was laid out. After a few minutes the viceroy and Lady Waverly appeared, and an informal tea was served. The political office and foreign ministry personnel were there, ready to provide the delegation with various information regarding Indo-Tibetan matters and so on. I accompanied our delegation to the Moghul Gardens and took some pictures. After tea Lord and Lady Waverly excused themselves, and the delegation was taken on a tour of the beautiful gardens. Afterward, they were ushered into a drawing room, from which I and other members of the press were asked to leave. The delegation returned about two hours later.

During our stay in Delhi I recall clearly that our delegation called on the Chinese ambassador to India. Our representatives must have done so because we were on our way to China. I also well remember that we called on the American ambassador, Mr. Charles Bowles, and conveyed our government's congratulations to him on his country's victory in World War II. He was also presented with gifts from the Tibetan government.

I once more attended in the capacity of cameraman. A few sightseeing tours notwithstanding, the delegation was invited to one particularly interesting event: a military tattoo at the newly built stadium across from the India Gate. Phala Wangchuk and I did not receive any invitations, but we were not deterred. Being a young man, I was very eager to see the show. We wore our silk Tibetan robes, and at the stadium we walked in confidently behind the rest of the delegation; nobody stopped us! Once inside, naturally we didn't have any seats, whereas our delegates were shown to their seats in the gallery by the hostesses. We just stood by, leaning on the gallery stand, and when a host or hostess appeared asking us for our cards we feigned ignorance of English, and gestured to convey that we were waiting for someone. Once they believed that we couldn't communicate they left us alone, and we had a wonderful time watching the entire superb performance, little hampered by our lack of seats. There were military parades, motorcycle-riding stunts, camel and horse cavalry displays of skill, airplanes flying overhead, soldiers dropping in parachutes, and infantry with cannons and machine guns, which they fired.

12. A BRIEF STOPOVER IN BOMBAY EN ROUTE TO CHINA

The official visit was over, and while most of the delegation proceeded to Calcutta after a few days of pilgrimage in Bodh Gaya, the Khemés decided to go to Bombay for five days and took me with them. They were not going for any particular reason but just to visit; it was a famous city, and few Tibetans had ever been there. We had also never seen the ocean, so we chose to stay in a hotel on Marine Drive, right across from the Indian Ocean.

The government officials in Delhi must have informed the state government in advance because upon our arrival, the governor of Bombay sent us an invitation to lunch for the very next day. As such, on the second day of our visit two cars arrived and brought us to the governor's residence, which stood in a beautiful location and had the most exquisite garden. The house was built on a piece of land projecting out into the water, and so we appeared to be standing over the sea. Down below we could hear the waves beating against the rocks on the edge of the shore. At lunch the governor was accompanied by his family, and we were the only guests. First, tea was served in the mansion. This was followed by lunch an hour later in a beautiful gazebo overlooking the ocean, with windows all around. While we dined, a band sitting on a raised platform nearby played music for us. We had a delicious lunch, and the governor and his family were very friendly and hospitable and curious about Tibet. The governor's son, a tall, young gentleman in uniform, told us that he was in the navy, and the governor suggested that he take us for a boat ride the following day. Dzasak Khemé readily accepted the invitation, and it was arranged that we would be picked up at two in the afternoon.

Unfortunately, by evening I was feeling feverish and unwell. The next morning since I hadn't improved, I had to write a note explaining my absence, and the Khemés had to go without an interpreter. They came back about an hour and a half later, and we had a good laugh over their account of how they tried to communicate to their host through plenty of smiles, gestures, and signs; some of these were very comical, to say the least! However, despite the lack of verbal communication, everyone got along fine. The gentleman who brought them back kindly offered to arrange medical help for me, but I declined as the medicine the hotel had provided had already begun to make me better. The Khemés were very anxious about my health, not least because they were completely helpless without me in communicating with non-Tibetans! Fortunately I was better the next day, and we were able to go on a shopping trip before finally departing for Calcutta by train.

We traveled first class and had a whole compartment to ourselves, so the journey was pleasant. In those days a journey by first-class train was very comfortable, with excellent meals. On arriving in Calcutta we went straight to the guesthouse of the Chinese consulate, where we found the other members of the delegation already present. We stayed in Calcutta for about ten days, during which my brother Lo Gedun came down from Kalimpong to visit us. Arrangements for the onward journey to China were being made by the Chinese consulate in conjunction with the Chinese trade agent for Lhasa, who had come to Calcutta for that purpose. Later we were also joined by Gyalo Thondup, elder brother of His Holiness the Dalai Lama, and his brother-in-law Phuntsok Tashi Taklha. I came to know that from Calcutta onward, the Chinese trade agent was to be the liaison officer for the Chinese government; he was to escort us to China.

13. TO CHINA WITH THE TIBETAN DELEGATION

We finally left for China in the first week of March 1946. The Chinese had chartered a Dakota plane, and the entire party consisted of about twenty-five people, including the servants. The plane appeared to be a military aircraft and had no individual seats like a regular passenger plane. Instead there were two long steel benches on either side of the fuselage, and all our luggage was piled up and strapped down in the middle between them. The interior of the plane was neither heated nor pressurized. As it flew higher and higher it became colder and colder, and our eardrums felt like they were bursting, unless we stuffed them full of cotton. Our first stop was at a remote spot in upper Burma, two hours from Calcutta, where the plane refueled and where we were served breakfast. Then, after a three-hour flight, we reached Kunming, the economic center of China's Yunnan province. We spent the night there and left early next morning for Nanjing, China's capital at the time. We reached Nanjing in three hours.

At the airport we were received by His Holiness the Dalai Lama's representative and some protocol officials of the Chinese government. Then we drove straight to a two-story building with a courtyard in the center that was to be our residence for many months to come. The entire compound was surrounded by a five-foot wall that provided security and privacy. The liaison officer lived in the building and had his office there. Also living in the building was an old Chinese lady whom we called Gyamo Achala, meaning our "Chinese older sister," who acted as interpreter. She had lived in Tibet for many years and spoke excellent Tibetan. While we were there two military jeeps along with their drivers were put at our disposal.

The weather in Nanjing was still quite cold, so to keep from sitting still, I took to walking around the city and the surrounding area. I found we were in the suburbs of Nanjing and that, though there were some residential houses nearby, most of the land was agricultural. Not far off there was a road under construction, and the labor force was made up entirely of Japanese prisoners of war. They were still wearing their military uniforms, and their caps were familiar to me from films I had seen of Japanese soldiers. Once when I passed by, the Japanese laborers bowed to me, though I couldn't understand why. Later on in my life I was often mistaken for being Japanese, so perhaps these men also mistook me for one of their countrymen.

The representative of His Holiness the Dalai Lama came over every day for frequent meetings. Gradually I came to know that our stay in China was going to be a long one, as there appeared to be difficulty in getting an appointment to meet General Chiang Kai-shek. In view of this, Dzasak Khemé and other members of the delegation decided to have Western clothes made, as Tibetan robes would be very uncomfortable during the summer months when the heat, we were told, could be very intense. However, since I myself already had plenty of Western clothes, I didn't need to add to my wardrobe. When we went out to shop or to dine in a restaurant, I became aware of the state of rampant inflation present in the country. The value of the yuan dropped virtually every day. When we first arrived, the exchange rate was 500 yuan to one Indian rupee. Only denominations of 500 or 1,000 yuan were counted, and all smaller denominations were simply tied into bundles of 10,000 each. It meant that when we went shopping we had the cumbersome task of carrying a bag full of paper currency along with us. Sometime later, the notes of small denominations disappeared altogether, and even 500-yuan notes became worthless. Then it was primarily the 5,000 and 10,000-yuan notes that could be seen in circulation.

A couple of weeks passed by, and still the delegation wasn't able to get an appointment to see the president. In the meantime they called on a few influential ministers, among whom was the president's brother-in-law, who was also minister of finance. We finally got an appointment about the third week of our stay. All of us attended, including Gyalo Thondup, Phuntsok Tashi Taklha, Phala, and myself, though none of us were part of the official delegation. We were taken to the official residence of the general of the armed forces, and while the meeting took place with the official delegates, the remaining four of us were ushered into a large drawing room to wait.

Lunch was served directly after the meeting. The famous Madame Chiang Kai-shek was also present, and she sat next to the heads of our delegation, exchanging pleasantries with them with the help of an interpreter. The president, dressed in full uniform, sat with Mrs. Khemé to his right,

Tibetan delegation to China, 1946. Formal portrait with General Chiang Kai-shek. Author is in the back row on the left. Gyalo Thondup, the Dalai Lama's brother, is in the front on the right.

followed by Gyalo Thondup. Lunch lasted for about an hour, followed by a group photo on the steps of the main entrance. I noted that the general always wore a long cape over his uniform, which I later heard was bullet-proof. All this experience was most interesting and educational for me, a Khampa boy not yet out of his teens.

It now seemed certain that we would have to stay in China until the winter. The National Assembly was going to convene in November, and the president and his government strongly urged the delegation to witness the winter session. Meanwhile the entire delegation was invited on a tour of well-known cities and other places of interest. The first place we visited was Shanghai, the commercial center of China and an overnight journey by train. Although I had seen large cities like Calcutta and Bombay, I found Shanghai to possess a charm of its own. It even had a road called Tibet Road!

Next we visited Hangzhou, a beautiful town with parks, large lakes, and a long range of hills in the background. There were several Buddhist monasteries built on these hills, and we visited some of them. Since Hangzhou was noted for its manufacture of silk, we visited some silk factories, where some of China's most beautiful silk products were made. One particular factory made Tibetan Buddhist *thangka* wall hangings, and I took the opportunity to buy some.

We went back to the Shanghai area to visit what was referred to as Nan-hai Potala, which was the southern end of a small island. The island itself was called Mount Putuo, or sometimes Mount Potalaka. It had striking hills and forests and was not only a center of retreat but also turned out to be a little vegetarian kingdom. We visited three to four temples, and in one of them we were served a grand lunch with a great many delicious dishes of what looked to be beef, pork, and chicken, along with a variety of vegetables. Later on I was amazed to find out that what had appeared to be meat was actually made solely out of flour and milk products. The temple cook was no doubt a true master at his craft.

The rest of the delegation went back to Nanjing, but Phala and I stayed back a couple of days to receive and pack some goods. When we reached Nanjing early in the morning, we didn't find anyone to meet us, so I asked Phala to mind the luggage while I phoned for a car. But when I returned ten minutes later I found a crowd of people clustered around our luggage and no Phala to be seen! A man in the center of this crowd seemed to be in charge, and he began to ask me a lot of prying questions. By this time I had picked up some Chinese, and I tried to the best of my abilities to explain to him who we were. I felt I wasn't getting very far and asked if anyone spoke English, but no one did. However, someone ran off and brought back a gentleman who could speak English; then I was able to explain exactly who we were and why we were in Nanjing. I learned then that the man asking all the impertinent questions was from the intelligence department. He had questioned Phala because he found him to look very much like a Japanese man, but Phala didn't respond and instead walked away. Later I found Phala outside the station and asked him why on earth he walked away. He told me that the man was talking a lot, and everyone was looking very hostile, so he got nervous and just walked away! I teased Phala about his behavior and told him he should be thankful because if I hadn't been there, he'd probably have landed in jail, where he would not only suffer an ordeal but be embarrassed too!

It was now summer and the weather was getting very hot. In the meantime, on the special advice of the president himself, Gyalo Thondup had shifted elsewhere to get schooling. There was some talk of us moving to a cooler place to avoid the heat and to sightsee. One evening we were in the midst of a game of mahjong when Mrs. Khemé complained of a headache and retired to bed. We continued with the game for half an hour more while Mrs. Khemé took a Chinese herbal-medicine powder for her headache. This brand was normally very effective, but this time it didn't help. She got worse and started feeling feverish and restless, and the liaison officer was asked to call a doctor.

The doctor came around ten o'clock that night. He gave her some medication for the fever and asked us to call him if she wasn't better in two hours. Not only was she not better after two hours passed, but she had grown worse and become almost delirious. The doctor was called again, and when he came this time he was joined by two other physicians who were endorsed by the president. There was considerable consultation between them, which made me realize that there was something seriously wrong with Mrs. Khemé. She was now in a lot of pain and had a high fever. The doctors said she might have had a brain hemorrhage and nothing could be done until the fever was brought down. They prescribed ice packs and arranged for a nurse to monitor temperature every half an hour. We were now all very agitated, and Phala and I stayed by her bedside to help the nurse. No matter how much ice we used, we simply could not control the fever. I watched in dismay as her temperature gradually climbed. After two hours more her temperature reached 105°, and Mrs. Khemé became delirious. After only another two hours it reached 108°, and she went into a coma. We were all very apprehensive and fretfully discussed the situation. Finally, as a last resort, we decided to call the American military headquarters and seek their help. At that time General Marshall was posted in Nanjing, and he sent over the best doctor they had. The military doctor examined the patient and said the very same thing the other doctors had said: we had to bring down her temperature first. He also found the patient had become dehydrated and injected two large bottles of glucose. Other than that, there was nothing he could do.

It was early the next morning, around six, when I saw her head move slightly, give a sudden jerk, and then fall to the left. I quickly called the nurse, who pronounced the patient dead. Phala and I were the only ones in the room. We could hardly believe it and didn't know quite what to do. Finally Phala went to inform the monk official who was head of the delegation and asked him to break the news to the Khemé family.

Dzasak Khemé and his brother-in-law were heartbroken when told the news. Both were so grief-stricken that they fainted and their bodies became immovably stiff. Some senior members of our delegation knew how to treat this with Tibetan herbal medicine they had brought with them. They burned the herbal powder on a fire, and when the smoke was put near the noses of the two gentlemen, they inhaled it and came to with a start, regaining consciousness immediately. Using a Tibetan technique, hot butter was applied to the crown of the head, palms of the hands, and soles of the feet. This treatment is a tremendous help in preventing fainting spells. Having never been in such a situation, I was absolutely amazed at how people could be so strongly affected by the death of a loved one. I felt very sorry and also sad for the Khemés, who were very kind people indeed.

Had the tragedy taken place in Lhasa there would have been more relief for the family as many religious rites could be performed to their satisfaction. In China this was not possible in the same way. The body was kept in the room for three days while certain religious rites were performed, and on the fourth day Mrs. Khemé was cremated. The liaison officer, on his own initiative, had arranged some twenty Chinese professional mourners, who accompanied us to the cremation ground. These people were clad in white with sackcloth covering their heads, and they made a dreadful noise with all their wailing. Such practices were normal in China, but I found it all rather distasteful. At the cremation ground Phala and I represented the Khemé family, and there were a few other junior officials too.

According to Tibetan custom, religious rites and special prayers for the deceased begin on the seventh day and last for seven weeks. This forty-nine-day period is considered vital. Being the time of the intermediate state between death and rebirth, the deceased must be exhorted to maintain the right frame of consciousness in order to gain a positive rebirth. Immediately after Mrs. Khemé passed away, we were very concerned about the physical health of Dzasak and Rimshi Khemé, as they could neither eat nor sleep properly. We feared they might go into a deep depression, as every time they even saw an article belonging to Mrs. Khemé, they were reduced to tears. However, as the weeks passed they gradually improved, and they began to spend a great deal of time in prayer.

As soon as the rites of the forty-ninth day were over, it was decided that the Khemés should go to a resort to convalesce, and Beijing was chosen as the most suitable place. After arrangements were made, six of us—Dzasak and Rimshi Khemé, Phala and I, and two servants—left on a long train journey to the north. When we arrived at the station, we were received by a government officer and taken to a pleasant single-story house with a garden, right in the heart of the city. It was around late July, and the weather was pleasant and cool after the exacting heat of Nanjing.

Beijing was not very big at that time. It was clean and beautiful, not congested like Nanjing. There were many houses with gardens and long avenues with trees planted on both sides. We spent a leisurely time there playing *mikmang*, a Chinese game similar to chess, and occasionally going out to visit parks or to tour famous places like the emperor's palace. Phala and I, being young, used to go out more than the others, often on shopping trips, as we found many things we couldn't get in Tibet. Beijing in those days didn't have many taxis, or many motor vehicles at all for that matter, but there were plenty of cycle rickshaws that we could hire. After a month, the Khemés had recuperated well and were almost back to their normal selves. However, we stayed on for one more month before returning to Nanjing. Once we finally returned to Nanjing, the rest of the delegation welcomed us back. They were pleased to find the Khemés had recovered so well.

We continued to wait in Nanjing for the National Assembly to convene. We had nothing important to do in the meanwhile, so we used to frequent the many tea shops in the city in the evenings. Once we went to see a Chinese opera performance by the famous actor Mei Lan-fang. He played the part of a lady and was impressive in his portrayal. One thing quite noticeable on our return was the rampant inflation. One Indian rupee was now not 500 but 5,000 yuan! According to the newspapers gold prices were soaring because of the staggering inflation. It was rumored that the finance minister himself was buying gold in large quantities, knowing that the Chinese currency was becoming worthless. We had to now carry a small suitcase of paper currency when we went shopping or to a restaurant!

By early November, as the date drew near for the National Assembly to convene, we began to see some new Tibetan faces in town. They were Khampas, Bapas, and Amdowas from northeastern Tibet. They were guests of the Chinese government and had been invited to attend the National Assembly. The most prominent among them was Geshe Sherab Gyatso, one of the most accomplished scholars of Buddhist philosophy, who was famous for being able to compose poetry on any subject. His knowledge of literature was unsurpassed. He had many students from among the nobility in Lhasa, and the Khemés were well acquainted with him. They took me to visit him once, and Dzasak Khemé requested Geshe Rinpoche to compose a poem on each of our names. Amazingly he did this with great ease and delivered the poems extemporaneously there and then.

The day of the National Assembly finally came. That morning all of the

members of the delegation dressed in the traditional robes of Tibetan officials and were escorted by a few Chinese representatives to the meeting.
Phala and I also went along and were seated in the public gallery, whereas
the delegation sat in the observers' gallery. We returned after only a couple
of hours, but the delegation continued to attend the Assembly sessions for
several days. It was not made clear to me what instructions our delegation
had from the Tibetan Government, but they kept in close contact with
Lhasa by means of coded wireless messages.

Even after the Assembly we continued to stay on for another three
months, mostly in Nanjing but with a visit or two to Shanghai. I was now
getting anxious that I might not be able to return in time for the start of
the new school year. Finally we left for India in the first week of March. The
Chinese government provided the delegation transportation in a special aircraft: a four-engine Constellation, which the Chinese had newly acquired.
It was one of the most modern commercial aircrafts of its time. It had a
pressurized cabin and was soundproof, making it a lot more comfortable
than the Dakota of the earlier journey. The return was a direct flight, and
in five hours we were at Dum Dum airport in Calcutta. Once more the
Chinese consulate was our host. After a few days of rest, we at long last
proceeded to Kalimpong.

14. BACK IN KALIMPONG

It had been exactly a year since I had left for China, and I was glad to be back home. My eldest brother and his wife, Tseyang, were both home in Kalimpong, along with my eldest cousin, Sochö, who had come on pilgrimage. I came home determined to go back to school, but it turned out that this was not to be. My relatives were very grim when I met them, and I soon learned of some unfortunate incidents that had taken place in Lhasa. They explained to me that the former regent Reting Rinpoche, who was Tseyang's maternal uncle, had been arrested by the Tibetan government under the regency of Takdrak Rinpoche. The five thousand or so monks of Sera Monastery had risen up in armed rebellion, for Reting Rinpoche had received his monastic education at Sera. The government quelled the rebellion but also started retaliating against suspected allies of the rebels. Since we were connected through marriage to Reting Rinpoche, our family became unfortunate suspects. My cousin Gyurme had been arrested, and our house in Lhasa was put under government seal, with soldiers guarding it twenty-four hours a day. In spite of this, some two to three hundred monks from Sera came and raided the house in the hopes of obtaining arms and ammunition, and this added to our already existing problems. Being a big trading house,

Reting Rinpoche, regent of Tibet 1934–41.
He recognized the present Dalai Lama in 1939.

we always kept a few dozen guns on hand for the protection of our traders whenever they had to go to remote areas on business.

My relatives were now apprehensively looking for some means by which our family members might be released from custody. They were, of course, also looking to redress this gross injustice against us, as we had nothing to do with the Sera rebellion. My family sought the advice of Dzasak and Rim-shi Khemé. Meanwhile, a Tibetan delegation to the Asian Conference in

New Delhi arrived, led by Theiji Sampho. At that time India was very near to getting full independence from British rule, and the Indian Congress Party, led by Pandit Jawaharlal Nehru, called the conference to exchange ideas about India's future. The Khemés, Theiji's in-laws, were able to get some honest firsthand information about the latest news from Lhasa. After being apprised by the Khemés, my cousin and my brother discussed the pros and cons and finally decided that they should both return to Lhasa. They asked Dzasak Khemé, who was highly educated and capable, to draft a suitable appeal and then left at once, not wanting to waste any more time.

In view of all these developments, I was asked to abandon the idea of returning to school and to instead take responsibility for the family business in Kalimpong. Given the seriousness of the situation, I had little choice but to accept the wishes of my elders. I had no idea at that time, but I believe the Khemés and other officials of the delegation also came to know, possibly through wireless messages, of further serious developments in Lhasa, for the Khemés and the rest all left straightaway. Tseyang was left behind in Kalimpong as a precautionary measure, as the situation was volatile.

While we waited anxiously for news from Lhasa, I didn't have much difficulty in adjusting to my new duties. My brother had given me a good briefing before he left. Besides, my working knowledge of Tibetan and good command of English made my work easier in all respects. It didn't take me long to become familiar with the wool business.

We were now exporting wool directly to the U.S.A. and to England. Our secretary, Kancha, was still with us, and he briefed me on the foreign contacts we had as well as those we had in India. When I went through some of his correspondence, both older and more recent, I realized with some embarrassment how poor his English was! My unwitting relatives, having no clue when it came to the English language, simply signed their names on them. Our buyers in the U.S.A. and England must have had a thoroughly difficult time trying to decipher them! At any rate, I now drafted all the letters myself and made Kancha type them out. Our accounts were all kept in Tibetan, and for that purpose we had three accountants who kept the books and who also dealt with Tibetan correspondence. I had no problem supervising this team of employees thanks to my years of schooling in Lhasa.

The main Tibetan business houses dealing with the export of wool and the import of Indian commodities were Pandatsang, Sadutshang, and Retingtsang. Then there were about five or six Indian businessmen who were our counterparts in the wool trade. Mr. Odling, a veteran British soldier who had lost his left foot and now ran a handicrafts production house, acted as agent for the foreign wool buyers, especially the British. I kept in constant touch with all these associates.

The majority of our wool was obtained by sending traders to all wool-producing areas in Tibet, where they bartered other commodities for raw wool. No doubt Pandatsang and Retingtsang did likewise. The best quality wool came from eastern and northern Tibet. Wool from western Tibet was shorter in hair length and was therefore considered a lower grade. Many smaller Tibetan traders, who collected wool and dispatched it to Kalimpong, sold their wool to the highest bidder. If we had already made a prior deal

Khampa trading group with chief guest Dzasak Surkhang Surpa
seated in the center, 1940. To the right of him is Sochö Sadutshang and
to the left is Lo Gedun Sadutshang.

with one of our foreign buyers, then we purchased large volumes of wool from suppliers and traders both in Tibet and in Kalimpong. Many of these smaller traders sold us their wool because of the good credit we gave them and because of our reliability in other business dealings. We also gave them the option of taking their payment in Tibet, instead of in Kalimpong, if they so desired. All the Indian businessmen were Marwaris, originally from Rajasthan and famous for their shrewdness and business acumen. They were also said to be not entirely ethical in their approach, and we Tibetans, who thought of ourselves as simpler people, felt we had to be very careful when dealing with them. It was said that they even went to the extent of bribing the postman to show them telegrams sent to other businessmen so that they knew the kind of offers that were being made.

By the end of April the wool business would wind down for the year, as the wool supply from Tibet came to a standstill. We would then have to speed up the sorting and packing of wool in bales so that everything could be shipped before the summer heat set in. Everything was dispatched by ropeway to Gelkhola and then shipped by rail to the Calcutta docks. From there it was all finally sent by sea to the respective destinations. We had an agent in Calcutta who took care of all these proceedings.

In the summer, though there was a lull in the wool business, we were kept busy trading in other commodities like textiles from India, for which there was a high demand in Tibet. There was also a demand for food items. Many types of consumer items were exported from India to Tibet, and of them rice was especially popular, since Tibet produced no rice at all. Tibet also produced no tea, whereas the beverage was drunk there in huge quantities. But the tea most in demand was not the kind produced in India but in China. Certain types of Chinese tea molded into ball shapes were even imported from Yunnan via Burma to Calcutta and thence to Tibet.

Transportation was the major problem for those in the export and import business in Tibet, as there were no motorable roads in our country. Everything had to be carried by mule, yak, or donkey. Coming into India from Tibet, the last stage for animal transport was either Gangtok in Sikkim or Kalimpong. Wool coming from distant eastern Tibet or nearby western

Tibet could take up to two or three months to reach these destinations. Communication by letter was made faster thanks to the postal service, but that too took weeks. By this time, however, the quickest means of communication had become the telegraphic service. India and other foreign countries used the Bentley code system that was common at that time. For Tibet we devised our own personal code, consisting of five-digit numbers. I remember improving our idiosyncratic system by substituting a single code number for frequently used words and phrases, or even recurring messages such as, "Pack mules with a total of 230 loads arrived safely and will return in three days." I was happy to contribute a little something to make our system simpler and more cost effective.

It was almost two months after my cousin and brother left Kalimpong that we got the good news that my cousin Gyurme had been released; it was a great relief to us all. However, Tseyang was still very anxious, as there was no news of the fate of her uncle, Reting Rinpoche. A month or so later we received the almost unbelievable news that Reting Rinpoche had passed away while under detention in a prison cell at the Potala Palace. The Tibetan government claimed that the death was from natural causes, but few believed this to be true; it was suspected that the former regent had been murdered by his adversaries. Poor Tseyang was grief-stricken, as she was very close to her uncle. I tried to console her as much as I could and encouraged her to put her mind into learning English, as that would distract her and further her education.

After the release of my relative, all the Sadutshang properties that had been seized by the government at various trade points in Tibet were simultaneously released and given back into our possession. It took several months for my absentee relatives to reestablish the entire business in Tibet, so I was left holding the fort in Kalimpong for virtually the entire year. During that time Tseyang and I became very close. Though two years older than me, she was nonetheless young and attractive. While I was engaged in business, she looked after our household affairs. She was kind and supportive, and in time we became attracted to one another. As the months passed our relationship became more intimate, and we began to cohabit. This was totally acceptable within our customs and way of life; polyandry was practiced in Tibet and especially in Kham, where it was not uncommon for the male members of a family to be away from home for long periods. In many Khampa families, the sons were nearly always on business, but each took a turn to stay at home with the bride and look after affairs at home. So there was really no need for more than one housewife in a family at any given time. My family is a prime example.

My brother Wangdor was a monk, and my brother Lo Nyendak had separated from the family. As I mentioned above, the family sent him to an English boarding school in Kalimpong called Dr. Graham's Homes, but he ran away from school. Prior to that they had tried sending him on a business trip to western Tibet with a manager, but that didn't work out either. Eventually my brother decided that he'd had enough of listening to his elders and opted to leave the family to live life on his own terms. This he did in a most colorful and flamboyant way, with many women in his life. It helped that he was dashing and well dressed. In the case of my immediate family, then, only two sons were involved with family affairs, Lo Gedun and myself.

Given this situation and the Tibetan custom of polyandry, when my brother Lo Gedun returned to Kalimpong in November and became aware of the relationship between Tseyang and myself, he accepted it as completely natural and encouraged us to maintain it.

Tseyang and I both waited anxiously to hear from Lo Gedun about details of the tragic death of Reting Rinpoche. The entire turn of events that had taken place was extremely sad and unfortunate. The Thirteenth Dalai Lama had given many indications that Reting Rinpoche would be the regent after his death. These indications have been documented elsewhere. Beyond that, Reting Rinpoche justified the Thirteenth Dalai Lama's choice through his achievements, the greatest of which was to successfully recognize the Fourteenth Dalai Lama and bring him to Lhasa. The enthronement of the Fourteenth Dalai Lama, who is in my mind the greatest of all of the Dalai Lamas, as the spiritual and temporal leader of our country was made possible thanks to Reting Rinpoche. It was a great disgrace that such intrigue should have taken place at all under the regency of Takdrak Rinpoche, who had been personally appointed by Reting Rinpoche himself. Takdrak Rinpoche was appointed to be acting regent for a period of only three years, but after this period was up, Takdrak Rinpoche refused to relinquish the reins of government.

Both the lamas were highly respected religious leaders, so undoubtedly it was the men serving under them, men who wielded a lot of influence, who were responsible for the misfeasance and for fueling suspicion and disharmony between the two regencies in order to safeguard their own personal ambitions. This led ultimately to the death of Reting Rinpoche, an incarnate lama who in his childhood had shown indisputably clear signs of being an extraordinary person. This evidence was on full display both in his native homeland and in the Potala Palace, at least until the advent of the Chinese occupation. The betrayal and the infighting between the two regencies precipitated the shelling of Sera Monastery by the Tibetan government and the massacre of many monks. Such a tragedy was unprecedented in the history of Buddhist Tibet. What was especially sad was knowing that people who were otherwise devout Buddhists, when blinded by political and material gain, could go completely against the teachings of the Buddha and disregard, without hesitation, all thought of karma, of cause and effect.

In the turmoil following the death of Reting Rinpoche, the Sadutshang family suffered significant losses in business, prestige, and property, for no just reason and through no fault of our own. When everything had subsided, the family decided to appeal to the government and request compensation for the extensive damage. The family proposed that the government indemnify us by exempting us from both tea and wool taxes for the next ten years. After due consideration the government rejected this request. However, they also said that they appreciated that the claims submitted over losses incurred had been genuine. In lieu of compensation they would, as a special consideration, allow one member of the family to join the Tibetan government as either a lay or a monk official. Now it should be noted that all government officials, barring a few monks, had to come from nobility. Therefore it was considered a great privilege to have one of our own enter this elite service as a lay official. This would also undoubtedly enhance our family's prestige.

My brother Lo Gedun related to me that the family was seriously considering the offer but had yet to come to a decision. He told me I might have to be the one to take up the post. Many of our friends, especially those from noble families like the Khemés, had suggested my name. In January Lo Gedun returned to Lhasa, and I continued to manage the family business in Kalimpong, waiting to hear the final outcome of this new development.

Before my brother left for Lhasa he told me that he had over two hundred loads of textiles stowed in Kathmandu. I should, he instructed, undertake a trip there in order to dispose of the goods. January and February were the peak months of the wool-trade season, and I was kept busy buying and shipping consignments to our foreign buyers. By mid-March I was more free, so I decided to make the trip to Kathmandu then. I traveled by train from Siliguri to Raxaul, which was the nearest railhead to the Nepal-India border. From Raxaul I had to board a local bus, which took me to Biratnagar, about fifty kilometers away. There I had to spend the night in a village hut, as no other accommodation was available. From Biratnagar, I was told, I had to either go by foot or hire a palanquin carried by two porters, as there were two big hills and no motorable roads. I didn't like the idea of humans carrying me, but I also didn't think I could withstand the journey on foot, so I reluctantly hired a palanquin.

Soon after Biratnagar we began the ascent, and I tried to walk as much as I could to spare the porters the burden of my weight. We reached our stop for the day in the late afternoon, and once again, with no lodgings to be found, I spent the night in a village hut, where I shared with the residents their simple meal. We continued on our long and slow journey early the next morning, descending halfway down by eleven o'clock. After that our descent was quick. By early afternoon we had reached the foothills, which ended my palanquin ride. Here I found a bus station, where I managed to get a seat on the bus that left once a day for Kathmandu. The journey was rough owing to the poor condition of the road, but it was a relief compared to the arduous journey from Biratnagar.

I reached Kathmandu after a two-hour journey and easily located the house of the Nepalese trader who had stored our goods in his warehouse. There I found Rapgay, our employee, had already arrived from Lhasa, having been sent by my eldest brother to assist me. The trader and his son welcomed me to their home and were very helpful to me, a stranger in their country, when I sought to dispose of my entire stock of goods to the highest bidder. Having accomplished my task, I stayed on for a few more days in order to visit two sacred Buddhist sites: the stupas at Boudhanath and Swayambhunath. The day I visited the latter I was exceptionally fortunate because I witnessed a religious function called Samyak that only took place every twelve years. After our pilgrimage, Rapgay and I left for India by the same route I had taken earlier.

When I reached home in Kalimpong, after a brief sojourn in Calcutta for business purposes, there was a letter and news from my brother Lo Gedun. He wrote to say that the family had decided that I should enroll myself as a lay official of the Tibetan government and that I should come to Lhasa by May, as they had arranged for my enrollment in June. I was not at all happy about this decision but was powerless to counter it. I wanted to continue my education in India. What's more I did not like the system of governance in my own country and so didn't want to be part of it. I did not like the idea of the nobility having a monopoly on government service, and I thought that the huge gap between the privileged and the common people was unacceptable. Now that I am much older and more mature, I am inclined to look more kindly at the way my country was governed then, which is the way it had been for centuries. At any rate, decisions had been made about my future by my elders with the welfare of the whole family in mind, and custom dictated that I had no personal say in the matter.

Meanwhile I continued with my responsibilities in Kalimpong. Around this time we got news of a big fire at the docks in Calcutta that had damaged the wool shipments of a few of the traders from our area. I quickly made inquiries, as we had consignments awaiting shipment and found that some of our consignments to New York had been damaged. So I left immediately for Calcutta to deal with the problem. Fortunately we always insured our shipments up to their destination, so our goods were fully covered. After about a week of completing formalities, the insurance company reimbursed us at the market rate for the full amount lost. I came to know that one Indian trader in Kalimpong by the name of Kaluram had lost over a hundred bales in the fire and, not being covered by insurance, his loss was total. Feeling bad for him, I paid him a visit and found him distraught.

Back in Kalimpong I took the necessary steps to hand over the business to one of our managers until my brother Lo Gedun arrived in late autumn. I also had to make preparations for Tseyang and me to travel to Lhasa. We had a fair amount of shopping to do, as henceforth I would be residing in Lhasa permanently. Finally we departed in early May via Gangtok, and since it was summer, the journey was not very arduous. The banks of the rivers were lush and green, so we picnicked a couple of times and even spent an extra day camping by a riverbank. This gave all of us, including the animals, some extra rest and a chance to wash our clothes and bathe in the river. It took us eighteen days to reach Lhasa. My brother Lo Gedun and about half a dozen other friends came to receive us five kilometers or so outside the city. They brought plenty of Tibetan tea and snacks, so we picnicked with them in an open field. We rode home along the Lingkhor, or the Ring Road, avoiding the streets of central Lhasa. When we got home I found our cousin Gyurme was there, but my cousin Sochö had retired from his worldly duties and taken up a spiritual life at the hermitage called Chösang Ritö beyond Sera Monastery.

PART TWO

Enormous, Imminent Changes in Tibet

15. AN OFFICIAL IN THE
TIBETAN GOVERNMENT

Soon after Tseyang and I settled down in Lhasa, I was briefed about the enrollment process into the Tibetan government and began preparing for it. First, numerous different types of official garb, both for winter and for summer, had to be tailored from silk. In addition, there were special sartorial requirements for my attendant, who had to accompany me whenever I went, whether to the office or to any official function. The customary requirements dictated the types and styles of dress, hats, and boots he was to wear. I was also required to have a horse. Even the horse had to be outfitted in a certain way, as prescribed by the government's protocol!

What concerned me more than being dressed correctly, however, was learning the general rules and regulations for the various official functions, not to mention the conventions of procedure and conduct. My relatives and I decided it would be best to request our good friend Dzasak Khemé to coach me in such matters, as I had already known him for a year in India and China and could discuss everything freely with him, dispensing with any formality. My brother-in-law Goshampa, who was a fourth-rank official, was also very helpful in many ways, but the education I received from Dzasak Khemé was invaluable.

I was told that before I could be inducted into government service, I had to complete one formality: I had to be admitted to the finance ministry as an apprentice. To be admitted I had to pass a test in accounting, which was very simple and easy. However, the accounting method utilized in this test was so unbelievably archaic that I had to actually spend time becoming proficient in this outdated system in order to pass an otherwise simple test. In this system, one had to do all the mathematics using dry seeds, stone chips, broken china, and the like to represent single units, tens, hundreds, and so forth. Additionally one had to have a partner, usually an official or a senior apprentice, who would read everything out figure by figure. One would select the traditional token that properly represented the dictated value and place it in front of his partner. One had to do all this while repeating the figures back in a singsong voice, ending each little numeric melody by intoning the Tibetan word for "plus," "minus," "times," or "divided by" in order to indicate the operation performed. The method was painfully slow, and it took me quite a while to learn the tune, as music is not one of my talents. However, the accounting in and of itself was so simple that the whole thing was really nothing more than a formality.

There were a couple of additional things in which I needed a little training and practice before I joined government service. Since I would be wearing a small round hat called a *boktho* as part of my official dress, I had to learn not only how to properly wear it but how to take it off and hold it in my hand in a certain way when bowing in salutation to senior officials. I also had to learn how to get off of my horse and bow down whenever I encountered a minister or a high lama on the road.

The date on which I would formally be enrolled into government service was determined by astrologers, who calculated an auspicious date on the basis of the stars under which I was born. Then an application had to be made to the Dronyer Chenmo, or the lord chamberlain, of His Holiness the Dalai Lama. For on the day one enrolled, one was formally presented to His Holiness, and the Dronyer Chenmo was responsible for conducting all functions where His Holiness the Dalai Lama would be present. This application had to be made six weeks in advance, but the approval letter came promptly. Meanwhile I had to formally apply for apprenticeship into the finance ministry. It was a relatively easy process. I had to offer Tibetan tea and *droma dresil* to the finance secretaries, to other officials under them, and to the other apprentices. This was followed by the accounting test I mentioned above.

The date chosen by the astrologer was the sixth day of the sixth month in the Tibetan year of the mouse, sometime in July 1948 according to the Western calendar. In keeping with the astrologer's calculations, I had to begin my first day of office by leaving my house at a certain auspicious time, which turned out to be before dawn. I was then to make offerings at the Tsuklakhang, Lhasa's central cathedral. I had three servants with me, who carried plenty of greeting scarves and a large pail of melted butter to place in the butter lamps as offerings. At the Tsuklakhang I offered scarves and butter lamps to the Buddha statue and other sacred images. I also made aspirational prayers, praying that I would be able to serve His Holiness the Dalai Lama and my country to the best of my ability. Then we proceeded to my enrollment ceremony at the Norbulingka, the summer palace of His Holiness, which lies about five kilometers west of Lhasa. On the way, my servants gave greeting scarves to anyone carrying water or milk, as these were considered auspicious signs.

My activities at the temple had to be completed early enough to allow me to arrive in time for the morning tea ceremony at seven. This ceremony was to be a departure from the normal daily tea ceremony that was attended only by monk officials. Special occasions like this one featured a large assembly of officials along with the predictable pomp and circumstance. I arrived too early and waited for a while at the main gate. Then, as had been prearranged, I went straight to the residence of the Dronyer Chenmo, who came from the noble family of Phala. The Dronyer Chenmo sent one of his attendants to take me to one of his secretaries. They in turn guided me to my seat as the officials began to assemble for the tea ceremony.

I was seated in the row where the fifth-rank officials sat, as I was to be accorded the fifth rank upon enrollment. My seat was in a courtyard facing a raised pavilion. In the center of this pavilion was a door that led to the main hall, the *nangmakhang*, which was reserved for ceremonies and meant for His Holiness, his tutors, and the highest of officials. On either side of this entrance sat huge monk-guards, or *zimgak*, on raised seats. Near the guard, on the left, sat a few third-rank officials, or *dzasak*, and facing them sat the fourth-rank officials, or *rimshi*. Near the right guard sat the Dronyer Chenmo and all his secretaries. Facing them, below the platform, sat the fifth-rank officials, both monk and lay, and I sat in the last row of this section. Behind us sat all officials of lower rank. Monk officials, even of equal rank, always sat ahead of lay officials.

I was well briefed about how to conduct myself at the ceremony. The procedure was not difficult to follow, but there was one part in it where I had to be sure to exercise utmost care. This moment was called *solsel*, the tea-tasting ceremony, where I would have to taste a sip of the tea made for His Holiness the Dalai Lama. This was done before the master of the tea ceremony poured the tea into His Holiness's cup in order to ensure that it contained no poison. First I was to take off my hat, place it on the floor a little distance away from His Holiness's throne, unfold a shawl from my left shoulder, and do three prostrations to His Holiness. Then I had to get up, place the shawl back over my left shoulder, kneel on my right knee, take my teacup out of a case strapped to the right side of the belt that hung around my waist, remove the cup from its silk wrapping, and hold it up for the master of the tea ceremony. The master of the tea ceremony would then proceed to pour a little tea into my cup and I was to drink it immediately. Only then would the master of the tea ceremony turn and pour tea into His Holiness's cup. During this moment, when His Holiness's teacup was being filled, I had to quickly wipe my cup clean with its silk wrapping and put it back into its case.

I was warned of the possibility of making a fool of myself during the solsel ceremony because of the hat known as an *arkong* that I had to wear. It was made of thin white cotton stiffly starched and pleated into a semicircular turban. The arkong derives from the days of the great Dharma king Songtsen Gampo, who wears one in all his representations. Since this hat was very light, the air stirred by the movement of my shawl being unfolded from my left shoulder or being placed back sometimes blew it across the floor, away from the spot near His Holiness's throne where it had been ceremoniously placed. Then the unfortunate owner would have to chase after it in a most undignified way, right amid this solemn ceremony! Such a hapless soul would be the object of gales of laughter and the mirth of all present. To add to the ignominy, the stiff hat always made a silly rattling sound when blown across the floor, which amused everyone all the more!

By a stroke of luck, and to my great relief, I was spared the solsel ceremony! When I was called into the inner chamber for the ceremony, one of the monk secretaries informed me that Ling Rinpoche, senior tutor to His Holiness the Dalai Lama, having been newly appointed the abbot of Ganden Monastery's north college, had also come that morning for his scarf presentation ceremony. It would be he who would perform the solsel. After Ling Rinpoche finished I was called up for my turn. I made three prostrations to His Holiness and then made a "mandala" offering that consisted of presenting him a statue of the Buddha, a scriptural text, and a small stupa: symbols representing the Buddha's body, speech, and mind. These were presented to me one at a time by a monk secretary to the left of the throne. As the secretary gave them to me, I accepted them with both hands, in which I also held a long white greeting scarf. I presented the three symbols in turn to His Holiness with bowed head and great respect, and His Holiness handed them over to another monk secretary to the right of the throne. Finally I placed my long white scarf on the table in front of His Holiness and took off my hat to receive his blessing, which he gave by lightly touching my head with his hand. I then walked along the wall of the chamber and went outside to take my seat.

According to custom, newly enrolled officials, as well as officials newly promoted, threw a party to celebrate. Many friends, both from noble families and from others, had come to offer congratulatory scarves, and they gave me many gifts. A record of the people who came and the nature of their gifts was kept, so that my family could reciprocate in kind when the occasion arose. This also helped us to draw up a list of the people I needed to invite to my celebration party, which would take place three weeks after the enrollment. The guests were divided into three groups: government officials, businessmen and acquaintances, and relatives and very close friends. I threw separate parties for each of these groups, so the celebration turned out to be a three-day event. What's more, they were all-day affairs, since Tibetan parties started with lunch, followed by afternoon tea, and ended only after dinner! In addition, relatives and close friends were expected to attend all three days.

Extensive preparations had to be made, and as was customary, a person with experience had to oversee the overall management of such affairs. Three chefs we called *gyasé machen*, meaning "chefs of Chinese cuisine," were hired for the occasion, and they brought their own assistants with them. Extra crockery and such were borrowed, as we expected to entertain between eighty and a hundred people each day. A messenger was sent door to door extending invitations; there was no custom of printed invitation cards. The guests were requested to check "yes" or "regret" next to their names on the list so we would have a good idea of how many to expect. It was customary to send these invitations three days before a party and then send a reminder by way of messenger on the eve of the event.

The first-day party was important for me, as all of the government officials who would attend would come on the first day, including some very senior ones. I waited at the door to welcome and invite the guests in, and in the case of very senior officials, I went to receive them at the outermost door, where they dismounted from their horses. I also accompanied these guests inside and to the sitting room. First tea was served to the guests. Tea was followed by lunch at one o'clock and dinner later, at seven. At both lunch and dinner, I as the host attended to each table where senior officials sat. After the first two or three dishes were served, I went table to table, took off my hat, bowed, and respectfully requested them to kindly enjoy the meal, urging them to do so without any hesitation.

After lunch the guests played mahjong, *bakchen*, which is a Chinese game of dominoes, or *mikmang*, the Chinese game similar to chess that I mentioned above. Those who didn't play these games, mostly the elderly, sat around and talked or walked about in the garden. Some guests listened to music or danced in one of the rooms in the house that had been prepared for that purpose.

In the evening, about an hour after tea, we served *chang*, a homemade barley beer. Hard liquor such as whiskey was never served at Tibetan parties unless there happened to be foreign guests. The party ended at about ten o'clock, and as the host, I went to the door to thank my guests for coming, offering a farewell scarf to each. Relatives and close friends who were coming the next day weren't given farewell scarves. The second and third days were much more informal and relaxed, but I was glad when the three days finally came to a successful end.

After I had finally completed enrollment into government service, a month passed, and I still hadn't been assigned any work. Dzasak Khemé, whom I frequently met in order to familiarize myself with official customs and regulations, told me I would definitely be put in the department that dealt with foreign affairs. His elder brother was the minister of foreign affairs. Not long after Dzasak Khemé's prescient words, I received instruction to report for work as early as possible at the foreign affairs ministry. Once more I consulted an astrologer for an auspicious date to join work, which turned out to be a few days later.

Dzasak Liushar and Dzasak Surkhang Surpa were the ministers in charge of the department, with the former being the monk official and the latter the lay official. In every department of the Tibetan government, posts were dually held by one monk and one lay official of equal rank. In my office there were eight other officials: two of fourth rank, three of fifth rank, and four of sixth rank, with the sixth rank being the lowest. (Second-rank officials in the Tibetan government were the *kalons*, or ministers, and the first-rank official was the prime minister, the *kalon tripa*. Above them was the Dalai Lama or a regent acting in his stead.)

On my first day of work in the foreign affairs ministry, I first went to pay my respects to the ministers. Afterward I greeted the rest of the officials with whom I was then given a seat. At the foreign affairs ministry, as with the other departments, office hours were between ten in the morning and five in the afternoon. However, most officials, including ministers, were rarely punctual. There was no lunch break, so we ate a big meal before coming to work and contented ourselves with the copious amount of Tibetan tea that was served in the office throughout the day.

My work consisted mostly of translation from English to Tibetan and vice versa. Occasionally I had to act as an interpreter when officials of the Indian trade mission called upon the ministers. I had almost no assignment that involved documentation, as my written Tibetan was not up to the required standard. I was conscious of this shortcoming and began to improve my classical Tibetan in earnest with much help from Dzasak Khemé.

There were only three foreign representatives in Lhasa: the Indian trade mission, the Nepalese representative, and the Bhutanese representative. The latter two were deemed less important and were dealt with by another office in accord with whatever understanding there was between our respective governments. Nevertheless, our office did maintain an official trained in Nepali, in case the need should arise. The Nepalese representative also had a slightly higher status than his Bhutanese counterpart. As for the Bhutanese, there was little problem with the language, as their script is the same as Tibetan, and in general their language is very similar to ours. At certain functions all foreign representatives were invited, and during those times a representative of the Tibetan Muslim community, a people descended from Kashmiri traders who had married Tibetan women and settled in Lhasa, was also invited. The lunar New Year, for example, was one of the occasions upon which they were invited to attend celebrations at the Potala Palace.

My work at the foreign affairs ministry was not difficult, and I really didn't have all that much to do. There was one urgent occasion, however, when I had to put in a lot of hours translating, hours that went well beyond office hours. One evening, late that summer, after I got home from work, a man came to see me saying he had been sent by the Chakdzö Chenmo, the principal assistant to the regent. At that time, the regent was Takdrak Rinpoche. The man held in his hand a copy of *Life* magazine and told me that he'd been instructed to have me translate the entirety of the magazine's contents. Since this wasn't an official job, and since it entailed tedious work that was not of obvious importance, I wasn't happy about it. I told him this would take time, that I was quite busy, and that I would complete the work when I was more free. At that time I was rather busy with family business matters. I was vaguely aware that the Chakdzö Chenmo was a man of importance but didn't really attach much significance to it.

Later that evening when my cousin Gyurme came home, I mentioned to him what happened. He reacted immediately with great alarm! He told me that this Chakdzö Chenmo was the most powerful man in all of Tibet and that he had tremendous influence over the regent, making virtually all of his decisions for him. Gyurme was very upset that I hadn't handled the situation correctly and hadn't treated the messenger with more courtesy. If the Chakdzö Chenmo was angered, Gyurme lamented, then he had the capacity to bring about the ruin of our entire family! He told me that I must begin the translation immediately. I must personally go and deliver it within the shortest time possible and apologize for any inconvenience caused.

I did as I was told, spending every moment I could spare on the translation. It was a tedious job for me, as my Tibetan was not up to scratch, and I found myself often running to Dzasak Khemé for help. I finished the translation in six days and personally went to deliver it. After a short wait I was taken into a room where I came face to face with the man everybody feared. He greeted me with a big smile and accepted my apology courteously, saying no inconvenience had been caused. He said he appreciated my work and even offered me a cup of tea. Outwardly he seemed a pleasant person, and I would never have imagined that this genial exterior concealed a very shrewd and even treacherous personality. Alas, these were qualities I would come to know intimately.

When I first joined the foreign affairs ministry, I was not the only person there who had been educated outside Tibet. Rimshi Kyibuk, an officer from a good noble family, had not only been to school in India in the early 1930s but had also studied at the famous Rugby boarding school in England. He was much my senior and a pleasant person to work with. Though there were two of us fluent in English in my office, I found there was little to do that involved the English language. There was virtually no English-language correspondence of any kind on the diplomatic level, since we only dealt with the Indian trade mission at Dekyilingka, a suburb of Lhasa. I do not recall any written correspondence taking place between our two offices. Most of the time, the head of the trade mission came to our office only after having made a prior appointment, and he brought his own translators. At times, if the Tibetan government wanted to communicate something to the government of India, it was done through the Indian trade mission. As far as I can recollect, our office had no direct written communication with any other government during my time there. It remained that way until the Chinese Communist invasion of my country in early 1950.

Soon after I assumed my new position, I found out to my surprise that we had to deal with legal cases too! These cases were assigned to us by the Kashag, Tibet's council of ministers. I discovered that the legal system in Tibet was a rather peculiar one. While minor legal matters were handled by local authorities, all cases involving serious charges and all manners of appeal were filed with the Kashag. In Lhasa itself, for example, the mayor dealt with all minor criminal cases, and a separate tribunal took care of other minor legal cases. However, if the verdict of a district commissioner was found to be unsatisfactory by either party, an appeal could be made to the Kashag. The result was that the Kashag had a surfeit of cases and was forced to delegate a portion of them to various governmental departments, especially those that didn't require much work.

Though my first year in the service of the Tibetan government passed without any significant events taking place and the office work was not difficult, acquainting myself with the correct ceremonial procedures was tiresome. The three most important ceremonies were those that took place on the Tibetan New Year, on the commemoration of the Lord Buddha, and on the commemoration of Je Tsongkhapa. The fifteenth day of the fourth month was celebrated as the day of the birth, enlightenment, and death of the Lord Buddha. On that day a special ceremony took place at the Potala Palace. That was also the day when all government servants officially changed into their summer dress. The twenty-fifth day of the tenth month commemorated the death anniversary of Je Tsongkhapa, the founder of the Geluk sect, which is headed by the Ganden Tripa, or abbot of Ganden. That entire day was spent in prayer, led by His Holiness the Dalai Lama, at the Potala Palace. That was also the day when the government servants officially changed from summer to winter dress. Since there was much I had to learn about formal ceremonial etiquette, being a Khampa and not being born of Lhasa nobility, I often had to turn to help from our good friends the Khemés as well as my brother-in-law Goshampa.

Around this time there was another noble family, the Phalas, with whom I also became close friends. I was already well acquainted with the second Phala son, Phala Kuding, who also went by Phala Wangchuk, from our time together in India and China. I was introduced to the rest of the family by Dzasak Khemé, whose sister-in-law was married to the youngest Phala son. Phala Wangchuk was not in government service but looked after the family estates in Gyantse. He did this very ably, and whenever I visited, I was very impressed with his accomplishments. Most nobility, both big and small in wealth and status, were typically less than benevolent when it came to their subjects. Phala Wangchuk, on the other hand, was an exception. What impressed me was that he had established a school for the children on his estate, taking special interest in seeing that the quality of education imparted was of the highest caliber. At the same time he also encouraged children to take up sports and physical exercise. In all likelihood he introduced this emphasis after his visits to India and China.

The head of the Phala family, the eldest son, was the Dronyer Chenmo I mentioned above. Dronyer Chenmo Phala was a tall, dignified monk, always impeccably dressed. He was also a man of great integrity, very capable and decisive and therefore well suited to the important position he held. He was in charge of all government ceremonies involving the Dalai Lama at the Potala Palace, the Norbulingka Palace, or anywhere else. All instructions from His Holiness, whether public or private, whether at a formal function or during an audience, were conveyed through him. Similarly, all official appointments, promotions, and demotions were announced by him. He was the only person of authority who had access to the Dalai Lama on a day-to-day basis, seven days a week. He normally had four to five secretaries working under him in the office he maintained just outside the ceremonial hall of the Potala Palace. He was among the most influential officials in the private secretariat of His Holiness the Dalai Lama.

16. THE ENEMY AT OUR DOOR

S oon after I completed my first year of government service, major politi-
cal changes began taking place in China. The military gains of the
People's Liberation Army were mounting with amazing speed, and the
Kuomintang government was on the verge of collapse. That autumn the
Communist party gained complete control of China, and General Chiang
Kai-shek fled to Taiwan with trusted members of his party. In October 1949
the Communist Party of China was formally installed, and a few months
later they began to broadcast over the radio that they would liberate Tibet.
If there had been any questions before, these radio broadcasts left no doubt
as to the seriousness of the threat the recent developments in China posed
to Tibet. It was decided that all prominent international news broadcasts
should be monitored daily. Heinrich Harrer, the Austrian who wrote *Seven
Years in Tibet*, was given the task of monitoring English-language broadcasts, and I was assigned the task of translating them. Phuntsok Tashi Taklha, the brother-in-law of His Holiness the Dalai Lama, had by now become
a member of the foreign affairs ministry. He was directed to monitor the
Chinese-language broadcasts.

The newly installed Chinese Communist government claimed that Tibet was a part of China and that it must be "liberated" from foreign domination. The foreign power from which we needed to be liberated, however, was a mystery to us. As time went on, broadcasts emphasizing the need for our liberation became more and more frequent. The Tibetan government decided to air some broadcasts of their own, refuting these claims and appealing to the outside world for help should the Chinese decide to take military action against Tibet. These broadcasts were made in both English and Tibetan. The Kashag at this point was in constant touch with the government of India through their consulate in Lhasa, where Hugh Richardson was the consul general. However, there was no discernable reaction from any foreign country whatsoever. Even as months went by, there was no change in our situation. The Chinese threat of so-called liberation continued with increasing stridency.

It was early in 1950 when news came that the Chinese army had entered eastern Tibet into a region we called Dotö or Kham, which the Simla Accord of 1914, signed by Britain, China (who later withdrew from the accord), and Tibet, termed Outer Tibet. Under the terms of the accord, the region was to be administered by Tibet while officially under Chinese suzerainty. The strong, well-equipped, and by now very experienced Chinese military found no significant resistance from the Khampas, despite the Khampas' reputation for combat bravery. The Khampas had simply never encountered such a large, disciplined, and modern army. The threat of the invasion was now not only imminent, but manifest.

When the Chinese army first crossed over into Dotö, the governor of eastern Tibet was headquartered in Chamdo. The governor, Kalon Lhalu, was known to be very shrewd and was thus looked upon favorably by the regent. Lhalu immediately realized the larger implications of the Chinese incursion. He was only two years into his three-year tenure as governor, but he quickly made moves to get himself relieved of the post. Everybody knew that he did this to avoid blame for a no-win situation, but he was well connected and got what he wanted. Ngabo Ngawang Jigme, who had been finance minister up until then, was tapped to replace him. Ngabo objected to this appointment on two grounds. First, officials were required to serve only a single three-year term in Chamdo, and he had already done his stint as paymaster under a previous governor. Secondly, Lhalu had not fulfilled the required three years. His arguments were valid, but the government would not lift the pressure and insisted he must accept the promotion. In the end a compromise was reached. Ngabo would accept the post but only on the condition that he share it as a joint position with Lhalu. It was agreed, and he left immediately for Chamdo.

Many years later, in 1994, I had a chance to meet Ngabo Ngawang Jigme, and I asked him what happened when he arrived in Chamdo. He said he found an extremely nervous Lhalu, who was very glad to see him. Lhalu had only about six regiments, around three thousand soldiers total. To bolster these numbers, he was preparing to assemble local militia from all of the territories under him. These military units were known as *chopgye druknga,* which literally means "eighteen to sixty-five," the age restriction on such drafts. In essence, this meant that every able-bodied male would be forced to join the army, causing great hardship to the villagers, as there would be no men left to help with the day-to-day work. Ngabo said that he himself was of the opinion that a militia of this nature, which is to say, one without proper training, a reliable food supply, or adequate arms, would never be able to resist the might of the Chinese army. He felt that resistance served no purpose and would only cause misery and suffering to the local people. However, he couldn't suggest disbanding the newly formed militia, as Lhalu was very intent on this action. As time passed and the Chinese drew nearer and nearer, Lhalu, Ngabo said, grew desperate and wanted to leave Chamdo, despite orders to stay. Ngabo then suggested a way out for Lhalu: he could go up to Kongpo Gyamda and create a second post there, thus remaining governor while nevertheless leaving Chamdo. Ngabo said Lhalu thanked him heartily and left within days, a very relieved man indeed. Once Lhalu had gone, Ngabo immediately disbanded the militia, a move deeply appreciated by the local people.

The Chinese army had by this time amassed along the border, and this alarming development was communicated to the Kashag through messages sent by pony express. The Kashag's first move was to apprise the regent and then call a meeting of the Drungtsi, an eight-member committee comprised of four monk officials at the secretary level and four lay officials with the finance ministry. At this meeting it was decided that the National Assembly must be convened immediately. The National Assembly was comprised of all government officials, the abbots of the three biggest monasteries of Drepung, Sera, and Ganden, representatives of various guilds of craftsmen, and representatives from the local community. The National Assembly was presided over by the Drungtsi but not attended by the Kashag.

The meeting of the National Assembly was well attended, and as was customary Ta-Lama, the monk official who ranked senior-most among the secretaries, led the meeting. He explained the serious developments taking place in eastern Tibet and the grave danger of an impending Chinese invasion. He suggested that everyone should express their unfiltered opinions so that the Assembly could make resolutions that would be in the best interests of the people and the country. Numerous views were put forth from various sections of the Assembly. Some of these views were well informed and pragmatic. Others showed complete ignorance about how big and powerful China was and how much fighting experience they had accumulated in the preceding years. The one thing that was clear to all was that Tibet had fewer than ten thousand regular soldiers, and without exception, these soldiers were utterly untrained in modern warfare. What's more, they were equipped with outmoded British .303 rifles from World War II, a few hundred trench mortars and machine guns, and a couple of field howitzers. In the end it was generally agreed that Tibet must appeal for outside help and at the same time negotiate for a settlement through peaceful means. The Assembly then decided to pass the following resolutions, which would then be presented to the Kashag:

1. To make an appeal to the United Nations requesting help in restraining the Chinese from invading Tibet.

2. To send a delegation to the United Kingdom, the United States, India, and Nepal appealing for military support and/or mediation in dialogues with the Communist Party of China (CPC).

3. To send a delegation to Beijing to establish direct contact with the Chinese government.

The Kashag, after noting the Assembly's resolutions, had further discussions with the Drungtsi and then reported the results to the regent. Officials for each delegation were immediately appointed, and the countries to which they had been appointed were informed, indirectly, through the government of India. The delegations were instructed to leave forthwith, and the first to do so was the one tasked with establishing contact with the Chinese. Monk official Khenchung Thupten Gyalpo and lay official Tsipon Shakabpa were assigned to lead this delegation. I was appointed to accompany Theiji Dingja and Khenchung Thupten Sangye to the United States as their secretary and interpreter. However, before we or the delegations to the U.K., India, or Nepal could leave, messages arrived from all the four countries expressing regret over the inability to provide any military assistance. They spoke of the futility of such resistance and advised settlement through dialogue. This was very disheartening news indeed, and now there was nothing to do except to wait for news of any progress from the delegation that had left for Beijing via India and Hong Kong.

Hong Kong was considered a safe place to conduct preliminary discussions with the Chinese before proceeding to Beijing. Talks could be held via the head of Xinhua, the official state press agency of the People's Republic of China and de facto embassy for the PRC in Hong Kong. However, a visa to Hong Kong had to be obtained from the British government, and this proved to be extremely difficult, as it appears that the British were reluctant to facilitate any talks between the Tibetans and the Chinese.

Meanwhile an incident occurred in Kham that is worthy of mention. The Chinese army, which was on the verge of storming Kham, deputed an incarnate lama named Getak Rinpoche to negotiate with Kalon Lhalu. Getak Rinpoche was a high-ranking lama of a big monastery in Beru, very close to Karzé. He enjoyed very good relations with the Chinese People's Liberation Army because of assistance he had rendered to the Red Army some fifteen years earlier. During the Long March of 1935, when units of the Red Army in western China retreated northward, Getak Rinpoche had helped the Communist rebel soldiers under General Zhu De with food grain, having seen that they were close to starvation. He did this undoubtedly on grounds of compassion. The Communist leaders hadn't forgotten this, and when the PLA came to Kham in 1950, Getak Rinpoche was rewarded with a high title.

When Getak Rinpoche learned that the Chinese intended to proceed to Lhasa, he suggested a peaceful "liberation" of Tibet, knowing full well that Tibet had no means of fighting a Chinese invasion. He arrived in Chamdo and forwarded the Chinese proposal of a peaceful liberation of Tibet to Kalon Lhalu. Lhalu forwarded the proposal to the Kashag in Lhasa, who in turn instructed the governor to stall Getak Rinpoche for as long as possible. The Kashag, of course, was waiting to hear from Shakabpa.

Getak Rinpoche waited for several weeks and then became seriously ill with a stomach ailment. According to Ngabo, when I met him in 1994, a highly skilled Tibetan doctor first treated Getak Rinpoche but found his patient hadn't improved by the following day. Getak Rinpoche then insisted on taking some pills said to have been made by the famous physician-lama Dromo Geshe Rinpoche. These pills were renowned for their efficacy in treating all manner of illnesses. The doctor warned the lama, saying there were many pills said to be made by Dromo Geshe Rinpoche that were not genuine products. Should Getak Rinpoche take one of these, he cautioned, the result could be disastrous. However, Getak Rinpoche did not heed the warning, and by the next day his condition had grown even worse. The situation was desperate, and the English wireless operator, Robert Ford, who was in Chamdo, was asked for some of his Western medicine, probably penicillin. Ford initially refused, perhaps sensing the delicate state of affairs, but was ultimately persuaded to part with the medicine. Getak Rinpoche took Ford's medicine but unfortunately he expired soon afterward.

At the time there was a rumor saying that Lhalu had poisoned Getak Rinpoche. The rumor stemmed in part from the fact that Lhalu had invited him for dinner, and it was immediately after that dinner that Getak Rinpoche took ill. A few months later when the Chinese army marched into Chamdo, they made enquiries into Getak Rinpoche's death and even conducted a postmortem on his body. They concluded that the cause of death was poisoning and Ford was responsible. Ford was immediately arrested and sent to China, where he would unfortunately suffer nine years of imprisonment.

As the Tibetan government was beginning to fathom the futility of its attempts at dispatching delegations to Europe, North America, and China, the Communist Party of China (CPC) continued to broadcast their threat of "liberation" and continued to amass troops across our border in the east of Tibet. On October 7, 1950, while the annual five-day cabinet party called the *kashag thokto* was in progress, we received the alarming news that the Chinese army had entered Tibetan territory on six fronts. They had captured our wireless checkpoint at Dema Chökhorgon, and the wireless operator, Sonam Dorje, had been taken prisoner. This distressing news was a huge jolt that awakened the government to the enormity of the situation. A series of meetings was held among the Kashag, the Drungtsi, and the regent.

Ultimately the Kashag decided to consult high lamas and the state oracle for guidance, a move that was supported by the National Assembly. The state oracle, it was said, demanded that the reins of government be handed over to the young Dalai Lama. Although only sixteen years old, His Holiness was fully aware of the corruption and the inefficiency of the long period during which the regents ruled. This period had proven disastrous for the country, and now the Chinese had crossed over into Tibet. Despite his youth, His Holiness had no option but to accept. Regent Takdrak Rinpoche immediately announced that he would be handing over the government to His Holiness. It was a tellingly convenient timing for the regency, and especially the powerful Chakdzö Chenmo and his cronies, to be freed of responsibility. All the same, on the eighth day of the tenth month, in 2077, the year of the iron tiger, November 17, 1950, by the Western calendar, all powers of government were invested in His Holiness the Dalai Lama by way of a traditional ceremony and celebration. On his part, His Holiness the Dalai Lama marked the occasion by proclaiming a general amnesty, and all convicts were immediately granted their freedom.

Meanwhile the Chinese army advanced farther and farther into Tibet and attacked Chamdo, the seat of the governor in eastern Tibet. In the face of swift advances made by the Chinese, the governor abandoned his post and retreated to Tho Drugu Monastery several kilometers to the west of Chamdo. However, he and his soldiers were soon outflanked by the versatile Chinese troops and had to surrender. The situation had now become critical, and there was still no word from Khenchung Thupten Gyalpo and Tsipon Shakabpa, who had reached Kalimpong several months earlier in March 1950. They evidently encountered a problem in Calcutta and were stuck there. It later became clear what the problem was. The Chinese wanted to meet the delegation in Hong Kong, but the British were apprehensive and delayed issuing the Hong Kong visas. Shakabpa went to Delhi and tried to persuade the British. At the same time he also tried to get the support of the government of India. Mr. K. P. S. Menon, then the foreign secretary of India, had his own ideas. He wanted the talks to take place in Delhi. He advised the Tibetan delegation to wait for the new Chinese ambassador, who was to arrive shortly. When the new ambassador arrived, Shakabpa met with him. However, the ambassador put forward three conditions that had to be agreed upon before formal talks could begin. The conditions to be agreed to in advance were:

1. Tibet must be recognized as a part of China.
2. All of Tibet's foreign affairs must be handled by China.
3. All defense matters must be handled by China.

If all these conditions were met, then and only then could the talks be held in Beijing. Shakabpa forwarded these conditions to the Tibetan government in Lhasa and waited for instructions. In response, the Kashag deputed their foreign minister, Dzasak Surkhang Surpa, to proceed immediately to New Delhi to meet the Chinese ambassador. Once there he was to discuss terms for a peaceful settlement. I was appointed his assistant and interpreter.

17. TRAGEDY AT SHEGAR KHUNLUNG JANGTHANG

Before the account of my visit to India with Foreign Minister Surkhang Surpa, I should relate an incident that occurred during the height of the Chinese invasion threat. On April 1, 1950, Hugh Richardson, the head of the Indian mission in Lhasa, called on our foreign ministers, Dzasak Liushar and Dzasak Surkhang Surpa, to convey an urgent message. He said that the United States had informed Britain that the American vice consul of Tihwa (now Ürümqi), along with four others, had fled southeast from Xinjiang, China's northwest province, in the wake of the region's occupation by the People's Liberation Army. The fleeing party had now entered wild Tibetan territory, and the U.S. government requested formal permission for them to enter; they also requested assistance and protection for the group's onward journey to India. Richardson was assured that the request would be put before the Kashag immediately and everything would be done to provide the facilities and assistance the U.S. had asked for.

As soon as Richardson left, the two ministers met with the Kashag, and a half an hour later they had their approval. They immediately issued instructions for providing safe passage and all manner of assistance to the marooned consul and his companions. The Kashag's orders were to go straight to the *jangchi*, the commissioner for the northern area of Tibet, since the band of wayfarers had entered at Jangthang in the northern wastelands. The dispatch was first sent to the mayor of Shol, the village just below the Potala, and he arranged to have it delivered posthaste by pony express. The following day Richardson was duly informed of all that had been done and asked to convey as much to the American government.

Almost three weeks later we were shocked and deeply pained to receive the news that American Vice Consul Douglas Mackiernan and two others had been killed by our border guards. Two surviving men, American Frank Bessac and Russian Vasili Zvansov, were alive, but Zvansov was wounded in the left leg. Our two foreign ministers and the Kashag were deeply upset to hear of this tragedy. Orders were immediately issued to investigate why the Kashag's instructions were ignored and who was responsible for the killings. At the same time arrangements were made to send a doctor, along with two junior officials equipped with medical and food supplies, to the two survivors.

The area commander of the border post went to meet the survivors and escort them back to his headquarters in Shentsa. The district commissioner welcomed Bessac and Zvansov and apologized deeply for the terrible tragedy. Afterward, while every effort was being made to provide the two gentlemen with the best treatment possible, arrangements were made to recover some of the possessions of which they had been robbed. A week later, the doctor arrived, and Zvansov's leg wound was immediately treated. After a couple of days, when Zvansov was fit to travel, the party left for Lhasa, journeying at a slow pace. They finally arrived in Lhasa on June 11, 1950, and were met some five kilometers outside the city by an official of the foreign office named Tsesur. They were taken to Tredelingka guesthouse, and every effort was made to make their stay comfortable.

I was appointed liaison officer to attend to the foreign gentlemen, so the morning after their arrival I went and introduced myself. They were both in a cheerful mood and glad to be able to have someone with whom they could communicate directly. Bessac told me he had been a student in Mongolia studying the Mongolian language when he had to join the American consul group to escape the Communist invasion. Zvansov, I was told, was the wireless operator for the vice consul. I welcomed them on behalf of the Tibetan government and apologized to them for the dreadful experience they'd had at the border. I also explained to them that the lamentable actions of the border patrol had occurred owing to broken communication. I then invited them to meet the foreign minister on the following day and briefed them that they would be expected to give a firsthand verbal account of the whole episode; they would also need to provide a written one. Bessac came with me to the foreign office while Zvansov rested because of his bad leg. The meeting was a long one. The ministers expressed their profound regret at the turn of events and apologized on behalf of the Tibetan government. They also gave their assurance that a full investigation would be conducted and the guilty men severely punished.

The investigation revealed that a messenger had delayed his delivery of the instructions. What's worse, the border patrol had not only failed to act with discipline, they also acted criminally, assaulting the foreigners with the intent to rob them. These soldiers were identified and sentenced to three to five hundred lashes. In addition, the two main culprits were to have their ears cut off. I was instructed to convey this to Bessac, and he was invited to witness the lashing. I took Bessac to Shol, where the punishment was to be carried out in the courtyard of Shol Lekhung, the district mayor's office. We stayed there for only a few minutes, as Bessac was horrified to see such punishment. He also asked that the two main culprits be spared of losing their ears, and this request was granted.

The two men had been wandering through harsh terrain for months and were in need of fresh clothing and other requirements. They had in their possession some gold coins and small, flat gold bars that they wanted to sell so they could buy the things they wanted. In the process of doing so, a funny incident occurred that I should include. I was given one gold bar of about seventy grams and asked to sell it. I gave this to a servant to have it appraised. Two to three days passed, and my servant still gave me no word. Finally, when I questioned him, he told me a story that I found hard to believe. He told me that his puppy had swallowed the biscuit, and that he was trying to retrieve it by giving the dog laxatives! The next day he did hand over the gold biscuit, and I was left wondering whether or not the dog really had swallowed it. Anyway, I sold the gold myself and gave Bessac the money. However, he was a very tall man, at about two inches over six feet. He thus found it almost impossible to find clothes in Lhasa that fit him. At that time, fortunately for him, Sadutshang had a large stock of American Army surplus clothing. We had bought the clothing in India from traders who themselves had bought it at an auction in Calcutta at the end of World War II. I was happy to offer some of the clothing to Bessac.

After about six weeks Zvansov's leg wound was completely healed, and it was now time for the two men to leave our city. The vice consul and his two colleagues were given Christian burials at the foothill of a mountain east of Lhasa, with crosses bearing their names marking the graves. Photographs of the monuments were later sent to the U.S. embassy in Delhi. The Tibetan government saw to all the necessary arrangements for the two men's long journey ahead, making sure that it would be as comfortable as possible. Before leaving, our visitors offered their wireless hand generator as a small gift, which later became very useful to me. Bessac asked me if I wanted him to send anything once he was back home, and I asked for a Ronson cigarette lighter. After a couple of months, he kept this promise and sent me a cigarette case with a lighter. Although I gave up smoking in 1984, I still have the lighter.

18. IN INDIA WITH FOREIGN MINISTER SURKHANG SURPA

I n November of 1950 I was heading to New Delhi once again. The circumstances this time, however, were dire. The foreign minister summoned me to his house and instructed me to leave within the week. He also told me that I would have to travel separately to Phari. He would join me there on a date to be specified, and then we would travel together for the next three days up to Gangtok, the capital of Sikkim. I was also instructed to take delivery of two boxes containing important documents from the foreign office and make whatever arrangements necessary to bring these with me; I was told to do so with the utmost care. The minister then confided to me that these boxes contained original treaties made with neighboring countries, as well as other related documents. As such I was to keep the matter utterly confidential and ensure the safe arrival of these papers to their destination.

On returning home I immediately got down to preparations. I decided to take two servants, and I thus needed three horses and four pack mules. Apart from the important documents, we had to carry bedding and provisions to last the seventeen-day journey. Though it was late autumn, wet weather was a possibility, so I also had to take good canvas covers for protecting my important cargo. Like all Tibetan documents, these were handwritten in soluble black ink. Any water damage would ruin the papers entirely.

I left Lhasa four days later, and for the first two days of travel I kept to the normal stages of this journey. On the third day I decided to deviate from the typical circuit. The third day's stop was usually at Gampa Batsi, just across the Tsangpo River. However, I started early and decided to skip the overnight stay at Gampa Batsi, and I instead headed straight for Pedé Dzong, the final destination of what was typically the next stage of the journey. Pedé lay about twenty-seven kilometers away, on the far side of Gampa Pass along Yamdrok Turquoise Lake. We stopped at Gampa Batsi for an hour to rest and to eat lunch. Gampa Pass, at about 15,000 feet above sea level, passed over an extremely steep section of the mountains. It took about two and a half hours to reach the pass at the top of the mountain and then another hour to get down to the shores of Yamdrok Lake. We had to ride along the bank of the lake to reach Pedé, another two to three hours ride.

After riding for about an hour, I told Loda, one of my servants, to ride ahead to Pedé and arrange for our stay in a rest house for the night. I instructed him to also prepare tea and some food. My other servant Wangchuk and I followed at a slower pace because the journey had been long and the animals were tired. After some time I noticed that the canvas cover from one of the four pack mules was missing. Wangchuk was a somewhat clumsy, dreamy, and inexperienced young man, unlike Loda. He had not noticed a thing, though he was riding at the rear of the mules. I brought him out of his reverie and instructed him to backtrack to look for the canvas, as I didn't want anything to get wet in the case of rain.

It was getting late and the sun was about to set. An hour passed, and still Wangchuk had not returned. It was now dusk, and soon it would be dark. I reached a point where I had to start making my way around a long curve. The path was an extensive switchback that would have me nearly making a complete U-turn. I would eventually emerge heading the opposite direction, directly across the inlet. In the twilight I couldn't see very far, so I was making my way slowly when suddenly I heard someone shouting. As I looked across to the opposite side, a figure appeared, waving wildly. It was Loda! I recognized his voice as he shouted frantically to me to ride uphill because the animals were going into the water. I immediately spurred my horse on and went ahead to find that two of the pack mules had already gone into the water and were on the verge of getting their loads wet! Thoroughly alarmed, I immediately drove them out of the water and uphill toward the main track. I was extremely relieved to find that neither steel box had even touched the water. Exhausted and famished, as well as cross with Wangchuk for still not returning, I made my way along the curve and reached the point where I'd seen Loda shouting and waving. He had saved me from certain disaster.

When I got to the place where I had seen Loda, I was surprised to find he was no longer there, and this added somewhat to my bad mood. After a short while I entered the village of Pedé and saw Loda waiting for me at the door of a house where we were to stay for the night. I reprimanded him for not waiting for me, as I was alone and finding it difficult to manage the animals. But he denied ever shouting or waving to me from across the water; he insisted that he had never warned me. He said that he had only just finished making tea after having arranged lodgings. He came out only when he saw me approaching. I protested that I not only recognized his voice but also saw his figure and the long sword he always wore tucked through the sash that held up his robe. Still he denied ever having been there. Truly baffled, I went upstairs to enjoy a good cup of tea and some rest. Wangchuk arrived soon afterward, having retrieved the canvas. That night I thought over this strange but fortuitous incident for a long while, and the only explanation I could come up with was that our family protective deity had saved me from unquestionable disaster and failure of duty. That night I slept restfully with a profound sense of relief!

Traveling via the normal stages once again, we arrived in Phari five days later without further incident. There I reported to my superior, who advised me to go ahead and wait for him in Gangtok, as he was not feeling well and would thus be traveling at a slow pace. It took me four days to reach Gangtok, where monsoon rains were unfortunately still falling. Still, I was glad to be done with horseback riding.

Minister Surkhang Surpa arrived two days after I reached Gangtok. The next day we called on Indian Political Officer Apa Pant, who was already aware of our arrival. We briefed him about the latest situation in Tibet and about the Tibetan government's plans to deal with it. He was requested to convey to the external affairs ministry our approximate date of arrival in New Delhi and our request for an appointment to see the prime minister. We also asked that the two boxes of documents we had brought be temporarily kept in his custody, to which he kindly agreed. That afternoon I took the boxes and delivered them to the head clerk. Needless to say, I was tremendously relieved to leave them in someone else's safe hands.

The next day we left by car for Kalimpong, where the Tibetan government had a trade agent posted. Tsipon Shakabpa was also there at that time, and he reported to Minister Surkhang about the latest status of his mission. He reported that he had not succeeded in establishing a dialogue with the Chinese. I was not present at that meeting and came to know of the details only later. Two days later we were on our way to New Delhi, traveling first by car to Siliguri and then by train.

On arrival in New Delhi, in early November of 1950, I got in touch with the ministry of external affairs and enquired about our request for an appointment to meet the prime minister. I was told to contact them again the next day, which I did. I was informed that the prime minister was not available and that we should meet with Foreign Secretary K. P. S. Menon. When I told my minister this, he decided that we should call on the foreign secretary, as we were pressed for time and as it seemed uncertain that we would ever meet Prime Minister Nehru. The next morning we met Menon at ten at his office in the parliament building. Dzasak Surkhang Surpa conveyed greetings from His Holiness the Dalai Lama and the Kashag and explained the situation that Tibet was in. He said that before meeting with the Chinese ambassador in Delhi, it was our desire to solicit the government of India's advice, since the matter was not only of the gravest importance to Tibet but would also affect the interests of India. Menon responded by saying that India was indeed very much concerned by the developments taking place in Tibet and was of the opinion that a peaceful settlement was not only the best solution but the only one. He said that any further military advance by China into Tibet would be disastrous for the people of Tibet.

The sooner a settlement was reached, he suggested, the better it served the interests of all concerned.

We returned from the meeting very disappointed. Not only did Nehru not consider the meeting important enough to spare a little time, but the attitude of the Indian government was most unsupportive. It is my belief that, though Nehru was a great statesman and a man of enormous vision, he made a huge mistake in sacrificing Tibet to the Chinese. I am sure that he realized this when the Chinese invaded a wholly unprepared India along India's northern border in 1962.

We arranged to meet with the Chinese ambassador the following day, and the meeting went cordially enough. We agreed in principle to have a dialogue, but the venue became a problem. We wanted the meeting to take place in New Delhi, but the Chinese would not accept this at all. They insisted that the meeting take place in Beijing. Minister Surkhang then said that he would have to consult with his government, and so the matter was conveyed by wireless transmission to the Kashag. After a week we got instructions to agree to Beijing as the venue for talks. We were told that a delegation would be sent there as soon as possible. Meanwhile, on our insistence, the Chinese agreed that their army would not advance beyond Chamdo for the time being, at least while the talks were going on. They also agreed that they would release all prisoners from captivity.

While I was away in Delhi, crucial developments had taken place in Lhasa. After the fall of Chamdo, Governor Ngabo and all his staff had been taken prisoner, and a great feeling of insecurity was growing in Tibet. Once more the Kashag moved the National Assembly to convene in order to ascertain public opinion. The overwhelming opinion was that the danger of the Chinese army advancing to Lhasa could not be ruled out, and that the risk to the person of His Holiness was very much a possibility. Under the circumstances, it was thought that His Holiness and his cabinet ought to leave Lhasa temporarily and proceed to Yatung in Chumbi Valley, near the Indian border. This would not only reduce the risk of a Chinese invasion of Lhasa but also enable His Holiness to cross over to a safe haven in India should the need arise. When the cabinet approached His Holiness with this proposal, he was not happy with it at all. It took some time to convince him that this was the best alternative for the time being. His Holiness then gave the full responsibility of administering the country to two prime ministers: a senior monk official, Khenchung Lobsang Tashi, and veteran lay administrator Tsipon Lukhangwa, who was finance minister at that time. Only matters of the utmost importance were to be referred to His Holiness at Chumbi.

On December 19, 1950, His Holiness left Lhasa under complete secrecy accompanied by his family members, high lamas, and a large entourage of officials. About two hundred and fifty soldiers of the Drapchi regiment along with their two commanders, who were both fourth-rank officials, escorted His Holiness and his entourage to the Chumbi Valley. My brother Lo Gedun gathered a force of fifteen brave, well-armed Khampas and also volunteered to escort His Holiness to Chumbi, which he was permitted to do. He was a devout disciple of His Holiness the Dalai Lama and considered it a privilege to be able to provide this service, even if it endangered his own life.

The author's brother Lo Gedun, front center, with Khampas escorting
the Dalai Lama to Yatung from Lhasa, December 1951.

While various meetings were taking place in Lhasa, Ngabo, with the consent of the Chinese general overseeing occupied Chamdo, sent an emissary to Lhasa with a letter. In it he said that if the Lhasa government were able to get full support from foreign countries, then every effort should be made to overcome the invading Chinese forces. In this case factors like the lives of prisoners such as himself should not stand in the way. However, he said, if the support of foreign countries was not forthcoming, it would be best to negotiate a peaceful settlement. Toward this end, the letter stated, Ngabo himself was prepared to begin the dialogue, if so authorized. The reply to Ngabo's letter was sent immediately, authorizing him to head the delegation for peace talks. Two more senior officials, Khenchung Thupten Lekmon and Rimshi Sampho Tenzin Dondrup, were appointed as assistants to Ngabo with instructions to proceed to Beijing as soon as possible.

At this point it should be mentioned that earlier, after taking over the reins of government, His Holiness had sent a letter addressed to Chairman Mao Zedong through the commander occupying Chamdo. In that letter, His Holiness had said that he had recently taken charge of the government of Tibet and was willing to have talks in either Beijing or Lhasa on condition that all prisoners be released and that the Chinese army withdraw from the Tibetan border. No response to this letter was ever received.

Hearing news that His Holiness was on his way to Chumbi, Minister Surkhang and I waited in Kalimpong. When the time was right, the minister left to make his report to His Holiness and the cabinet. I did not accompany him this time, having asked for temporary leave, since my wife was expecting a baby any day. She had come to India to have the baby, as there were no proper Western medical facilities in Lhasa at that time. She had already suffered two miscarriages, so we were both anxious that she have a safe delivery. In those days in Tibet many women had miscarriages, and many even died in childbirth, owing to lack of safe medical care. Dr. Craig, a Scotsman at the Scottish Mission Hospital in Kalimpong, gave my wife frequent checkups. She finally delivered a healthy baby girl at home, on January 21, 1951.

In Chumbi Valley, after Dzasak Surkhang Surpa had reported his mission's outcome, the government decided to appoint two more senior

officials to assist Ngabo, our family friend Dzasak Khemé and a monk official, Khendrung Lhautara. Ngabo and his two assistants in Chamdo were
told to proceed to Beijing, where the two officials from Chumbi would join
them in due course. I received instructions to accompany the latter party
through India to China as English interpreter. Also traveling with us would
be the Dalai Lama's brother-in-law, Phuntsok Tashi Taklha, who had been
appointed Chinese interpreter. The officials arrived in Kalimpong within
days of my receiving these instructions. Two days later we left for Delhi via
Calcutta.

We spent a week in Delhi as the delegation had to meet the Indian
prime minister and of course the Chinese ambassador. On the third day
of our stay, we were able to get an appointment to meet with Prime Minister Nehru. Dzasak Khemé and Khendrung Lhautara handed over a letter
from the Tibetan cabinet and explained the purpose of their mission. In
accordance with the contents of the letter, they requested Nehru to mediate in the forthcoming negotiations between the Tibetans and the Chinese
and asked him for his guidance and advice in conducting them. Nehru
replied that a peaceful settlement was the only alternative and that mutually acceptable terms could be discussed. However, he declined to mediate
in the negotiations, as India had just attained her independence and was in
too weak a position to be effective. He strongly emphasized the importance
of not allowing the Chinese military occupation of Tibet. Nor, he added,
should we allow them to maintain a military base anywhere in our country.
We could of course see that such a situation was also not in the interests of
India.

We then met with the Chinese ambassador and discussed details about
the delegation's scheduled visit to Beijing. We were advised to inform the
Chinese consulate general in Calcutta about our date of departure for Hong
Kong so that necessary arrangements could be made to receive us, and to
arrange our onward journey to Beijing. In the evening the Chinese ambassador hosted a dinner for the Tibetan delegation.

The next day, Indian chief of army staff General K. M. Kariappa contacted us and invited the delegation to visit the Indian army headquarters
in Delhi the following day. The invitation included dinner in the evening.

Dzasak Khemé was then chief of army in Tibet, hence the protocol. The next afternoon General Kariappa sent a car with two pilot motorcycles, which took us to the army headquarters. Once there, a guard of honor was presented, and we were taken for a short tour of the headquarters. Afterward we attended a tea reception. Later in the evening there was a grand dinner, attended by many senior army officers. General Kariappa was an impressive personality, and he had a lot of sympathy for the Tibetans.

We left for Calcutta the following day and immediately made arrangements to fly to Hong Kong on the first available flight, a Pan American flight, two days later. We duly informed the Chinese consulate general of the date and time of our arrival in Hong Kong. When we reached Hong Kong the weather was very poor, and the plane made several circles waiting for clearance from air traffic control. Since there was no hope of improvement in the weather, however, the pilot was forced to divert the flight to Manila in the Philippines. The following morning the weather had improved, and we were able to fly safely to Hong Kong. We were received by two Chinese from the Xinhua news agency. They took us to a hotel, where we were later joined by the Chinese vice consul from Calcutta. The vice consul had arrived that very morning. He said he had specifically made this journey to find out our whereabouts, since he had received news that we did not arrive in Hong Kong at the appointed time. He told us it was very dangerous to travel by any American aircraft and warned us never to do so again! He probably assumed we would believe him, but of course we didn't. In all likelihood he actually believed it himself.

19. IN CHINA AS AN OFFICIAL WITH THE TIBETAN DELEGATION

The day after arriving in Hong Kong, we left for the city of Guandong by train. From Hong Kong it was only a half hour to the Chinese border, where we got off the train, walked about fifty meters, and transferred to a Chinese train to continue our journey. The next day we again changed trains and finally arrived in Beijing on April 26, 1951. At the railway station we were received by a group of about thirty Chinese officials, a party of schoolchildren, the Panchen Lama's resident official in Beijing, and Ngabo, who was accompanied by his two assistants from Lhasa. Among the Chinese officials there were Lin Beichui, a secretary level official, and Li Weihan, head of the Department of Nationalities. Ngabo and his party had arrived two days earlier and were staying at Peking Hotel, where we were also put up. After a short rest Dzasak Khemé and Khendrung Lhautara handed over to Ngabo a letter from His Holiness the Dalai Lama. They also conveyed a letter from the Tibetan government that authorized them to negotiate with the Chinese. Lastly, the two officials related certain verbal instructions and the pertinent details about our talks with Prime Minister Nehru.

On April 29th, the Tibetan delegation was asked to attend a meeting with Prime Minister Zhou Enlai and the Chinese delegation deputed for

Tibetan delegation to Beijing, May 1951. Dzasak Khemé, unknown lady,
Khendrung Lhautara, author, and Kalon Phuntsok Tashi Taklha.

the negotiations. At the meeting Zhou Enlai introduced to us the members
of his delegation: Li Weihan, Tan Chiwu, Tang Gohua, Sung Tingyuan,
and Bapa Phuntsok Wangyal. The latter was a communist Tibetan, and
he was to be the interpreter for the Chinese side. We in turn introduced
our delegation, and Zhou Enlai expressed to us his hopes and wishes for
a successful conclusion of the negotiations. Talks began a few days later,
and on the first day there was a brief discussion about the agenda. It was
agreed that the Chinese would prepare a draft of it in Tibetan, which Bapa
Phuntsok Wangyal did soon after. This draft had no mention of any matter pertaining to the Panchen Lama. However, a few days later, after the
candidate that the Chinese favored to be the Panchen Lama arrived in
Beijing, the Chinese wanted to include the status of the Panchen Lama on
the agenda. Ngabo explained that he and his delegation had no authority

to discuss such a matter. Furthermore, Ngabo explained, any matter concerning the Panchen Lama was an internal matter and could not be made part of negotiations between China and Tibet. The Chinese refused to accept this and insisted on discussing it. Finally the Chinese suggested the appointment of a committee to deal with this matter and appointed Tang Gohua, Sung Tingyuan, and Bapa Phuntsok Wangyal to be on this committee. The Tibetan side was represented by Khendrung Lhautara, Khenchung Thupten Lekmon, and Phuntsok Tashi Taklha. The committee had several meetings, and the Chinese were informed that there were already three proper candidates for the Panchen Lama. One of these three must be chosen following proper traditional procedures, and so the one in Beijing could never be officially recognized. The Chinese would not take no for an answer and insisted that the candidate they had brought to Beijing be recognized as the true Panchen Lama.

In light of this obduracy, the Tibetan delegation decided to refer this serious matter to the Tibetan government and request instructions on how to proceed. The Kashag in Lhasa reported to His Holiness in Chumbi, and the state oracle was consulted. The state oracle said that if the Chinese persisted, then the Beijing candidate may be accepted as the Panchen Lama. However, our delegation was also told by the Kashag that such recognition and matters concerning the Panchen Lama should not be incorporated into any agreement. They advised that the Chinese should be persuaded to accept a separate agreement on it. But now the Chinese not only wanted to include this matter in the overall agreement, but they also insisted that the status of the Panchen Lama be returned to the respected position it had enjoyed during the period of the Thirteenth Dalai Lama and the Ninth Panchen Lama. This was a time prior to certain recent problems between the two great lamas, a time when relations were very cordial between the two. The Chinese were unrelenting in their demands. With the Tibetan delegation being unable to accept such high-handedness, the talks broke off. After a lapse of more than a week, during which time Bapa Phuntsok Wangyal negotiated between the two sides, the committee met again. Ultimately, the Tibetan delegation was forced to accept most of the Chinese demands as far as the Panchen Lama's position was concerned.

Talks on the main issue continued alongside talks on the Panchen Lama. Not much progress could be made, however, as the Chinese stand on all matters was very rigid, and their approach was one of applying force until we conceded to their demands. One day, during discussions on the Chinese demand to appoint a military and political committee, the Tibetans expressed the view that, since Tibet was an independent country, such an administrative office was unnecessary. At this suggestion, the head of the Chinese delegation, Li Weihan, became red in the face with fury, and he practically scolded the Tibetans for claiming Tibet to be a sovereign state! Then he threatened them by saying that if they were so arrogant as to refuse to recognize Tibet as a part of China, then they could go back home any time they pleased. In that case, he assured them, all he need do was to send one, just one, single wireless message, and Chinese troops would advance immediately into Tibet. Then, he told them, they themselves would be responsible for the military liberation that would take place! So it was up to them to sign the agreement or else leave without a peaceful settlement. That day the meeting came to an abrupt end.

The Tibetan delegates, on returning to their hotel, immediately held prolonged discussions among themselves as to what they should do in the wake of such strong threats made by the Chinese. Ultimately, they came to the conclusion that they had absolutely no remaining options beyond accepting whatever the Chinese dictated; there was no way Tibet could risk a military invasion. However, they decided to place one condition on accepting the Chinese terms. They decided to tell the Chinese that they were not sure whether or not the Dalai Lama were still in Chumbi Valley and that in all probability he would have already crossed over to India. Therefore, while accepting the proposed agreement, an additional article should be inserted stating: "If and when the Dalai Lama returns to Tibet, he will be accorded the full recognition of status and authority that existed before he left." Meanwhile the Tibetan delegation concluded confidentially that it would be best for His Holiness to cross over to India. That way he could wait and watch to see how things developed after the agreement was signed. Moreover, they thought all efforts should be made to muster outside support for opposing Chinese occupation. If they received such support, then the treaty could be revoked by blaming the delegation for signing such an unacceptable agreement, without the full approval of His Holiness and the Tibetan government.

When this proposal was put forward at the next meeting, Li Weihan said that they were willing to incorporate such a statement, but that it would only be in the form of a note appended to the main agreement. He said that the note would state that the Dalai Lama, while staying in a foreign country, could witness the peaceful liberation of Tibet and see how the Communist Party of China implemented its policies in Tibet. In a few years' time, if the Dalai Lama were satisfied and decided to return to Tibet, he would be given full recognition of his previous status and authority. Thus the agreement was finalized. The Chinese, according to their custom, wanted the Tibetan delegation not only to sign but to put an official seal on the agreement. Although Ngabo had in fact brought with him the official Kashag seal, this was not disclosed to the Chinese. Therefore the Chinese went ahead and had a seal made for the delegation. On May 23, 1951, the agreement was signed in the presence of General Zhu De, vice chairman of the People's Republic of China and commander in chief of the People's Liberation Army, in the Great Hall of the People.

At this point I should add that during the entire negotiations, the delegation was in constant contact with the Kashag through wireless messages sent in code. This was true, even to the last moment. They had the full approval from the Kashag to sign the Seventeen-Point Agreement. I myself was not physically present during any of the talks. I was not a senior official and therefore not a member of the team that was responsible for holding the talks. What I have related here is what I learned firsthand from those who took part in the negotiations.

This, then, was the last day of Tibet's independence. Our sovereignty had been surrendered to the Chinese. Little did we know how terrible the repression that was to follow it would be. It is my belief that the irresponsibility on the part of the ruling Tibetan elite in carrying out their duties and obligations in the twenty-five years after the death of the Thirteenth Dalai Lama directly contributed to the subsequent indescribable suffering of the common people. In a prediction written before his death, the Thirteenth

Dalai Lama had issued a stern warning that, unless government officials worked collectively toward good governance and the security of the people of Tibet, our country would be overrun by communism. He warned that the ruling class themselves would be subject to untold misery and suffering. All of this came true, in every detail.

The day after the signing of the agreement, the long-standing request of the Tibetan delegation to meet Chairman Mao Zedong was granted. We met him and a number of other senior CPC members in the morning. Later, in the evening, an elaborate dinner was given to mark the signing of the agreement. The dinner was attended by Prime Minister Zhou Enlai, Communist Party General Secretary Liu Shaoqi, and many other senior party officials.

20. BACK TO TIBET AFTER THE SIGNING OF THE SEVENTEEN-POINT AGREEMENT

Four days after the ceremonial dinner engagement, we were on our way back home. Ngabo and those who came by land from eastern Tibet wanted to return home via India along with us, but the Chinese wouldn't agree to this. As a result, the delegation departed in two separate batches. Ngabo, along with Khenchung Thupten Lekmon and Lekmon's secretary, left for Kham. The rest of the delegation, including Rimshi Sampho Tenzin Dondrup, who was originally with Ngabo, traveled by train to Hong Kong and thereafter by air to Calcutta. We were also accompanied by Representative Zhang Jingwu, the Chinese representative in Tibet, his assistant Alo Butang, and twelve other young military personnel, of whom ten were security and two were medical officers. There was also one other Chinese man, a junior official of their New Delhi embassy, who was returning to India with a maid to help his pregnant wife. I mention this particular person because I would meet him again in New Delhi some twenty-nine years later, though under very different circumstances.

On our arrival in Hong Kong, we found it difficult to book reservations on flights to Calcutta for a group as large as ours, so we eventually had to split into four different groups and fly on different dates. I stayed behind to fly with the last group. My senior officials, Dzasak Khemé and Khendrung Lhautara, had each brought along a servant on this trip, and I put the servants in the third group along with two Chinese men. However, these two Tibetans were convinced that they would be kidnapped by the Chinese men and taken back to China, and they refused to travel without me! They were genuinely afraid and even wept, asking me to either come with them or let them stay behind and join me on the last flight. It took me considerable time to convince them that the plane would take them only to Calcutta and that there were other passengers bound for that destination too. When I arrived in Calcutta two days later, I learned that these two Tibetans had refused to get out of the plane. They thought their plane had not landed in Calcutta but in China! It was only after seeing that all the staff who came to speak to them were Indians that they finally agreed to disembark. The fact that the Tibetans spoke neither English nor Hindi added to the problem, which might have amused some but which clearly revealed how much the ordinary Tibetan distrusted and felt threatened by the Chinese.

Once in India, the members of both delegations assembled at the Chinese consulate general's guesthouse. Two days later the Tibetan officials, accompanied by the Chinese representative Zhang Jingwu, his assistant Alo Butang, and a few others, left for Kalimpong on their way to Chumbi Valley. I stayed behind with the remaining members of the second group and, once we were able to get seats on a plane to Bagdogra, the airport nearest to Kalimpong, we followed the first group. Soon after we arrived in Kalimpong, our Tibetan officials left for Chumbi with the Chinese representative and his assistants. I, on the other hand, was instructed to stay behind to accompany the rest of the Chinese, who numbered eight in all—one doctor and seven security personnel. There were preparations to be made for the long journey, and a week passed before we left. Meanwhile we had news that Zhang Jingwu had been granted an audience with His Holiness the Dalai Lama. Indeed, within a couple of days His Holiness left for Lhasa followed later by Zhang Jingwu.

My journey to Lhasa proved rather difficult, as I had to look after the welfare of eight Chinese men who had never in their lives, prior to this moment, ridden horses. In addition, I had to make arrangements for food and lodging for people entirely unfamiliar with our Tibetans ways and customs. Needless to say, we traveled at a slow pace. Thankfully, when we reached Phari, I was informed by the district commissioner's office that Chöphel Sonam, a monk official and district wool-tax collector, had been given instructions to accompany me as an assistant. He was very useful and eased my burden a great deal.

During our long journey, especially in the early stages, the Chinese men fell off their horses several times after dozing off. When their horses made sudden moves or jumped a bit, the sleeping riders inevitably became unbalanced and tumbled down. Fortunately there were no serious falls, and the cuts and bruises from the falls were easily taken care of by the doctor. Since it was summer, the warm weather made the journey much easier. When we crossed Nyasok Pass, there was a steep decline. I advised the Chinese men to dismount and walk slowly, but two of them didn't heed me and rushed downhill, despite my shouting to slow down. They continued to gain speed, and out of control, they finally tripped on an uneven surface and fell, rolling over several times. I quickly went down to check on them. Apart from being dazed, they were not hurt badly. Thereafter, all of them listened to what I had to say, and we zigzagged our way slowly down the hill. Four days later we reached Lhasa. After a long journey of three weeks, the Chinese, in particular, were greatly relieved, as all of them suffered from sunburn, sore bottoms, and aching bodies! I saw their broad smiles as the magnificent Potala Palace came in view because they knew they had now reached the end of their journey. Just before we reached Lhasa a messenger had come to tell me to take the Chinese to Trimon House, where Zhang Jingwu was being accommodated. I did as I was asked, and went home, tired and relieved.

Two weeks later, Ngabo and his staff arrived from Kham, and within a few days, the commander general of the southern army, Zhang Guohua, along with General Tan Guansan and three to four thousand troops, entered Lhasa. They were billeted at Makar Sarpa, or the "new garrison," south of Lhasa, and along the Kyichu River. A month later, General Fan Ming, commander of the northern sector, arrived with twenty thousand troops. A large park called Nortö Lingka, west of the Norbulingka, the Dalai Lama's summer palace, was requisitioned in order to provide a camp

H. H. the Dalai Lama meeting General Zhang Guohua at
the Norbulingka Palace, 1952.

for the troops. A sizeable number of Lhasa's people came to witness this
large number of soldiers march into the city. They clapped and shouted,
which the Chinese interpreted as a sign of welcome and approval, little
realizing that when Tibetans clap it is a form of disapproval intended to
ward off the unwelcome!

Rations for this sudden influx of troops soon became a major problem.
The Chinese demanded large quantities of grain to be loaned to them by the
Tibetan government. But the state granaries did not have sufficient grain, so
the government had to borrow from private sources and monasteries. Soon
all food items soared in price, and grain became ten times more expensive
than it was before the arrival of the Chinese troops. The Chinese demand
for various supplies kept on increasing, as more and more Chinese officials
and their staff kept coming to Lhasa. Soon all food items became scarce, and
the common people suffered as a result.

The common people began openly criticizing the Chinese for causing
this food shortage and called for the Chinese to return to their own country. The Chinese began to feel the heat of this opposition as people now

began to meet in large groups to express their anger. Representative Zhang Jingwu complained to the Tibetan government and demanded that such opposition be put down. He also demanded that since the Chinese had come to help develop Tibet, this should be conveyed to the Tibetans, and cooperation between the Chinese and Tibetan people should be fostered. The Tibetan government explained to the Chinese the real cause of the Tibetan people's outrage. The Tibetan government said that they were not in a position to meet the Chinese army's demands beyond the next six to eight months. Unless the Chinese made their own arrangements for the army's food requirements, the Tibetan government explained, the situation would go from bad to worse.

At this point the Chinese began a series of meetings with the Kashag and the two prime ministers. Instead of becoming more conciliatory, they made even more demands in various fields, all under the pretext of development. In the beginning, they were polite enough during the meetings, but gradually they became more and more arrogant in their attitude. They even became critical of Prime Minister Lukhangwa, who was not afraid to oppose some of the more unreasonable demands made by the Chinese. Around this time, the Chinese also began to organize many meetings and functions to propagate communism, by brainwashing the younger and more susceptible officials and youths of the city. However, opposition to the Chinese by the general public became more vociferous and open. The public made a strong representation to the Tibetan government, to demand the immediate withdrawal of all Chinese troops from Lhasa. The Chinese became furious at this and blamed the two prime ministers, who they said were responsible for fueling such public sentiments. The Chinese went so far as to demand that they resign forthwith. These demands were not met for some time, but the Chinese exerted so much pressure in many ways that before long, the Kashag had to finally recommend to His Holiness the Dalai Lama that the two prime ministers be asked to resign. It was with much sadness that His Holiness accepted their resignations. After this, the Chinese appeared to be very pleased at having their way.

The Seventeen-Point Agreement clearly stated that the Chinese authorities would not interfere with or seek to change the status and authority of the Dalai Lama and his administration. It also stated that no reforms would be introduced without the consent of the Dalai Lama. However, the Chinese authorities in Lhasa gradually began making various demands, including demands for vigorous land reforms. This was despite the fact that His Holiness had already established a reform office (*lekchö lekhung*) for the very purpose of redistribution of land to the common people. Reform had been initiated and was in progress before the Chinese began demanding it.

One of the early and most significant demands that the Chinese made was to merge our foreign ministry with the Chinese foreign department, which they had established about a year after their arrival in Lhasa. As a consequence, on September 6, 1952, our entire office and staff shifted to Sungphü House, where the Chinese had set up their foreign department. Thus our foreign ministers became colleagues of Yang Gongsu, who was

Tibet's foreign ministry, which was incorporated into the Chinese ministry, Lhasa 1952. In the front can be seen from the left: Kalon Shatra Surpa, Kalon Ngabo Ngawang Jigme, Kalon Rampa, General Zhang Guohua, and General Tan Guansan. In the third row, Dzasak Liushar is fifth from the left. To the right of him is Yang Gongsu, the Chinese officer in charge of the foreign office.

the Chinese official in charge of their foreign department. There were seven Chinese staff, including a Tibetan from Ba in eastern Tibet who acted as translator and six of us Tibetans. Among us was Phuntsok Tashi Taklha, brother-in-law of His Holiness, on whom we relied to translate for us, despite the Chinese always trying to insist on the use of their own translator. Yang Gongsu did not appear to me to be an experienced diplomat. He knew some English but was not fluent, whereas his wife, who was also on the staff, could express herself quite well in English. Among the Chinese was also a man of small stature who had studied Nepali and knew it quite well.

Our remuneration was fixed by the Chinese, and I was paid one hundred and eight yuan per month, a very modest salary. Earlier, in the Tibetan government, we were never paid in cash but in kind, in measures of barley. I was given two hundred and fifty *khel*, which is about eight hundred kilos per annum, also a very modest payment. All the officials, being from nobility, had their own estates. Therefore the size of the salary was not of much

Author (right) with Phuntsok Tashi Taklha, who married the
Dalai Lama's sister, in front of the Potala, 1952.

A group of journalists from Eastern Europe with the Dalai Lama at the Norbulingka Palace, 1952. Author is far right.

consequence. More important than salary was the prestige and the influence one could exert as a government official.

Soon after the merger of the Tibetan and Chinese foreign offices, the Chinese began to give us lectures on how to conduct ourselves in dealing with representatives of foreign countries. They cautioned us to be very alert and to guard ourselves from being influenced or exploited by "such people," as it might endanger China's interests. I was explicitly asked if I had any close friends among the Indian mission staff. It was hinted that if I did, then I should distance myself from them henceforth.

Another significant action that the Chinese took early on was to take charge of all important documents the Tibetan government possessed relating to trade agreements, border demarcation, and treaties with countries such as India, China, Outer Mongolia, Nepal, and Bhutan. The Chinese had absolutely no knowledge of these papers, a fact that clearly demonstrates that Tibet had dealt as a sovereign nation with other nations. The Chinese began an extensive study of these documents, and two of our senior Tibetan officials were assigned to help translate and explain the contents so that the Chinese could become acquainted with all of Tibet's international relations.

A few months after the merger of my department with our Chinese counterpart, the Chinese insisted that all government personnel and prominent persons traveling to India must now do so with a passport issued by our joint offices. Before the Chinese arrived in Tibet, all Tibetans traveled freely to India without any documents whatsoever. Indians likewise were permitted to travel without documents as far as Yatung, after which they had to obtain a permit. However, members of the Indian mission in Lhasa and their families could travel between towns like Gyantse and Yatung without any papers. On the implementation of this new procedure by the Chinese, the Indian government also introduced a policy of registering all Tibetans at border checkpoints.

In these and other such ways the Chinese gradually began to dominate all aspects of foreign policy and relations. Thereafter, Tibetan government officials had very little say in matters of foreign policy. Whenever they tried to oppose or object to anything, the Chinese would say that they'd received instructions directly from Beijing and so were powerless to make any changes.

One point of the Seventeen-Point Agreement stated that "The administration of the Autonomous Region of Tibet would be established as soon as possible." Representative Zhang Jingwu and his colleagues worked diligently to implement this, and by the end of 1952 they had more or less completed the task of forming what was called the Preparatory Committee of the Autonomous Region of Tibet. In the spring of 1953 the Chinese announced that this committee would be formally inaugurated in the summer, and that for the occasion Marshal Chen Yi would be coming to Lhasa as the representative of the Beijing government. Around this same time, all new lay officials of the Tibetan government appointed during the previous five years were notified that their examination in traditional riding and shooting skills would be held in June. It was scheduled to coincide with the opening of the Preparatory Committee, and Marshal Chen Yi was to be the chief guest.

This examination of riding and shooting skills dates back centuries to when Tibet was a more warlike nation. Of course the exam no longer served any practical purpose and instead was more of a traditional performance for entertaining the public. Such examinations took place every three or four years, whenever there was a group of about twenty to thirty new officials. The examination had two parts. The first tested one's ability to accurately fire a musket, shoot an arrow, and throw a spear. Three targets were placed in a line about fifty yards apart, and the contestant had to try and strike each target with its respective weapon from atop a galloping horse as the target sped by! The second part was a test of archery. Each contestant was to shoot an arrow as far as possible, and the ranks were announced publicly at the end of the contest, creating fierce competition, as no one wanted to be in the bottom ranks! Months of training and practice were invested, and the quality of your equipment also played an important part. Participants from well-known noble families usually had the best equipment so as to try and ensure a good ranking; this was for the sake of prestige, no doubt. Fortunately, during the test that year, the year in which I had to participate, the government changed the rules and said that there would be no formal ranking. This brought a lot of relief to the participants.

My family and friends were all worried about my performance, hoping that I would not disgrace myself! Sometimes unfortunate accidents did occur, like falling off a horse galloping at full speed. I discovered, however, that the faster your horse galloped, the better your balance. Galloping faster, then, made shooting at targets easier. I had a beautiful dark chestnut horse with a very fast gallop, so I was determined to do well. The day of the exam came, and when it was my turn I hit my gun target easily and my spear target too, without difficulty. Nevertheless I missed my arrow target by a few inches. When I shot my arrow I twirled it with my fingers first as a sign of my confidence; this was customary in those days. One hindrance for me was that I had to wear a large hat with red tassels, since I was a fifth-rank official. Fourth-rank officials had a much smaller hat, and this made it not only easier for them to sling the guns which they held, over their backs after shooting, but also gave them more time to shoot their arrow afterward.

There were five of us new officials who had formed a group to practice before our performance. All of us did well. One of us got the number one position, and I earned the second position. At the end of the day we were all satisfied and glad that this compulsory requirement was over. The officials and Chinese guests were well entertained, as were the people of Lhasa, who turned up in full strength to enjoy the festivities and some picnicking on the grounds below the Potala Palace.

By the end of 1953 the Chinese were well settled in Lhasa and the surrounding areas. The military had fully established their headquarters with a large contingent of troops at Makar Sarpa, just south of the city along the Kyichu River. The major contingent of the troops was concentrated in Nortö Lingka, about ten kilometers west of the Norbulingka, with some outlying garrisons in two areas across the Kyichu, about twenty kilometers east of Lhasa. However, as more and more Chinese officials arrived from China, accommodation became harder to come by. They brought large quantities of silver Chinese dollars, probably confiscated from the Kuomintang government when it fell. With this money they began to buy many large houses at exorbitant prices. They had no idea of the cost of property in Lhasa, nor did they attach much value to the silver dollars that had cost them nothing. Many Tibetans with large houses sold them. Likewise we too sold our large house and got a handsome price for it.

With the influx of Chinese silver dollars, inflation swelled rapidly, causing great hardship to the common people. Traders, however, did brisk business as the Chinese began to give big contracts for many items not locally available. Some of their essential needs like rice, sugar, flour, textiles, and medicines were not produced in Tibet and had to be imported from India, which was far nearer and much more accessible than China. There was no motorable road to China, and of course there wasn't a single airport in the whole of Tibet. The Chinese began constructing roads on two fronts soon after the occupation. They followed more or less the path of the old trade routes, from Kham to Lhasa in the east and from Amdo to Lhasa in the north.

Soon the traders also discovered that there was a huge market in China itself for items like toothbrushes, razor blades, and wristwatches. Swiss watches were greatly prized, but most people could only afford the cheaper varieties, of which the most popular brand was Roma. People with more money bought the brand called West End, but senior party members favored Rolex and Omega. When the traders sold their goods in China, they approached the Chinese authorities for assistance in transferring money through official channels, and usually the officials obliged. However, in keeping with their official policy, they tried in all their dealings to instill in as many traders as possible the communist way of thinking. Having sold their goods in China, traders usually bought merchandise like brick tea, silk, chinaware, and carpets, which were all in demand in Tibet.

The pressure created by Chinese occupation also began to be felt in quarters other than foreign affairs. The Chinese made many demands to the Tibetan administration for big reforms, such as the absorption of the Tibetan army into the People's Liberation Army and the replacement of the Tibetan flag with the Chinese one. The Tibetan public realized that such arrogant Chinese demands were not only creating great difficulties for the Kashag but, more importantly, were disrespectful to the Dalai Lama. Soon the people of Lhasa began to publicly show their anti-Chinese sentiments by singing songs, putting up posters, and holding public meetings. Beyond expressing their outrage, they demanded that the Chinese go back to their own country. The Tibetan government was forced to put a ban on public gatherings, but popular resentment grew even stronger still. At a large meeting in Lhasa, a memorandum was drawn up that drew attention to the precarious situation regarding food grains. The memorandum requested the Tibetan government to demand the immediate withdrawal of all Chinese troops. After submitting this memorandum to the Kashag, a copy was sent to the Chinese. The Chinese were incensed and were even prepared to use force if necessary to repress such movements. The Tibetan government in turn was deeply concerned that violence would erupt that would lead to destructive and even deadly repercussions for the people of Tibet.

During these unhappy times, one event brought gladness to everyone's heart. In May of 1954, His Holiness the Dalai Lama gave his first Kalachakra teaching at the request of Lhalu Lhacham, a lady of nobility from the family of Lhalu. In those times the Kalachakra teachings were rarely given, perhaps once or twice in a Dalai Lama's lifetime, so the people considered themselves incredibly fortunate to be receiving them. For the Sadutshangs it was an even more joyous occasion because in 1948 we had presented an amplifier and speakers (as well as a movie camera) to the Dalai Lama with the idea that they would be of use on just such occasions. My brother Lo Gedun had asked me to obtain these, and I was able to buy them when I was in Calcutta. Now, for the first time in the history of Tibet, the general public would be able to hear the voice of the Dalai Lama during a religious teaching. The teaching took place at Norbulingka and lasted for four days. There was a tremendous crowd present. I could see their faces, filled with awe and shining with happiness at hearing their beloved Dalai Lama's voice.

21. THE RETURN OF
THE PANCHEN LAMA

In terms of both religion and politics, the Dalai Lama and the Panchen Lama have long played prominent roles in the history of Tibet. The relationship between these two beloved figures is special and unique. Nevertheless, their respective statuses and the shifting terrain of the relationship between the two occasionally became a point of political tension. This is something that both the Chinese and British governments have attempted to exploit, with varying success. In each case the foreign power seized every opportunity to develop special relations with the Panchen Lama in order to use him politically as an opponent to the Dalai Lama. This was clearly a stratagem and not merely misguided diplomacy, since these nations were fully aware of the fact that the Panchen Lama was a religious leader of lesser status than the Dalai Lama and had no say in the political matters of Tibet. The Dalai Lama was clearly the undisputed spiritual and temporal head of Tibet, and any views that suggested the contrary were subterfuge, created by political institutions with vested interests. Any misunderstandings between the two lamas that arose from time to time were largely owing to these external interferences. But the advisers, officials, and attendants of the two lamas were not entirely free of blame.

In 1904 during the British expedition to Tibet led by Younghusband, the Ninth Panchen Lama is said to have collaborated with the British, who subsequently invited him to India. He spent more than a year in India, during which time he met Lord Minto, who later became viceroy of India, and also the Prince of Wales before he became King George V. The Panchen Lama tried to gain political influence in Tibet at that time but was unsuccessful. Meanwhile, the conflict of 1904 with the British and that of 1910 with the Chinese had cost the Tibetan government dearly. Funds were needed to raise a larger army for the sake of the future defense of the country, and there was no alternative but to raise money through the imposition of new taxes. New taxes were imposed on all monasteries' estates, including the Panchen Lama's own Tashi Lhunpo, which had the largest estates thanks to successive gifts from past Dalai Lamas. This created ill will between Tashi Lhunpo and the Tibetan government. When the Panchen Lama traveled to Lhasa to participate in the consecration of a large statue of the deity Bhairava that was sponsored by the Thirteenth Dalai Lama, the Panchen Lama tried to use this opportunity to plead for exemption from the new taxes. However, he never managed to speak to the Dalai Lama, for reasons unknown. On this occasion, the Panchen Lama's own officials behaved in a very arrogant manner. They carried on as if they belonged to a parallel government, refusing to recognize the authority of the central government over them.

In 1923 the Ninth Panchen Lama secretly traveled to Mongolia and sought Russian support but failed. Two years later he went to Beijing and was an honored guest of the Chinese Kuomintang government. He spent eight years in China, where he again tried to gain political recognition. In 1933 he came to Kham and stayed at the border town of Jyekundo. From there he sought permission from the Tibetan government to return home accompanied by an escort of five hundred Chinese soldiers. Naturally, this request was denied. While further negotiations were underway, the Dalai Lama unfortunately passed away. The Panchen Lama was forced to remain in Jyekundo until his own passing in 1937. Not long after the death of the Ninth Panchen Lama, the Fourteenth Dalai Lama was found.

In 1938 officials of the Panchen Lama claimed they had discovered his reincarnation in a village called Ngotsar in the Amdo region of Tibet. Officials in Lhasa, however, had launched their own search and favored a different candidate. In 1941, with no resolution to the conflict over the two candidates, the boy chosen by the Panchen Lama's officials was installed as the de facto Tenth Panchen Lama at Kumbum Jampaling Monastery and given the name Lobsang Trinlé Lhundrup Chökyi Gyaltsen by Alak Lakho Jigme Trinlé Rinpoche. Eight years later the Kuomintang declared their support of Chökyi Gyaltsen and sent Ma Bufang to preside over his official enthronement. This is, of course, the year when the Chinese Communist Party came to power. Despite his having allied himself with Ma Bufang and the Kuomintang only months earlier, the Tenth Panchen Lama immediately sent a telegram of congratulations in recognition of Mao Zedong and his government. The Chinese reciprocated by granting him official recognition as the Tenth Panchen Lama, effectively dispensing with the need to undergo formal tests with other candidates in Lhasa. Thus a new era set in, whereby the traditional and customary way of recognizing the Panchen Lama was done away with.

In 1951 the Panchen Lama and his retinue went to Beijing to meet officials of the Chinese government. He was present when the Tibetan delegation arrived to negotiate the Seventeen-Point Agreement. At that time the Panchen Lama demanded that certain rights pertaining to his position be incorporated into the agreement. The Tibetan government rejected this, leading to a stalemate. Two weeks later a separate document was signed with respect to this matter under strong pressure from the Chinese government, as I mentioned above.

In 1952 the Panchen Lama came to Lhasa for the first time. However, before his arrival, there were intense negotiations between the Tibetan government and the Chinese with regard to seating arrangements and other ceremonial procedures with respect to the lama's audience with the Dalai Lama. There is an established tradition with regard to these details, but the Chinese, on behalf of the Panchen Lama, demanded that his seating be on a level equal to that of the Dalai Lama. This the Tibetan government stoutly rejected. After several meetings a mutually acceptable solution was found. The Tibetan government then made elaborate arrangements to welcome the Panchen Lama.

The first reception was prepared in a huge tent five kilometers east of Lhasa. A group of fifty or so officials were assembled, headed by Kalon Rampa, the senior-most minister. He was accompanied by the Chikhyap Khenpo, or the chief ecclesiastical secretary, who represented the Dalai Lama. I happened to be there among the officials. When the Panchen Lama arrived, a ceremonial welcome was accorded with the offering of greeting scarves, tea, and so on. A half an hour later the Panchen Lama began a ceremonial ride in a palanquin, escorted by his officials and guards. We Lhasa officials rode on horseback in a single long line. The large Chinese military escort accompanying the Panchen Lama rode in two single-file lines on either side of us. Most of these soldiers were rough, uncouth men who behaved rudely. As we proceeded they would hit our horses with the butt of their guns if any of us were slightly out of line. They did this repeatedly, causing a commotion that could have turned into something ugly. I used to know Che Jigme, one of the senior-most officials of the Panchen Lama, and I complained to him. We Tibetan officials tried our best to be patient, but the behavior of the Chinese soldiers did not improve. Finally, we junior officials decided it would be best to move ahead of the main party and proceed straight to the Tsuklakhang, where the next reception was to take place.

The reception at the Tsuklakhang was even more elaborate and took about an hour. Afterward, the Panchen Lama proceeded to the Potala Palace. When he reached the top story of the Potala, he was escorted to the east ceremonial hall by the Dronyer Chenmo, or lord chamberlain. I was initially seated outside in the veranda along with other officials. However, I was very keen to witness the ceremony in the inner hall, so I took a chance and went in, even though officially I was not permitted. I stood behind the main door. High lamas and first- and second-rank officials were standing on both sides of the hall. His Holiness the Dalai Lama was standing on his throne and waiting, with a big smile on his face.

The Panchen Lama went forward toward the Dalai Lama's throne. He was led by the Dronyer Chenmo, who then stopped and stood beside a red silk covering on the floor. This indicated that it was time to prostrate. There was a slight hesitation on the part of the Panchen Lama. I noticed that he glanced at his attendants before he prostrated. The Panchen Lama was then handed a long, white silk scarf by one of his attendants, which he unfolded and held up to the Dalai Lama. The Dalai Lama took it with both hands and offered back a similar scarf, and the two touched foreheads. I noticed that the Dalai Lama was continually smiling, whereas the Panchen Lama looked solemn as he went to his own throne and climbed on to it. His throne faced east, whereas the Dalai Lama's was on a platform facing south. The Dalai Lama showed great warmth and hospitality and remained standing until the Panchen Lama was seated. I remember feeling very disappointed with the way in which the Panchen Lama seemed to ignore the warm, welcoming gestures of the Dalai Lama. I can only think that his officials must have coached him on how to behave. In the course of the proceedings I do not remember clearly whether the Panchen Lama made a "mandala" offering to the Dalai Lama or not, but I expect he did. After a while I left quietly and resumed my seat outside. To my relief no one noticed anything, including the two huge monk bodyguards who stood on either side of the door to the inner hall! Later I came to know that after the formal ceremony, the Dalai Lama led the Panchen Lama to the rooms behind the inner hall for an informal chat.

In 1954 the Panchen Lama went to China with the Dalai Lama to attend the National People's Congress. In the summer of 1956 he came back to Lhasa for the inauguration of the Preparatory Committee of the Autonomous Region of Tibet, of which he was appointed deputy chair. In the winter of that same year he accompanied the Dalai Lama to Delhi at the invitation of the Mahabodhi Society of India and attended the 2,500th anniversary of the passing away of Lord Buddha.

In 1959, after the Dalai Lama took refuge in India, the Panchen Lama was appointed chair of the Preparatory Committee of the Autonomous Region of Tibet. In 1961, on his journey home after a visit to China, the Panchen Lama traveled extensively in the Amdo region and other parts of Tibet in order to study the conditions of the common people. As a result of this he wrote his famous 70,000-character letter to the Chinese government, criticizing them harshly for their complete neglect of the hardships being suffered by the Tibetan people. Soon afterward the Cultural Revolution began, and the Panchen Lama became a victim of this immense upheaval, suffering imprisonment for nine years in China. But in 1978 he was reinstated into a position of status, and he returned to Tibet. Once more he took great interest in the development of his country and continued to fearlessly criticize the Chinese authorities with regard to their policy toward Tibet. He was able to visit a few countries like Nepal, Australia, and Bolivia, and in those countries he spoke about the Chinese policy toward the development of his country. At home he advised the Tibetans to take more interest in religious activities and encouraged them to revive their traditions and customs. He even openly supported the Dalai Lama and said that the Tibetans should continue to have full faith in him. Then suddenly, in 1989, he suffered a cardiac arrest in Tashi Lhunpo. A number of Chinese doctors attended to him, but he did not survive. Nobody knows for certain whether he genuinely died from heart failure or from some other medical cause. Many suspect foul play because of his harsh criticism of the Chinese authorities and open nationalist feelings for Tibet. The people of Tibet mourned his death deeply, as they found in him a champion for their cause during the troubled times they were going through.

Soon after the death of the Panchen Lama, the Chinese formed a committee to search for his reincarnation. The committee included Jadrel Rinpoche, who was the head of Tashi Lhunpo, as well as Ngabo Ngawang Jigme, Gungthang Rinpoche from Amdo, and eleven Chinese officials. In one of their meetings it is said that Ngabo Ngawang Jigme suggested that they should consult the Dalai Lama after the appropriate candidates were found. The sympathies of the entire Tibetan population were in the balance, and so it was important to ensure their support for the sake of future relations. Predictably, the Chinese rejected this suggestion. By 1996 Jadrel Rinpoche had found some suitable candidates, and in great secrecy he forwarded their names to the Dalai Lama in India, requesting approval of the correct reincarnation. The Dalai Lama identified one candidate as the Eleventh Panchen Lama and named him Gendun Chökyi Nyima. The Chinese soon discovered what happened and immediately arrested Jadrel Rinpoche, who is in prison to this day.

The Chinese hastily put forward a candidate of their own, declaring him the Eleventh Panchen. Meanwhile the six-year-old chosen by the Dalai Lama disappeared completely along with his family. Their whereabouts are still unknown. Through the years there have been many strong international appeals for the boy's release, but the Chinese have ignored these. In September 1998 Mary Robinson, head of the U.N. Human Rights Commission, visited Drapchi prison in Lhasa. During her visit she asked the Chinese authorities about the whereabouts of the Eleventh Panchen Lama, but she was given no clear information. Likewise, many other religious and political leaders have asked the same question to no avail.

For centuries, generations of children in Tibet grew up with the proverbial wisdom that the Dalai Lama and the Panchen Lama are the sun and the moon. The heart of the relationship between the two lamas has always been a unique and special spiritual one. Despite the grim circumstances of recent history, in the future this special relationship may once again flourish.

22. THE SADUTSHANG FAMILY SEPARATES

While immense changes were affecting the lives of everyone in Tibet, my family too was undergoing a major transformation. My cousin Gyurme complained to my brother Lo Gedun about my brother Lo Nyendak. Lo Nyendak had moved to Kham and built a beautiful house on a large forested property south of our ancestral home. This home cost a great deal of money. But Lo Nyendak had had no money of his own, so he took charge of two thousand boxes of tea that the family had imported from China. The tea had been in Dartsedo on its way to Lhasa when Lo Nyendak appropriated it and sold it off to pay for the cost of construction. Gyurme was especially unhappy because Lo Nyendak was no longer really part of the family, let alone the family business. Sparked primarily by this situation, Gyurme and Lo Gedun had a falling out, with Lo Gedun defending our brother. Gyurme and Lo Gedun concluded that the family should separate. Lo Gedun asked my opinion, and since he was my eldest brother, I said I would leave the decision entirely in his hands.

The separation didn't take long, and by early 1954 it was finalized. As for the assets, Lo Gedun said he was willing to accept whatever the two cousins, Gyurme and his eldest brother Sochö, decided. They offered us our ancestral home in Kham, which was by now rather old and dilapidated and not really worth much, especially as Kham was now under Chinese occupation. Then there was the new house Lo Nyendak had built. In Lhasa they offered us Changlochen, a house that the Sadutshangs had bought from a nobleman of that name. In addition they offered us a cash payout of five thousand *dotsé*, which was worth around ten thousand dollars at that time. As for the share my cousins kept, they had a newly built house in Lhasa, situated on prime property that had been part of my wife's dowry; houses in Shigatse, Nakchukha, and Phari; two buildings and a bungalow that sat on an acre of land in Kalimpong; a large amount of cash; and a huge amount of inventory. Both Lo Gedun and I knew approximately how much the family had by way of assets. I remember clearly that between 1952 and 1953 I did some business with the Chinese and imported medical supplies for them from India. I made a profit of forty thousand dollars from that one transaction alone. So it was a very unfair division by any standard, and my brother and I were deeply disappointed. Nevertheless, we decided not to contest it legally, as the scandal would only tarnish the reputation of the Sadutshang family.

What especially disappointed me at that time was my cousin Sochö's attitude. He had retired in 1947 and devoted himself to a religious life. He lived a life of meditation and seclusion in a hermitage. He should have been a much fairer person.

In retrospect, there is one more thing that I think could have influenced the separation. Toward the latter part of the 1940s, my brother Lo Gedun, being a devout Buddhist, decided to sponsor a *tsokpheb* during the annual Monlam prayer festival, which takes place soon after the Tibetan New Year. This entailed giving offerings to each monk of the three great Geluk monasteries: Drepung, Sera, and Ganden. His Holiness the Dalai Lama was to personally attend the prayer festival for a short while, meaning that offerings worthy of the occasion had to be made. As such, Lo Gedun arranged to give a brick of tea to each monk, which was considered an extremely generous offering and even became the talk of the town. As the monks numbered about sixteen thousand, the expense incurred must have been vast. But of course it would not have been proper for the other relatives to complain about money spent on religious activities. In any case the merit and the prestige would not belong to my brother alone but would be shared by the Sadutshang family as a whole.

23. TO CHINA WITH THE DALAI LAMA AND HIS ENTOURAGE

More than two years had passed now since the Chinese entered Lhasa. In China they were making preparations for the National People's Congress to frame a new constitution, which was to allot ten seats for Tibet. The Chinese extended an invitation to His Holiness to visit China and attend the National People's Congress in the fall of 1954. After some careful consideration the invitation was accepted. His Holiness, being fully aware of the existing problems between the Tibetan people and the Chinese occupiers, thought that this visit would give him an opportunity to speak directly to the top Chinese leaders to resolve these issues. However, the Tibetan public was deeply disturbed because they thought that if His Holiness went to China, he might never be allowed to return to Tibet. They pleaded with him not to travel to China. His Holiness promised to return within a year, and since this assurance came from him directly, the fears of the Tibetans were somewhat allayed.

The entourage accompanying His Holiness to China numbered 156, including His Holiness the Dalai Lama, his two tutors Yongzin Ling Rinpoche and Yongzin Trijang Rinpoche, two cabinet ministers, a large number of government officials of various ranks, heads of the various

His Holiness the Dalai Lama with ministers and other senior attendants,
China, 1954.

religious sects, abbots of all the large monasteries, and a few artists as well.
Apart from a special group of monk officials attending to His Holiness's
personal needs, including that of his kitchen, there were two other committees. One committee was responsible for all matters of transportation and
the other for organizing camping arrangements. I was assigned to the latter,
a committee of eight officials presided over by Dzasak Kundeling.

For the first sixteen days we had to travel on horseback and camp outdoors in tents when we rested. Thereafter we reached a motorable road built
by the Chinese, and from then on Chinese military vehicles were available
for the onward journey. Camping sites for each day had been determined
in advance, and all concerned Tibetan district heads had already received
instructions for arranging transport of animals, fodder, tables, mattresses,
carpets, firewood, and cooking utensils. Our camping arrangement committee also had the responsibility of transporting special tents and equipment for His Holiness's personal use, items that were assigned to us by

the government's tent department. We had to see to it that everything was arranged and ready several hours in advance of His Holiness's arrival. Since such advance preparations had to be made, we were divided into two groups. The first group traveled a day in advance and arranged the distribution of tables, mattresses, firewood, and such for each official member of the delegation. This group put name tags on the items they had made ready, so that there was no confusion on taking possession of these once the entourage arrived. The second group, to which I belonged, had to travel very early so that it reached the following day's campsite by late afternoon. This way, all preparations could be made ready by the next morning. His Holiness's kitchen staff also had the same alternate arrangement, and so we traveled together. As soon as we arrived, our foremost task was to select the best and most appropriate site for His Holiness's personal tent, making sure all the equipment was in place so that everything was ready the following morning. The Chinese insisted on taking full responsibility for His Holiness's personal security. A couple of Chinese security personnel would always arrive an hour or two in advance of His Holiness and check all that we had arranged, pulling everything apart and thus making us rearrange the entire setup. This of course was much to our annoyance!

His Holiness's historic journey to China began one fine, bright morning on July 11, 1954. His first stop was Ganden Monastery, which was one of the three largest of the Geluk lineage. Ganden was located on Mount Wangkur, about forty-five kilometers southeast of Lhasa. For the next three days His Holiness, accompanied by his tutors, traveled by car, as there was a fairly decent and level road. The rest of the delegation traveled on horseback, and it took them four days to reach Kongpo Gyamda, the last stop on the motorable road. I was given the privilege of driving the 1931 Ford convertible assigned to the two tutors. This car was of special significance because it was the first imported motor vehicle in Tibet and had been used by the Thirteenth Dalai Lama. The present Dalai Lama traveled in a newer car, a 1947 Austin. At the end of the motorable road I joined my original assignment and traveled on horseback for the next ten days. We passed through Kongpo, where the land was low lying and forested, enjoying plenty of rain. We encountered quite a few landslides, especially where the Chinese were constructing roads. Once we had to cross a spot where a landslide had recently taken place, wading through thick mud and loose stones. A few minutes later we heard rumbling and clatter and looked back to find stones falling down the hill at that very spot! This close call compelled us to stop until it was safe to proceed, around a half hour later.

Our hazardous journey ended seven days later at a place called Po Tamo, from where we could proceed by car. Here there was a large Chinese construction camp, and the Chinese gave His Holiness a warm welcome. However, we Tibetans were thoroughly shocked at the way they treated His Holiness, our ruler and spiritual leader, with familiarity and casualness, as if he were just an ordinary person. They shook hands with him and offered him Chinese tea in an ordinary enamel mug. What was worse, they didn't even hesitate to smoke in his presence. This made me angry and sad. At the same time I also felt helpless, because I couldn't do anything to stop it.

The Chinese had arranged army vehicles, Russian jeeps, and small World War II American trucks for our transport. Our journey began the next day with His Holiness, the two tutors, and high officials riding in jeeps. The rest of us had to ride in the trucks. On the second day we reached the town of Chamdo, the seat of the governor of eastern Tibet, where the Tibetans had formally surrendered to the People's Liberation Army three years ago. It was decided that there would be a rest period of two days, which I welcomed gladly.

When I left Lhasa, my wife was expecting her fifth child. I naturally was anxious to know how she was doing. I managed to get a telephone link through the post office and got the wonderful news that she had given birth to twin girls! Both mother and babies were doing well, I was told, and I was greatly relieved. In Chamdo we also got the news that a disastrous flood had taken place in Gyantse, the second largest town in western Tibet. Many lives had been lost, including Rai Bahadur Tempa, the gentleman in charge of the Indian trade mission, and his wife, who were known to my family. Tibet never had floods, as rainfall was so scarce. This was a freak incident caused by an avalanche that burst a big lake in the mountains southwest of Gyantse. Some forty kilometers north of the town, the floodwaters joined the Tsangpo River, which merges with the Kyichu River. This river finally enters Assam in India, where it becomes the famous Brahmaputra.

After Chamdo our next major stop was at Jomda. The next day we crossed the famous Drichu River, known as the Yangtse to non-Tibetans, and entered the region called Dergé. This area had now been named Dhardo Tibetan Autonomous Region by the Chinese. Here, the deputy chair of the local government, an ex-abbot of Sera Je College in Lhasa, came to welcome His Holiness and his entourage. We rested for a short while here and then proceeded on. Eventually we had to cross the treacherous Dergé Tro Pass, a feat that took us almost four hours. Our next stop was at Yilhung Lhatso, which is surely one of the most beautiful spots in all of Tibet. A vast, deep blue lake was surrounded on all sides by beautiful pine forests, and in the background, mountains topped with snow ranged from east to west. To the north of this lake we found lush, open grassland: a paradise for us campers!

On crossing the Dergé Tro, we entered the Trehor province of Kham, the region from which my family came. Yilhung Lhatso, in fact, was only about sixty kilometers from my ancestral home. I arrived early, as I had to proceed to the next stop to make preparations. But my brother Lo Nyendak had arrived even earlier and was there to welcome me with a group of friends and servants. I was surprised to see that he had driven up on a motorcycle with a sidecar, something very unusual for this part of the country. I told him that I would not be able to spend any time at home during this trip, as I had my duties to perform, but that I would perhaps get a chance to stay for a day or two on my return.

Our next stop was the town of Karzé. But before that, His Holiness was scheduled to make a short stop at Dargye Monastery, which was on the way. Dargye Monastery is just two kilometers west of my ancestral home and fifteen kilometers away from Karzé. My colleague and I arrived at the monastery on the previous evening to make advance preparations. I spent the night at my late cousin Chözé Talha's apartment, which was still kept for him at the monastery. As I had always regarded my cousin with the highest respect, I was very happy to be able to stay in this apartment.

His Holiness arrived at about ten in the morning, and in addition to all the monks, there was a huge crowd of local people waiting at the main gate to welcome him. A formal tea ceremony was held in the central hall of the monastery, and this was followed by His Holiness conferring his blessing on the 1,800 or so monks and approximately 1,500 villagers of the locality. As

His Holiness blessed each person individually, this took almost two hours. We left in the afternoon and reached Karzé an hour later. Karzé was the largest town in the area, and Karzé Monastery was where all our accommodations were prepared.

Our next day's journey started early. There was a short stop on a hilltop, about thirty kilometers from Karzé, where the surrounding monasteries in the valley had put up an exceedingly beautiful tent to greet His Holiness. After a welcome tea he gave all the monks and the local nomads his blessings. They were overjoyed, as it was the first time they had ever received blessings from a Dalai Lama. Our next stop was Tau Monastery deep in the green valley, and from there we proceeded to Dartsedo, the most important trade center between Tibet and China.

The following day we had to cross the extremely high pass called Erlang, which was the historical border between Tibet and China, centuries back. Late that afternoon we reached Chengdu, the capital of the Sichuan province of China and a large commercial center. The next day His Holiness and a small group flew to Xian while the rest traveled by train. At the airport the provincial head and officials were there to welcome His Holiness's party. Rampa, the head of the Dalai Lama's Beijing office, and some of his staff were also there to receive His Holiness and his entourage. Accommodation for His Holiness had been arranged at a brand new hotel. Once there I met Tara-la, also of our Beijing office, for the first time. Later in India, when we became refugees, I would work with him.

The Panchen Lama arrived the next day and stayed in the same hotel as the Dalai Lama. When the Panchen Lama arrived, His Holiness the Dalai Lama went down to the lobby to greet him with a traditional greeting scarf. A special train was arranged by the Chinese to take the entire Tibetan party to Beijing. The Dalai Lama and the Panchen Lama, as well as their respective families, rode in a special coach. His Holiness's two tutors and some senior officials were also included in that coach. We reached Beijing the following morning. At the station, Zhou Enlai, the army chief Zhu De, and senior Chinese officials were there to greet us with a Chinese military band. A large group of Tibetan students and other Tibetans also gave us a rousing welcome.

In Beijing a spacious bungalow called Yu Kha-chao had been arranged as accommodation for the Dalai Lama, his two tutors, and two of Tibet's top ministers. The Panchen Lama and his entourage were accommodated separately. The rest of us were put up in various apartments elsewhere. In the evening a grand dinner reception was given by the Chinese government. Zhu De gave a welcome speech, followed by speeches from the Dalai Lama and the Panchen Lama.

The main purpose of the Dalai Lama's visit was to attend the National People's Congress. It started a few days later, and His Holiness was kept busy for the next week or so, attending not only the main session but also various committees. There were a significant number of Tibetans participating as members of the National People's Congress, including His Holiness and some of his officials, the Panchen Lama and some of his officials, and a number of other Tibetans from Kham, Amdo, and other regions. In addition to the formal meetings that took place throughout the day, there were

The Dalai Lama, the Panchen Lama, and two other representatives from
Tibet at the Chinese National Assembly, Beijing, 1954.

numerous evening engagements: dinners, cultural shows, and the like. On the whole it was rather tiring for the Dalai Lama, who was taking part in such political and social activities for the first time in his life. Such activity would be considered unimaginable in the past. Quite a few senior Tibetan officials also attended the National People's Congress as observers, and for them I think it was a very good experience.

The Dalai Lama met several foreign diplomats during the course of these evening engagements. For example, even though the encounter was a brief one at a reception, he met Nehru, the Indian prime minister, who was in Beijing on an official visit. Although His Holiness was very anxious to speak with Nehru, the Chinese made sure this never happened. In any case, even if he had managed an opportunity, the conversation would have been interpreted through a Chinese translator. Thus it would have been impossible to discuss important matters in confidence.

Two weeks after our arrival in Beijing, His Holiness the Dalai Lama and the entire entourage were taken for a tour of important cities and industries. First we visited a large steel factory at Dongbei, known to most as Manchuria. Since most of my fellow Tibetans had never seen a steel plant in their lives, much less a large one, they were very impressed. Before every tour the Chinese always briefed us about what we were going to see, and we were always told about how much improvement there had been since the Communists took over. Our guides claimed that all the machinery in the plants had been manufactured by the Chinese themselves, and since most of the Tibetans present could not read English, they didn't doubt it. However, I could read plainly the words "made in U.K." or "made in U.S.A." on most of the machinery. The Chinese seemed to be unaware that among us there were those who could read English and who had seen similar machinery elsewhere. As such they didn't hesitate to blatantly lie. I told my colleagues what I had seen written on the machinery, and we had a good laugh about the Chinese attempts to fool us.

Leaving this industrial belt we were next taken to a small town called Shenyang in Manchuria. It appeared as though this area must have once been part of Korea, as the entire population was Korean. We found the

Koreans to be very friendly, and they seemed to us to resemble us Tibetans too. There was really not much to see at this stop. The Chinese merely wanted to show us how this town had grown and developed since the Communists came to power. During these tours a colleague of mine and I had to travel a day ahead of the others in order to prepare and allot accommodation for all the people in the entourage. In Shenyang I saw how the Koreans had a novel way of warming themselves during the harsh winter months. They used a special coal stove that they put under the bed. The small stove was enclosed on all sides except for a small sliding door on one side for putting coals in. They also used a piece of wood for a pillow, which left me wondering how one could ever possibly get used to it.

We journeyed on southward to a couple of well-known places. The most significant visit was to the city of Shanghai. My fellow Tibetans were very impressed by the size of the city, especially of the tall buildings that went up as high as fifteen stories. In fact, we were taken to dinner at a large restaurant with a beautiful open terrace, on the fourteenth floor of a hotel called Hotel Gochi. Since I had been to Shanghai in 1946, soon after World War II, it didn't make much of an impression on me. Neither did I see any distinct improvement in the city since then. In fact, with an overall appearance of neglect about it, it seemed to have deteriorated since I last saw it. On my earlier visit I remembered shopping at the well-known British department store Whiteway. I remembered being greeted by a tall turbaned Sikh doorman in a grand uniform. I also remembered that I had visited Xizhang-lu, or Tibet Road, right in the center of the city.

From Shanghai we were taken to Hangzhou, famous for its beauty and its silk factories. I had visited this city too in 1946 and recalled a pilgrimage to a few Buddhist monasteries on the hill. But this time we were not taken to any monasteries. Instead the Chinese took us to some homes for the elderly. In one of these we saw senior citizens enjoying themselves, playing mahjong, cards, and other games in a prettily decorated hall. After our visit there, one of our colleagues had to go back to retrieve something he'd left behind and was amazed to find the entire hall empty and deserted, the same hall that, until a short time ago, was lively and filled with happy old people!

The whole thing had been staged for us; the Chinese clearly had no qualms about resorting to deceit. In the same manner, they continued to brief us and feed us propaganda, distorting all the facts, no doubt.

After a long and exhausting tour of many places, some of which were truly enjoyable, we returned to Beijing a few weeks before the Tibetan New Year in early 1955. It was decided that a customary New Year ceremony would be held at the Dalai Lama's Beijing office, where already a special suite existed for His Holiness. There was also a hall that could be used for the ceremony. His Holiness moved into his suite at the Beijing office on New Year's eve.

The New Year ceremony was conducted in its traditional manner, with all the Tibetan officials dressed in special robes. In keeping with tradition, new officials were inducted that day, two monks and one lay. In the evening the Dalai Lama hosted a dinner for the Chinese leaders at Renmin Daihuitang, the Great Hall of the People, inside the erstwhile Chinese emperor's palace compound. I was among the officials assigned to make preparations for the dinner at seven in the evening. The Panchen Lama arrived early and exchanged greeting scarves with the Dalai Lama, and they touched their foreheads. The first Chinese leader to arrive was Zhu De, followed by Liu Shaoqi, a high-ranking CPC secretary. Then came Premier Zhou Enlai, followed soon afterward by Mao Zedong. We had arranged individual tables for the top leaders, each with a *dega*, which is a stack of Tibetan New Year pastries, *droma dresil*, and of course the indispensable butter tea. As soon as Mao arrived, the Dalai Lama and the Panchen Lama received him at the door, and they exchanged scarves. When they were seated butter tea was served, followed by an offering of *chema*, which is roasted barley flour, or *tsampa*, mixed with butter and set firmly in an ornamental wooden container. The Dalai Lama explained to his guests that when chema is offered, auspicious words are uttered, and one throws some of this tsampa in the air. Then the guests were escorted to the dinner table. There were altogether two hundred people, which included about thirty Tibetan representatives to the National People's Congress from various parts of Kham and Amdo, forty officials of the Tibetan government in Lhasa, and the Panchen Lama. The remaining guests were all Chinese officials.

24. THE RETURN HOME

We'd been in China for almost eight months when the time came to return home. A committee of officials was busy preparing the program for the return journey. Meanwhile a large number of Tibetan representatives from Kham and Amdo came to Beijing to request the Dalai Lama to give teachings in their various monasteries along the way. Since it was of course impossible to stop at all of these monasteries, it was decided that His Holiness would stop for a day or two in all the monasteries close to his route. However, with respect to three of the areas in Kham that were too far from the motorable road His Holiness was to travel, he decided to send as his representatives his junior tutor Trijang Rinpoche, Karmapa Rinpoche, and Minling Chung Rinpoche.

The Dalai Lama's first stop in Amdo was going to be at Tashi Labrang. From there he would go to Kumbum Monastery, some other major monasteries, and would also visit his birthplace, Taktser. A group belonging to the preparatory committee, which included our superior Dzasak Kundeling, two officials of the treasury, and myself, was instructed to proceed directly to Dartsedo and beyond to make necessary arrangements at various stops where His Holiness would give teachings. We traveled to Hunan from

Beijing and from there boarded a ferry that took us up the Yangtse River until we reached Chongqing, the wartime capital of China. Next we stopped at Chengdu, and then we drove to Dartsedo, where we stopped for two days. On our second day there, there was a big earthquake that destroyed several houses. Landslides also occurred from the hills into the valley where Dartsedo was situated, so we moved out from our residence into the open compound. We witnessed several Chinese offices being vacated and their equipment being loaded onto trucks. There were numerous aftershocks too, but by evening everything had more or less subsided.

We left the next morning, though with some trepidation, as we had to travel along the river in the valley and faced the possibility of more landslides. We started very early, and after crossing a high pass we journeyed down to a small monastery called Ba Chödé in Minyak, reaching it at eight o'clock. We were given a warm welcome and were taken to the top of the monastery, where tables had been laid for our breakfast in a veranda. We sat there for a few minutes and then decided to move down to the courtyard, which was more spacious and open. We had just finished having some tea when we heard thunderous booms in the far distance to the south. None of us had any idea what it was. It was only a couple of minutes later when the earth began to shake that we realized it was an earthquake! A few seconds later the intensity began to increase, and soon it was very strong. We witnessed a large pile of wood stacked some fifty yards away collapse, and more frightening still, I watched the wooden monastery rooftop structure come apart and then realign itself back to its original shape! All in all this lasted for about forty seconds. The huge earthquake that had occurred in Dartsedo earlier was not yet over. We were all very relieved to have moved down to the monastery courtyard. There were some aftershocks, and then it seemed that everything was over. But even as we were driving, after we had left, we felt some more aftershocks.

After a journey of a couple of hours we came to a very large monastery called Tau Nyatso. Here we again gave instructions about the preparations required for His Holiness's arrival. Likewise we stopped at Drango Monastery, Jori Monastery, Tongkhor Monastery, and finally Karzé, giving similar instructions. Since Karzé was a major town, we stopped there for a week, during which time we visited Dargye Monastery, close to my home, to also give instructions. I was then able to spend a day at home with my brother Lo Nyendak, like I promised him earlier. This short stay gave me the opportunity to visit the place where I was born and to see the house built nearby by my brother on a beautiful piece of open ground. Lots of trees had been planted, and a plentiful water supply was assured by building a connection to a clear stream a little farther north. My brother was present when the Chinese Communists first entered Kham in 1950. During my brief stay at home, I met many of our relatives as well as several loyal servants who had been working devotedly for the family for years. I had no idea at that time that I would not see my ancestral home again for several decades.

After completing the necessary preparations in Karzé and at Dargye Monastery, we traced our journey back to the town of Dartsedo. From here the Dalai Lama was scheduled to visit all the monasteries situated along the motor highway. I was then given an additional responsibility: setting up the portable amplifier and speakers, operated by a small hand generator, at all the monasteries. I must mention that this hand generator was the one given to us by Vasili Zvansov, the wireless operator of the U.S. consulate in Xinjiang I mentioned above. The amplifier and speakers were the ones my family had offered to the Dalai Lama and had been used for the Kalachakra teachings in Lhasa. I used the amplifier for the first time during this journey at Drango Monastery, where the Dalai Lama stayed overnight and gave teachings to all the monks as well as laymen of the surrounding area. All along the way, all those who received teachings from His Holiness were overjoyed because it was a once-in-a-lifetime opportunity for them, one they treasured dearly. The type of religious teachings given depended on the request of each individual monastery, and the duration of stay depended on the location and the size of the population of the surrounding area. The stays ranged from one to three days usually. Stops we made were at the following monasteries: Dartsedo Ngachö, Minyak Ra Nga Khar, Tau Nyatso, Drango, Jori, Tongkhor, Karzé, Dargye, Beru, Yilhung, Dergé, Rongsum, Jomda, Kyishung, and Chamdo. From here onward there were no monasteries until Lhasa, and so we proceeded ahead with stops at three places on the way. The last stop was at Ganden, where we stayed for an extra day so that proper arrangements could be completed for the entry into Lhasa; the entire population of the city would certainly turn out to welcome His Holiness.

The journey home proved to be as hazardous as our forward journey. Leaving Chamdo, as we were reaching Po Tamo, a densely wooded area, there was very heavy rainfall. A bridge across the river we had to ford suddenly collapsed as the convoy was progressing across it, to our shock and dismay! Most fortunately, the jeeps carrying the Dalai Lama, his tutors, and higher officials had been able to cross the bridge to safety in the nick of time. You can imagine our great relief. The last jeep in that group was at the end of the bridge when it collapsed. But the driver managed to react swiftly enough when he heard the splintering of the wooden supports below him and drove immediately to safety; thanks to his alertness he was saved.

The immediate problem we now faced was getting His Holiness's personal baggage, which included his bedding, across to the other side. We decided to make a ropeway, first throwing a thin rope and then attaching a thicker one to it with the help of a stone tied to the end. However, the distance was too great—the bridge was a hundred and fifty feet long. Then we decided to make a bow and arrow and shoot the rope across, and it worked! We got quite a bit of baggage across in this way. Meanwhile, the Chinese had sent a messenger to the next road construction camp, which wasn't far away. A gang of laborers and engineers turned up, and the engineers worked on the technical repairs while the laborers and carpenters cut the logs needed to restore the bridge. They worked late into the night while we slept in our trucks. The next morning we witnessed how hard and well they had worked through the night. When the bridge was fully repaired by late that following afternoon, we immediately crossed it and tried to catch up with the rest of the party ahead of us.

It took us another day to reach Ganden Monastery. From there we proceeded to Tsel Gungthang, where there were the remains of an ancient monastery built seven hundred years earlier. His Holiness camped there for a short rest. Early the next morning we started on the final leg of our journey. The day was a bright and clear. We crossed a new bridge over the Kyichu River, which the Chinese had built in our absence. As soon as we crossed, we found people from all walks of life lining both sides of the road, bearing scarves and incense sticks. The throngs extended the entire length of the twelve-kilometer route to the Dalai Lama's summer palace, Norbulingka. It seemed as though the entire population of Lhasa, including all the monks from the various monasteries, had come that day to welcome His Holiness. There were tears in all their eyes, tears of joy for having their ruler and spiritual leader back home and also tears of relief, for many feared that the Chinese would prevent the Dalai Lama's return.

For myself personally, it was such a joy to be back home and to see my newborn twin daughters. The elder one was healthy, but the younger one, born over two hours later, looked rather thin. My wife told me that the doctor at the hospital told her that the younger one was so weak she might not survive. However, my wife gave the weaker child her twenty-four-hour devotion and care and managed to beat the odds and give her renewed life.

25. TENSE TIMES IN LHASA

After a break of a few days, I resumed my duties at the office, but there wasn't much work there. Meanwhile the political situation in Lhasa appeared to be changing, with people in the city expressing open anti-Communist sentiments. News trickled in from Kham that the Chinese authorities had arrested many lamas and local chiefs for resisting Chinese domination. To substantiate this, many groups of Khampas began to arrive in Lhasa, and soon accommodation became scarce. Many of these Khampas had to camp outside the city. They brought with them stories of Chinese atrocities. Many of them had rebelled and fought Chinese soldiers. Some had even managed to kill several Chinese and were then compelled to flee their homes, with their families or by themselves. As more and more groups of Khampas began to come to Lhasa from various parts of Kham, the Chinese authorities began to take notice of these armed and rebellious people. They began to put pressure on the Tibetan government to disarm them and send them back to Kham. This caused the Khampas to group and organize themselves and get away from Lhasa to escape the Chinese threat. Months later we heard the news that the Khampas had formed an organization called Chushi Gangdruk, or "four rivers and six ranges," signifying the land of their origin. They had made their base in Chongé, about a hundred kilometers south of Lhasa. All this naturally affected even the Khampas residing in Lhasa, including my family. A year after my last visit home in Kham, my brother Lo Nyendak arrived from Kham with no intention of returning. The situation there was becoming more and more oppressive and unbearable.

The foreign ministry, where I worked, was headed by Dzasak Liushar and Dzasak Surkhang Surpa. By the time the Chinese took control of our office, however, Surkhang Surpa had passed away, leaving us with only Liushar. His Chinese counterpart was Yang Gongsu, a middle-aged man. He could understand English but refused to speak it, always using an interpreter when talking with the Indian or Nepalese consulates in Lhasa. In the Indian mission I had a couple of friends I used to visit from time to time. Noting this, the Chinese colleagues in my office asked me not to repeat these visits, as they were objectionable! I naturally took exception to their attitude and told them I couldn't see what there was that was undesirable in these visits. After all, they were not official visits but of a purely private nature. They, however, didn't agree with me.

In the spring of 1956 I was told that the Maharaj Kumar of Sikkim would be visiting Lhasa and that the Kashag had appointed me his liaison officer. Arrangements for his stay were made at Shekarlingpa House. On the day of his arrival, I went to receive him at an appointed spot near Drepung Monastery, where he had a short rest for refreshments. I knew the Maharaj Kumar from my school days, when we used to know him as Gyalsey Lama, or the "lama prince," because he was a prince of Sikkim and also the reincarnation of a lama. He had come to Tibet on behalf of the Mahabodhi Society of India, of which he was president, to extend an invitation to the Dalai Lama to attend the 2,500th anniversary of Lord Buddha's birth. Two days after his arrival, a private audience was arranged for him at the Potala Palace. During this audience the Maharaj Kumar also informed His Holiness that Sikkim had established the Tashi Namgyal Institute of Tibetology and would be deeply appreciative if His Holiness would contribute a complete set of the Kangyur and Tengyur texts to the institute. The Kangyur, with one hundred and eight volumes, is the teachings of the Buddha. The Tengyur has over two hundred volumes of commentaries on these teachings. His Holiness consented and not only contributed the texts that were requested but many other important scriptures too. All these were printed at the Shol Parkhang press, situated just below the Potala Palace. They were dispatched to Sikkim some months later. His Holiness also told the Maharaj Kumar that he would be very pleased to accept his invitation and would send a formal reply at a later date.

One odd incident during the Maharaj Kumar's visit shows how nervous the Chinese were about any foreign contact and the sometimes ridiculous lengths they would go to make things difficult for foreign dignitaries visiting Tibet. The Maharaj Kumar had come to Lhasa with two jeeps. The Chinese said that, since the drivers of these had no clearance from the transport department, they must undergo a driving test and obtain driver's licenses. This was unexpected and annoying, but there was nothing we could do, as the Chinese were insistent. I had done the driving test before and knew it was very difficult. The Maharaj Kumar's driver, Phiku, was an accomplished driver and managed to pass the test, but unfortunately his master failed. However, in a gesture of supposed magnanimity, the Chinese decided to treat this as a special case and issued him a license. The Maharaj Kumar also requested permission to visit the Kongpo region, about eighty kilometers south of Lhasa, but the Chinese refused to allow him to use the highway. He returned to Sikkim after about a week's stay in Lhasa.

26. THE DALAI LAMA VISITS INDIA FOR THE BUDDHA JAYANTI

The news that the Dalai Lama had been invited to the Buddha Jayanti festival in India was welcomed by all Tibetans, as it was such an important and holy occasion for Buddhists. However, I learned that once more the Chinese objected to His Holiness going, regardless of how eager he was to participate in this important event. Their excuse was that it posed a security problem, but such excuses seemed absurd to us Tibetans. Owing to the Chinese objection, it was decided that Trijang Rinpoche, junior tutor to the Dalai Lama, would attend the function as his representative. At that time I was in India on a private visit and suddenly received instructions from our trade mission in Kalimpong that I would have to accompany Trijang Rinpoche as his interpreter and assistant. Accordingly I went to Nathula Pass in Sikkim in late November to receive Trijang Rinpoche. My family was very pleased that I would have to accompany Rinpoche, as they were his devoted disciples. He rested for a few days in Kalimpong, but before we had even started on our way, we received the joyful news that the Dalai Lama and the Panchen Lama would now both be coming to the Buddha Jayanti festival. A few days later Trijang Rinpoche and I went to Gangtok and joined the entourage of over twenty officials of both the Dalai Lama and the Panchen Lama as well as about five Chinese officials.

The Dalai Lama and the Panchen Lama arriving in Gangtok and being
greeted by the king of Sikkim, Chögyal Tashi Namgyal, 1956.

Apa Pant, the political officer in Sikkim, was the liaison assigned to our
entourage, and he looked after us for all our engagements. He was an officer
of the Indian external affairs ministry stationed in Gangtok. He had to deal
with all matters concerning not only Sikkim but also Tibet and Bhutan.
His Holiness the Dalai Lama and the entourage arrived in New Delhi by
air on November 24, 1956. At the airport Vice President Radhakrishnan and
Prime Minister Nehru were both there to receive His Holiness, and they
gave him a warm welcome. From the airport His Holiness drove with the
vice president straight to Rashtrapati Bhavan to meet the president of India,
Dr. Rajendra Prasad. The meeting with the president was cordial and warm.
I believe both the president and his wife to be deeply religious people from
the way they responded to His Holiness. They called on him several times
during his stay in Delhi. The Dalai Lama's official residence during his visit
was Hyderabad House, built by the Nizam of Hyderabad. It was a beautiful and spacious mansion with a huge garden, something that His Holiness
always liked.

His Holiness the Dalai Lama calls on the Indian president Rajendra Prasad and the vice president Radhakrishnan at the Rashtrapati Bhavan, New Delhi, 1956.

The Dalai Lama's first engagement was to visit the Rajghat memorial and pay homage to the remains of Mahatma Gandhi by offering flowers at the site. During the course of the next few days, many dignitaries came to see him, including the president and office bearers of the Mahabodhi Society. The Buddha Jayanti celebrations were attended by an enormous gathering of important religious leaders as well as diplomats from India and other countries. His Holiness delivered a speech about how peace was such a strong feature of the Lord Buddha's teachings. Once the Buddha Jayanti festival was over, His Holiness visited Bodh Gaya, the most sacred of all pilgrimage sites for Buddhists, being the place where the Buddha attained enlightenment. He also visited the Buddhist holy sites of Nalanda and Rajgir. It so happened that during His Holiness's stay at Bodh Gaya, the Chinese premier, Zhou Enlai, was visiting Rajgir to formally hand over to the prime minister of India a relic of the Buddha that up to that time had been in China. There was a big reception for the occasion, which the Dalai Lama also attended. There he met Zhou Enlai for the second time in India, for

The Dalai Lama, Prime Minister Nehru, and the Panchen Lama, front center, surrounded by the heads of all the delegations who participated in
the Buddha Jayanti celebrations, December 1956.

several days earlier he had met him in Delhi during the premier's official
visit to capital.

During this reception I was abruptly called upon to perform a special
duty. I was instructed to go immediately to Kalimpong and bring Nechung Kuten, the state oracle, to Delhi by the very next day through whatever means necessary. Nechung Kuten was in Kalimpong being treated for
arthritis at the Scottish Mission hospital. I left immediately by train and
then traveled by plane from Calcutta to Bagdogra. I made airline reservations for four people—Nechung Kuten, his two attendants, and myself—
for the flight from Bagdogra to Calcutta and then for a connecting flight to
Delhi, which was scheduled to depart only an hour after we landed. After
doing all of this, I still managed to reach Kalimpong that same night.

On arriving in Kalimpong, I immediately made arrangements for dis-
charging Nechung Kuten from the hospital. We left early the next day.
Unfortunately our flight was delayed two hours, making it impossible for
us to catch our connecting flight. I talked to the Indian Airlines chief at

Seated is His Holiness the Dalai Lama flanked by his two tutors, Ling Rinpoche and Trijang Rinpoche. Behind them is the whole Tibetan entourage at the Buddha Jayanti celebrations, 1956. The author is first on the right in the second-to-last row.

Bagdogra and explained that I had a V.I.P. with me who must reach Delhi that very day. I made the case that the chief must ask Calcutta to delay the connecting flight. He was very cooperative and did everything I asked for. When we finally arrived in Calcutta and boarded our plane to Delhi, we found all the passengers on board waiting for us with looks of annoyance on their faces!

I was able to deliver Nechung Kuten to Hyderabad House that very evening, completing my duty successfully. I knew, of course, that something important was going on. Earlier I had heard some talk of His Holiness's elder brother Gyalo Thondup, Tsipon Shakabpa, and other senior officials suggesting that His Holiness not return to Tibet for the time being, at least till the situation was more stable. Three other ministers accompanying His Holiness—Surkhang, Ngabo, and Ragasha—were not supportive of this idea. I therefore assumed that the Nechung had to be consulted on this matter. Such a decision, however, would not be based solely on the prediction of the state oracle. When His Holiness ultimately made the final decision regarding his return to Tibet, it was based on the specific assurances of Zhou Enlai, who told him that the Chinese authorities in Lhasa would adhere to the proper implementation of the Seventeen-Point Agreement and that changes would be made only as and when the Tibetan people agreed to them.

The evening I arrived in Delhi with Nechung Kuten, I learned that His Holiness and entourage had arrived an hour before by train from Bodh Gaya, but he had yet to arrive at Hyderabad House, and no one knew exactly where he was. Our senior officials were pacing about in great anxiety, and the Indian officials, to whom they turned for an explanation, were also at a complete loss. After many queries and telephone calls made by the security officials, we finally traced His Holiness to the Chinese embassy! It came to light that when the train arrived at the New Delhi station, all the Tibetan officials went directly to the vehicles assigned to them. They all assumed that His Holiness would be escorted by the Indian liaison officer to Hyderabad House. This, however, did not happen. It seems the Chinese ambassador, without informing the Indian officials, had escorted His Holiness to the ambassador's own car and then driven off, straight to his embassy. The senior Tibetan officials were also not informed by the Chinese of this change of plans. When the entourage arrived at Hyderabad House from the railway station, Dronyer Chenmo Phala had gone up immediately to His Holiness's rooms to attend to his duties and found that they were empty. Everyone was thoroughly disturbed and distressed at this unprecedented turn of events, and the Tibetan officials learned a vital lesson in breaches of security arrangements.

After His Holiness's second visit to Delhi, a plan was made for him to visit the important Buddhist pilgrimage sites of Varanasi, Sanchi, the Ajanta and Ellora caves, Rewalsar near Mandi in Kulu Valley, said to be the birthplace of Guru Padmasambhava, and finally Nagarjunakonda in South India, the seat of the renowned Buddhist master Nagarjuna. I was grateful to be able to see the remains of Nagarjunakonda and the many sacred statues and writings housed in a museum there. I was very fortunate, because, from what I understand, two years later that entire area went under water owing to the construction of a huge dam.

In between the pilgrimage sites, His Holiness was also able to do some sightseeing. On the way to Rewalsar we saw Nangal Dam, one of India's biggest dams. On the way back His Holiness visited the hill resort of Mussoorie as well as the Indian Military Academy in Dehradun. He also visited the metropolitan cities of Bombay, Madras, and Calcutta. When traveling to Calcutta we were taken to Jamshedpur to see the Tata Steel Industry, where in addition to the steel factories we also saw the Tata Mercedes truck factory. Here His Holiness was offered trucks at concessional rates, so our government decided to buy ten trucks.

Our last stop at the end of this long tour was Gangtok. But before that we stopped in Kalimpong. The Indian government was not too happy with this stop, as Kalimpong was said to be a hotbed of covert political activity of all kinds; it was allegedly full of spies as well. His Holiness was keen to visit Kalimpong simply because the Thirteenth Dalai Lama had stayed there for some time between 1911 and 1912, during the Chinese invasion. The Thirteenth Dalai Lama had stayed at the beautiful Bhutan House at the invitation of the grandmother of the late prime minister of Bhutan, Jigme Dorji; she was a deeply religious lady. Ever since then, as I mentioned above, Bhutan House came to be known to Tibetans as Kalimpong Phodrang, or Kalimpong Palace. During His Holiness's three-day stay, he gave teachings and public audiences to all the Tibetans and local Buddhists in the Darjeeling district.

Two days before His Holiness's departure for home, I was instructed by the Kashag to stay behind and take delivery of the ten trucks the government had bought earlier. I was also to take charge of an Ambassador car, gifted to His Holiness by Nehru. I was quite happy to get this assignment, as my family was in Kalimpong at that time. It took me two weeks to take delivery of these vehicles. I sent them directly to Gangtok, where they had to be dismantled and then carried by porters across the Nathula Pass and up to Yatung. The porters who carried the Ambassador parts were delighted, as they knew the vehicle was for the Dalai Lama. When the dismantled parts reached Yatung, His Holiness's personal chauffeur, Tashi Tsering, had the task of re-assembling them. He was given a team of assistants, but even so it would take him a long time. I might add that, in addition to the vehicles,

I also had to arrange for sufficient fuel, both diesel and petrol, to be trans-
ported to Yatung from Gangtok. It was almost two months before I could
proceed to Lhasa with the reassembled vehicles. I arranged for my family to
go back to Lhasa in the meantime, and in late summer I joined them.

27. LAST DAYS IN LHASA

S oon after I finally returned to Lhasa, I joined my office at Zunbö House, a house belonging to a Tibetan nobleman and bought by the Chinese authorities. Not long afterward, Dzasak Liushar summoned me to his house. I went the next day. Liushar offered me tea and then told me that the Chinese officials objected to my working at the foreign office. They claimed that I had close relations with the Indian consulate at Dekyilingka and that I was also engaged in business activities. They demanded that my relations with the Indian consulate be terminated if I wished to continue working at the foreign office. I was quite astounded with these Chinese demands but certainly not at a loss for words to explain myself to Liushar. I told him, "As you know, my family is a family engaged in business and trading. I cannot abandon this activity, as our livelihood depends on it. My family and I cannot survive on the meager salary that I receive from the government. Besides, I do my own private business work in my own time, after office hours, and at my own expense. As for my connection with Dekyilingka, it is purely private in nature. I go there once in a while, as I have Sikkimese friends who work there. In any event, as you are fully aware, I am an employee of the Tibetan government and not of the Chinese government. My present position is that of a Tibetan government official assigned to the foreign office by the Kashag. If the Chinese do not approve of me and are making things difficult for you, I wish to be relieved of this post. I request you to inform the Kashag of this and also ask that I may be posted to some other Tibetan government office." Liushar said he would take the matter up with the Kashag, and thereafter I stopped going to work at the foreign office.

A few weeks later I was summoned by the Kashag and appointed head of the transport department along with a monk official, Dombor Tsedon Nga-wang Rigdol. We were given two junior officials and some additional staff. Our main responsibility was to transport government grain from various granaries across the country to points from which they would be distributed as payment to officials and soldiers. The ten Tata trucks that I had brought over from India were handed over to my department for this purpose. Since there were no drivers for these trucks, we recruited ten soldiers from the bodyguard regiment with the consent of the government and asked Tashi Tsering to give driving lessons to these young men. They learned fast, and within a month they were ready for work. I was quite happy with my new work and got on well with my colleague, whom I already knew well; he had a tremendous sense of humor. We managed also to cut costs for the government by letting the trucks carry loads for private traders for a fee when these trucks were going empty to the granaries. This income helped to offset the exorbitant cost of fuel. When our trucks were not needed for government use, we also sent them to Yatung and hired them out to private businesses.

When I returned home in the summer of 1957, I found the overall situation in Lhasa tense. Yet more Khampas were fleeing their homeland, and people in town talked of more and more Communist oppression in Kham. There were also rumors that Khampa resistance in the south was getting stronger and stronger. That winter rumors began to float about that Khampa resistance groups were raiding villages, pillaging and robbing. This was entirely untrue. What really happened was that the Chinese employed tactics of deception in order to malign the resistance fighters. They employed miscreants and also dressed their own people in Khampa clothes, sending them to loot villages in order to turn the local people against the Khampas.

My brother Lo Nyendak had been in Lhasa a year now. While in Kham he had been warned by a sympathetic Chinese friend who worked for the Chinese government that reforms were soon going to be introduced that would change everything drastically. He warned that it would be in my brother's best interest to leave Kham, proceed to Lhasa, and then to India. Lo Nyendak decided to heed this advice and so moved to Lhasa. A year later, when the Chushi Gangdruk resistance movement led by Andruk Gonpo Tashi was started, my brother joined up, along with thirty-eight well-armed relatives and friends of the family. My brother went on to become one of the top leaders of the Chushi Gangdruk.

The three top leaders of the Chushi Gangdruk Khampa resistance organization, 1958. Lo Nyendak Sadutshang, Andruk Gonpo Tashi, and Namgyal Dorje Chagotsang.

Since our family was Khampa, we were also fully aware that we were being closely watched in Lhasa. That we were under suspicion was made startlingly clear in the late autumn of 1957. One afternoon while my eldest brother Lo Gedun and the women and children were at home, a group of about ten armed Chinese soldiers showed up suddenly and forcefully entered our house. They searched all the rooms and even looked behind the cupboards! When questioned, they said that some dangerous prisoners had just escaped and were thought to have entered our gate. But of course, they were lying to disguise their true motive; it wasn't difficult to see through their lies. They were looking for weapons, and when they were satisfied we had none, they went away.

The people of Lhasa, especially the monks in the nearby monasteries, were now becoming restive, and people's groups were formed in secret. The people were strongly opposed to the Chinese demands for merging the Tibetan army with the Chinese People's Liberation Army and for replacing the Tibetan flag with the Chinese one. They were also angered over the Chinese interference in the administration of the Tibetan government. They filed several petitions to the Kashag, requesting it not to give in to the demands of the Chinese.

By the beginning of 1958 relations between the Tibetans and the Chinese had deteriorated even further, and there were more and more instances of open and public aversion toward the Chinese presence in Tibet. Noticing the uncertainty of the times, I made up my mind to send my family to India, where in any case I wanted my children to be educated. My two eldest daughters were already in Kalimpong, studying at St. Joseph's Convent. Now I arranged to have my wife, our two sons, and a daughter taken to Yatung in my jeep. I made arrangements for them to travel onward from Yatung on horseback with a mule caravan transporting wool to India. Fortunately, since they were only women and children, the Chinese checkpoint at the border didn't create any problems. I told my wife that under no circumstance was she and the children to return to Lhasa without my express approval. I thought that it would be far easier for me to deal with any untoward situation, should it arise, if my family were not around.

A couple of months later, we in the transport department learned that our vehicles needed several spare parts not available in Lhasa. It was decided that I should go to India to buy these parts and also to make arrangements for regular fuel transports to Lhasa. The Kashag gave us their official approval, and the foreign office was asked to issue me the necessary travel documents. This had become a routine procedure after our Tibetan government foreign office had merged with the Chinese foreign office. I went over to my old department and handed over the letter from the Kashag. After consulting with his Chinese colleague, the Tibetan official dealing with my case told me that they couldn't issue me a passport without clearance from the office of the United Front, which was a Chinese government department that dealt with a variety of issues, including minorities, and that was known to covertly gather information about us. I was surprised as this was not the practice during my days at the foreign office. I knew this with certainty, because I was the one who dealt with passports. I waited for a month for the clearance, but nothing happened. I decided then to go and see the senior Chinese officer, Li Kuotang, whom I knew well. I explained my problem to him and asked him for his help, as I needed to go to India urgently. He spoke with his colleague, the officer responsible for these matters, and then told me that the problem was that it was not safe to travel on the route to Yatung because of the activities of the Khampa rebels. They could not, I was told, guarantee me safety. I assured him that his office need not take any responsibility for my safety, but he would not agree to this either. Then I reminded him that Rimshi Taring, another government officer, had recently been issued a passport and was due to leave for India soon. This took him by surprise, and he didn't have a ready explanation to give me. He then ended our meeting by advising me to wait for some time longer. It was now clear to me that the Chinese were not going to give me a passport, but I was determined to go anyhow and to discharge my duties to the Kashag.

My fruitless interactions with the foreign office all took place during the autumn. In the winter all the officials would be busy, as His Holiness was due to take his oral examinations at the Monlam Chenmo, the Great Prayer Festival. The Monlam Chenmo always takes place on the third day of the Tibetan lunar year and ends twelve days later on the fifteenth. Dzasak Taring, older brother of Rimshi Taring, was given the assignment of taking photographs and movies during this important ceremonial function, and I was to assist him. I was also instructed to arrange the amplifier and speakers on the final day of the festival, the day when His Holiness would be giving a religious teaching to the public. I told my colleagues at my office that I would like to leave for India immediately after completing my duties at the Monlam Chenmo, and they agreed with my decision. They also agreed that if the Chinese did not issue me a passport before then, I should travel to India without one.

The Tibetan New Year came. I attended the usual ceremonies on the first and second day of the New Year holiday at the Potala Palace. On the third day, His Holiness journeyed from the Potala Palace to the Tsuklakhang in the center of Lhasa. All the government officials, dressed in their silk robes, accompanied him in a long, colorful procession, and the entire population of Lhasa turned up to greet him and to get his blessings. Over sixteen thousand monks from Drepung, Sera, and Ganden were gathered at the Tsuklakhang, forming an amazing sea of red. I was kept busy assisting Dzasak Taring with taking photographs. During His Holiness's stay at the Tsuklakhang, all officials had to attend the morning tea ceremony just outside the inner hall, the chamber where certain ceremonies took place and where His Holiness came each day to give special audiences.

The seventh day of the New Year festivities was the most important, as it was the day His Holiness would undergo his examination for the *geshe* degree. The examination was actually an intensive debate on all aspects of Buddhist philosophy, and all the most famous geshes of the three monasteries participated in this debate with His Holiness. Being a most rare and important occasion, the geshes even pushed and shoved in quite an undignified fashion in order to get even a minute to debate with His Holiness! For them it was a great honor and a blessing to be able to do this. The debate took over an hour to finish, and His Holiness, conducting himself in a most able and exemplary way, graduated successfully. He was awarded the title of *geshe lharampa*, the highest degree of academic honor attainable in the Geluk tradition.

Some readers might be interested to know a bit more about the occasion of His Holiness's geshe examination. Ganden Tri Rinpoche, head of the Geluk sect, was the senior-most participant and head of the ceremony. His Holiness's two tutors were next in rank and were seated together with many important rinpoches facing south. All the senior geshes were seated in the front row facing north, east, and west. In the middle was an open space about fifteen feet wide. In this open space His Holiness sat on a mattress with his hat on. The senior-most geshe began the debate by putting forth an argument to His Holiness, and the other geshes followed suit. In the second part of the debate His Holiness put forward questions to the geshe, who in turn had to answer them. All this took place in a large square called the Sung Chöra outside the Tsuklakhang. The square had an elevated area in the north with a high throne for His Holiness in the center. To the right of His Holiness's throne was another throne of lesser height for Ganden Tri Rinpoche, and two similar thrones were on the left for the two tutors. The entire ceremony took about two hours to complete. It was a solemn, holy, and sacred occasion, one that comes only once in a lifetime. I felt very blessed and fortunate to be there, and especially to be so close to the center of the entire proceedings.

The rest of the Monlam festival continued for another week. On the fifteenth day of the new year, I reached the Sung Chöra by seven in the morning to recheck the wiring of all the speakers on the adjoining roofs of the buildings, to examine the positioning of the amplifier and the connections of the microphones, and also to carry out a test. I made sure to check and see that there were sufficient batteries, as the teachings could last up to three hours. His Holiness arrived at eight, and the prayers started. This was followed by the main teaching, a first by His Holiness at the Sung Chöra. The entire area and even the streets were tightly packed with people. When the teaching was over it was still difficult to move around because of the dense crowds, so I had to wait for an hour to wind things up.

28. FAREWELL TO LHASA

I left Lhasa the day after the last day of the Monlam Chenmo. I left my house early, just before dawn, since that same day I had to reach Shigatse two hundred kilometers away. I stopped in Shigatse for the night and then left for my second stop at Phari, one hundred and thirty kilometers beyond that. From Phari it was only a two-and-a-half-hour descent to Yatung. At some two thousand feet lower than Phari, Yatung was far warmer, and I welcomed the change. I stayed in Yatung five days, trying to devise a way to proceed to India without drawing any suspicion from the Chinese. I already had a good excuse for coming to Yatung, as some of the trucks from my department had been driven here to transport some goods. I knew the Chinese were watching me, because I noticed a man in the house opposite my lodgings tracking my coming and going.

I considered various options for going to India. One was to travel to Bhutan by following a short route south of Phari. Another option was again to go to Bhutan but through another route, traveling twenty kilometers down the river from Yatung, proceeding south, climbing up a mountain, and then crossing the border to the Ha estate of the Dorji family in Bhutan, the family of the prime minister, Jigme Dorji. As my family was close to this family, I knew I wouldn't have any problem getting permission to travel to India through their territory. The third option, the one that appealed to me the most, was to follow the shortest route, crossing over to Sikkim via the Nathula Pass. However, this meant getting through the Chinese checkpoint two kilometers beyond Yatung. Since I was under surveillance, I had to come up with a good plan to overcome this obstacle.

It so happened that one of the head muleteers in my family business, a very loyal man by the name of Lodrö Gyaltsen, was married to a local woman of Yatung. They lived about five kilometers away in a village called Rinchengang. I asked him to come and see me and took him into confidence. I told him that I had to go to India but didn't possess a Chinese passport. The escape I had planned entailed traveling along the forested valley between two ridges that ended at the foothills below Nathula. The second and final Chinese checkpoint was on the right-hand ridge at Chöphithang, a thousand feet above the valley and about six kilometers from the Nathula foothills. Beyond that lay Indian territory. I told Lodrö that I would somehow evade the first Chinese checkpoint and come to his house in the evening. I asked him to have a horse and a servant ready. I planned on taking a path through the forest and avoid the second Chinese checkpoint. He told me not to worry and assured me that he would make all the necessary arrangements.

Just across from the first Chinese checkpoint lay a bridge with a river running below it. Beyond that was Drochi Khang, once the residence of the Tibetan commissioner. It also contained quarters for a garrison of Tibetan soldiers, who provided security for the commissioner. There was no commissioner in residence, as the post was no longer functional. The garrison remained, however, and the sergeant stationed there was a friend who often visited me. I asked him to come over the next day and suggested that we then ride back to his residence on bicycles, as I wanted to later go farther and visit Lodrö Gyaltsen together. I needed the company of the sergeant in case the guards at the Chinese checkpoint created any problems. I did what I could to ward off suspicion. The post and telegraph had been taken over by the Chinese, so two days earlier I had sent a telegram to my wife in Kalimpong informing her of my plans for returning to Lhasa. I hoped that it would be enough to allay any alarm about my intentions. I was now all set to put my plan into action.

My sergeant friend arrived punctually at four in the afternoon, and we hired bicycles from an Indian shop nearby. My personal manservant, a young man named Dondrup Dorje, was completely unaware of my plans. Since he was young and inexperienced in life, I thought it best not to take him into confidence, lest any indiscretion from him jeopardize my plans. I told him I'd be back home for dinner and left without taking anything with me except some money and a revolver, which I hid in my pocket. We left, riding our bicycles leisurely, came to the checkpoint, crossed the bridge, and went straight to the sergeant's house. After a cup of tea there and a half-hour stay, we rode back across the bridge, and turned left toward Rinchengang. There we met two Chinese soldiers hanging about, but they didn't say anything. We reached Rinchengang without any incident, but just as we were about to enter the village, we saw a group of people coming toward us. They turned out to be members of the village council, dispersing after a meeting. Unfortunately, the person who was spying on me was among them. This was rather disturbing, as he was sure to report my presence in Rinchengang. However, since there was nothing I could do about it, I rode past them in as natural a manner as possible and smiled, as I knew most of them. When I reached Lodrö's house I told the sergeant that since it was getting late, I thought I'd spend the night with Lodrö. I invited him in but he declined and left.

I told Lodrö about the encounter with the *gungdü*, the village council. We discussed the next day's journey and came to the conclusion that I should start very early in the morning, at three o'clock, so that I could reach the pass by seven. The next morning Lodrö insisted that he also accompany me along with the servant he had provided, at least to the checkpoint. It had started snowing heavily the night before, and this unexpected change in the weather proved a significant obstacle for me. We rode as quickly as possible, knowing that the snow would get deeper and deeper as we climbed up toward the pass. With the darkness and the thick snow covering the path, it became treacherous indeed. However, we safely managed to reach a spot just below the checkpoint, about one thousand feet above Rinchengang, just as dawn was about to break. I told Lodrö he should go back. Earlier I had briefed him about what to say to the Chinese in the event they came looking for me. My spy neighbor would surely report to the Chinese that he had seen me in Rinchengang the previous evening and that I had not returned to my lodgings that night. I told Lodrö there was no point denying that I had come to see him. He should tell the Chinese that I'd come to his house but left after dinner and that I was a little drunk when I left.

I rode slowly now, looking up every now and then to see if I could see anything going on at the checkpoint above, but there was no sign of movement. The trees were getting thinner, and an hour later my servant and I reached the end of the forest at the foot of Nathula Pass. The entire mountain was covered with a thick blanket of snow, and everything was a brilliant white. As we moved slowly onward, I saw about five or six mules with loads ahead of us. A man in front of the first mule was thrusting a stick into the ground to test whether he was on a safe track. We immediately fell in line behind them and were led by this guide. The sky was clearing, and the sun was about to come up as we left the checkpoint far behind.

As we got farther away, I glanced back and saw no sign of any human activity still. It took about an hour to negotiate the pass with the mules and my fellow traveler, who later turned out to be the Indian postman from Yatung. This last hour was an anxious one for me, and I kept looking back to see if there were any signs of Chinese soldiers following us. To this day I have no doubt that my protective deities helped me in my hour of need.

We reached the top of Nathula Pass at about nine in the morning to a clear blue sky and bright sunlight. My feet were very cold, so I got off my horse and started walking. Our progress was slow, as the road was icy. We finally reached Tsogo Lake after about two hours. After another two hours we reached a rest stop called Fifteenth Mile, where travelers from Gangtok usually stopped before crossing the pass into Tibet. I rested here for a while and had something to eat.

Since it was still early afternoon, I decided to move on to the next stop, Fourth Mile, which had a dak bungalow guesthouse. Thanks to my fluent Nepali from my school days, I managed to persuade the Nepalese watchman to give me accommodation in spite of the fact that I didn't possess a permit to stay there. I had him light a good fire and bring me a cup of hot tea, which was very comforting after my long journey.

As it wasn't dark yet I went out for a stroll. That's when I noticed the lights of a car approaching the village below. I got the watchman to go down to the village and find out if the vehicle could be hired to take me to Gangtok. He came back after a while and told me that the vehicle was a jeep belonging to the Barmiok Kazi. It had come in search of some mules that they had lost. I immediately went out again to see if I could catch up with the jeep, but it had already turned and was going away. I was rather disappointed as I knew the Barmiok Kazi, the senior-most official of the maharaja of Sikkim. His eldest son, Jigdal, had been with me at school in Darjeeling and was a friend. Had I met him, he would not only have given me a lift to Gangtok, he would also have invited me to stay at his house for the night. Missing this connection, however, proved to be the best thing that could have happened.

I got up very early the next day in order to reach first Gangtok and then Kalimpong, my final destination, all within a single day. My family would be hugely surprised to see me. My servant and the horses were accommodated in the village below, so I went to call them. I reached the village, but before I could trace my servant I heard the sound of a vehicle coming toward the village. I thought it was probably a truck coming to pick up firewood and planned to offer a handsome fare to get a ride to Gangtok. As the vehicle came closer I saw that it was a private jeep. I went toward it as it slowed to a stop, and to my complete surprise, my cousin Jiga got out. In amazement I immediately asked him how he came to know that I was here; I assumed that he'd come to receive me. Then to my utter shock my wife suddenly got out of the jeep! She told me that she'd received my telegram saying I was going back to Lhasa and decided to come quickly to Yatung to see me before I left for Lhasa. This was a totally unexpected encounter, and she beamed with delight.

My wife told me how she had intended to bring the jeep up to precisely the point where we were right then before she continued on horseback to Yatung. A couple of mules had already been hired to carry provisions, and they were coming behind her. I at once traced my servant, thanked him, and told him he could return home with the horses. I instructed him to tell Lodrö Gyaltsen that I'd had a safe journey. When the muleteer with my wife's provisions arrived, I told him the trip to Yatung had been canceled and sent him back to Gangtok with the loads. We then got into the jeep and headed for Gangtok.

On the way to Gangtok I thought of how my protective deities had once again saved me. Had I reached the Barmiok's jeep in time, I would not have met my wife nor known about her traveling to Yatung. By the time I learned of her plan, she would have already crossed the Nathula Pass, and the Chinese would have certainly held her hostage. I could say this with certainty because of the report I later heard from Lodrö.

As soon as he got back home, a Chinese officer and a few armed soldiers forcefully entered his house and demanded to know where Sadu Rinchen was. He told them that I had left for my lodgings the previous night; I was a bit drunk and insisted on going home. The Chinese officer looked at Lodrö's muddy boots, said in an accusatory tone that the road to Nathula Pass was slushy and demanded that Lodrö explain himself. Lodrö had the presence of mind to say he'd just returned from his potato fields, "Hence the mud." The Chinese officer warned him that he should tell the truth and that the consequences would be very grave if he didn't. The extent of the punishment Lodrö faced was all the more serious, he threatened, because Sadu Rinchen was an American spy! He told Lodrö to think over the matter very carefully, warning him again to cooperate. The officer said he would come again later to see if Lodrö changed his mind. In fact, Lodrö was called to the Chinese office several times, but he stuck to his story and never caved to the Chinese.

A couple of months later, after the uprising in Lhasa and when everything was in turmoil, Lodrö and his family crossed over into Gangtok and lived there in safety, though as refugees.

PART THREE

A Refugee and Stateless in India

29. A REFUGEE IN INDIA

After a few hours rest in Gangtok, we made it to Kalimpong that day. My children were thrilled to see me, and each one was eager to tell me about school. It was at this time that I learned my brother Lo Nyendak and other relatives had joined the Chushi Gangdruk rebels. Since the Bhutanese prime minister was a family friend, my brother and eight others had been able to travel via Bhutan to safely reach the Chushi Gangdruk headquarters in Tibet.

I stayed a few days in Kalimpong and then went to Calcutta to buy the various spare parts that my department needed for our trucks. On my second day in Calcutta, I opened the newspaper to the front-page headline "REVOLT IN LHASA." I was shocked, as I had expected trouble but not a revolt by the entire city. In light of this crisis, I flew back home immediately so that I could get more news firsthand. I also wanted to discuss the matter with senior officials already in Kalimpong like Yuthok, Tsipon Shakabpa, and His Holiness's brother Gyalo Thondup.

One of the first things I did on reaching Kalimpong was to get in touch with N. Chakravarti, a wireless officer under the political officer in Gangtok. I had known him when he was at Dekyilingka, the Indian mission in Lhasa.

He would still be in daily touch with Dekyilingka, which was close by the Norbulingka, the Dalai Lama's summer palace and the center of the storm. Mr. Chakravarti told me that the situation was very tense. His Holiness the Dalai Lama had been invited to the PLA's regional military headquarters for a theatrical performance. News of this invitation had sparked a near revolt. Huge crowds thronged the main gate of the Norbulingka, and even more still pouring in, all demanding that His Holiness not go to the military base. There was a deep fear that once His Holiness stepped inside the military headquarters, he would be abducted. The Chinese general had demanded that the Dalai Lama be accompanied by only two unarmed bodyguards.

The Kashag, along with other senior officials and heads of monasteries, were engaged in hectic meetings and were trying desperately to calm the rising emotions of the protesters. In Kalimpong, meetings were organized by all the Tibetan officials present and the heads of different local Tibetan organizations. It was decided that a contingent of this group should go immediately to Delhi and make a representation to the Indian government, requesting them to intervene and to help assure the safety of the Dalai Lama. Two days later the group, of which I was a part, arrived in Delhi. The senior Tibetan officials and Gyalo Thondup were not able to meet with Prime Minister Nehru, but they were able to hand over a letter to the foreign secretary at the external affairs ministry. They were told that the Indian government would study the contents of the letter and give the matter sympathetic consideration. There was no point in waiting, and since we could not know how long it would be before a formal reply was given, it was decided that we should return to Kalimpong.

A few days after our return, we received the incredible news that the Dalai Lama had left his summer palace and was traveling south! Everybody assumed that he would be traveling under the protection of the Chushi Gangdruk rebels, who now held large areas of southern Tibet under their control. Soon we learned that His Holiness and his party appeared to be heading toward the Indian border. The entire international media was focused on this important news, and they published daily reports about the progress of His Holiness's journey. The government of India was no doubt aware of everything and keeping a close watch on this development.

Meanwhile, Tibetans in India were performing prayers and hoisting prayer flags on hilltops for the safety of the Dalai Lama. About a week later, some newspapers reported that His Holiness had fallen ill, and this caused great concern and anxiety among us Tibetans, but this report turned out to be not entirely accurate. Another startling piece of news followed. An airplane was seen hovering over the south of Lhasa that everyone suspected was a Chinese plane search for the Dalai Lama. This greatly upset all Tibetans, so we prayed still more fervently for his safety.

Later I learned that the events in Lhasa in March 1959 included tragedy for my family. My brother Lo Gedun was shot and killed by Chinese soldiers while crossing the Kyichu River. Lo Gedun along with my brother Wangdor, my nephew Gonpo Chimey Gyapontsang, and many family friends had volunteered to defend the Norbulingka. The day after the Dalai Lama fled, they too left Lhasa for India, but Lo Gedun never made it into exile, along with many other Tibetans crossing the river near the Norbulingka. They had been spotted by a group of Chinese soldiers perched on a hilltop on the far side. The soldiers opened fire on the Tibetans with rifles and Bren machine guns.

Around this time we received news that a temporary government had been established at Lhuntse Dzong in eastern Bhutan. As to His Holiness's progress, a decision had been made within his camp, prompted by the sighting of the Chinese plane, to proceed more quickly to India than planned. The Dalai Lama first sent an advance delegation to India with an official request for asylum. When he arrived at Mangmang, a town two days from the border with the Indian state of Arunachal Pradesh, an official who had been sent in advance came back to report that the government of India would welcome His Holiness and his entourage. The official said that he had personally witnessed the preparations underway to welcome His Holiness. Everyone was very relieved.

Several days later His Holiness finally crossed the border at Khenzimana Pass to a place called Chudangmo in the Indian state of Arunachal Pradesh. He was officially welcomed by Deputy Secretary P. N. Menon. His Holiness had met Menon during his 1956 visit to India, and Menon had also been the consul in Lhasa during the mid-1950s. The deputy secretary had brought with him a Sikkimese gentleman by the name of Kazi Sonam Topgyal as interpreter. He had been the government of India's official interpreter during that same visit to India, so both gentlemen were familiar to His Holiness. Menon brought with him an official letter from Prime Minister Nehru that stated:

> My colleagues and I welcome you, your family and entourage to reside in India. The people of India, who hold you in great veneration, will no doubt accord their traditional respect to your personage. Kind regards to you.

When news went out that His Holiness had crossed the border and entered India safely, Tibetans everywhere were thrilled. More than a hundred news reporters had proceeded to Tezpur, a small town in northeast India, when they learned that the Dalai Lama would meet the press there. We officials in Kalimpong also made our way to Tezpur to await His Holiness's arrival. A small and remote town, Tezpur didn't have a modern telecommunications system, but the government of India had made special arrangements to satisfy the media. His Holiness arrived in Tezpur to an enthusiastic welcome. He received over a thousand telegrams from all over the world wishing him well. The press was hoping he would address them and take questions. Under the circumstances, this was judged to be not prudent. Instead, a press statement was issued outlining the events compelling His Holiness to leave his country and seek asylum in India. He also thanked all those who had sent him their messages of goodwill. Heinrich Harrer was there among the reporters, hoping to get an interview, but he too was denied. Only the Tibetan officials from Kalimpong were given a special audience. At this audience, I was instructed to make whatever arrangements necessary and then catch up with the entourage, who were headed to Mussoorie many hundreds of miles away.

His Holiness and his entourage left by a special train the very next day. I returned to Kalimpong and made preparations right away to join them in Mussoorie, where I would be required to stay more or less permanently. Only two of us officials could speak English, and I could foresee a dire need of interpreters. On arriving in Mussoorie I found that everyone was residing in an area called Happy Valley, ironic considering the frame of mind of the entourage, who had just become refugees in a strange land. His Holiness and family were staying at Birla House, a two-story house belonging to the Birla family, wealthy Indian industrialists. The Indian government had requisitioned the house temporarily. The Kashag and senior officials were lodged in a few houses close by, and a short distance away more houses were arranged for other officials and attendants. I was given a room to share with one other official.

A special secretariat for His Holiness had been opened, and I began work there as translator and interpreter. P. N. Menon acted as a liaison for the external affairs ministry of India, and we had to deal with him for all matters. I was well acquainted with him from his days as the Indian consul in Lhasa and during His Holiness's 1956 visit to India. Reporters had followed

Author with Kalon Gadrang and Ngawang Rigdol at Birla House,
Mussoorie, India, 1959.

His Holiness to Mussoorie and were waiting for an opportunity to interview him. Heinrich Harrer was there, too, and he hoped we'd grant him special access owing to his long association with Tibet. If I remember correctly, Harrer represented the *London Times*. He waited for several days, but when he could make no progress, he finally wrote His Holiness a letter in transliterated Tibetan. We had to write back to say no interviews would be granted to anyone. Finally Harrer left Mussoorie.

His Holiness and the entourage gradually settled down, and there were many meetings and discussions about the future course of action. Gyalo Thondup, His Holiness's elder brother, was a strong presence. So was Tsipon Shakabpa, the former finance minister, who had by then been living in India for a couple of years.

Soon after His Holiness settled in Mussoorie, Prime Minister Nehru came to meet him. They had a long discussion, and Nehru was briefed in detail about the entire course of events that took place after His Holiness returned to Tibet from India in 1956, when Zhou Enlai assured His Holiness that he would be given full authority to make any changes he wished in keeping with the Seventeen-Point Agreement. Nehru had advised His Holiness to return to Tibet at that time, as Zhou Enlai had to all appearances addressed the major concerns.

At ten in the morning on June 20, 1959, His Holiness gave his first press conference in Mussoorie on the lawns of Birla House to a crowd of reporters. First he detailed the critical events since the Chinese invasion of 1950. He emphasized the need to restore the status Tibet enjoyed before the Chinese invasion. He said the Seventeen-Point Agreement was no longer valid, as it had been violated time and again by the Chinese. His Holiness also claimed that the Tibetan people would recognize the seat of the true government of their country to be wherever he resided with his ministers. Although he did not clearly outline his future course of actions, he did speak of the possibility of approaching the United Nations. He strongly emphasized that the stark truth of what had happened in Tibet and the ongoing suffering of the Tibetan people must be understood by the world. He called for the attention of the world to focus on the problem of Tibet.

The Dalai Lama's press statement was followed by a question-and-answer session that lasted for well over an hour. During this session a question was raised about His Holiness's 1956 visit to India: had he considered not returning to Tibet at that time? The Dalai Lama confirmed that he had indeed decided not to return to Tibet but had changed his mind on Premier Zhou Enlai's assurance that the present method of Chinese reforms would be postponed for as long as the Dalai Lama wished; changes could be made in any manner His Holiness desired, he was told.

Around this time the International Commission of Jurists sent two of its members, Dr. Donald Thompson and Purushottam Trikamdas, to investigate the events in Tibet that led to a mass exodus of Tibetans to India. The International Commission of Jurists was founded after World War II to mobilize world legal opinion whenever there appears to be a systematic violation of the rule of law. The two jurists went separately to various places inhabited by Tibetan refugees to interview them individually. I accompanied Trikamdas while Dr. Thompson had George Taring to help him. Thousands of Tibetan refugees were interviewed, and after several months of studying these interviews, as well as press and radio reports, in both Hindi and in Chinese, the jurists brought out a detailed report in which they reached the following conclusions:

1. From 1950 onward, a practically independent country had been turned by force into a Chinese province.

2. The terms of the Seventeen-Point Agreement of May 23, 1951, which guaranteed broad autonomy to Tibet, had been consistently disregarded.

3. There had been arbitrary confiscation of property belonging to monasteries, private individuals, and the Tibetan government.

4. Freedom of religion had been denied to the Tibetans, and the Chinese had been actively trying to destroy the Buddhist religion of the people.

5. Tibetans had been denied the freedom of information.

6. Human rights abuses in Tibet included the systemic killing, imprisonment, and deportation of those opposed to the Communist regime.

In Mussoorie after several months of discussion and consultation with
sympathetic politicians and international lawyers, it was decided that a representation should be made to the United Nations. One of our advisors was
D. K. Sen, an international lawyer responsible for helping Bhutan draw up
its treaty with India. A preliminary representation was addressed to U.N.
Secretary General Dag Hammarskjöld. This was followed by a decision to
send a delegation to the next General Assembly in September. His Holiness
informed the government of India of this intention and requested their
formal support when he visited New Delhi in September 1959. The Indian
government thought this course of action would not be of much help and
declined to lend its support. We, however, moved ahead with our plans, and
Gyalo Thondup, Shakabpa, and myself in the capacity of translator were
appointed to the delegation. We were instructed to proceed to New York to
represent our case, and we left in the third week of September via Europe. I
should stress that we had diplomatic visas issued by the American embassy.
On the way, we stopped in London for two days and tried to enlist the
support of the British government. They were reluctant, however, to make
any commitment at that time. But our time in Britain was not a complete
waste. We were able to meet with and gain valuable assistance from Vijaya
Lakshmi Pandit, who was not only high commissioner of India to Britain
and sister of Prime Minister Nehru, she had also earlier presided over the
U.N. General Assembly as its president.

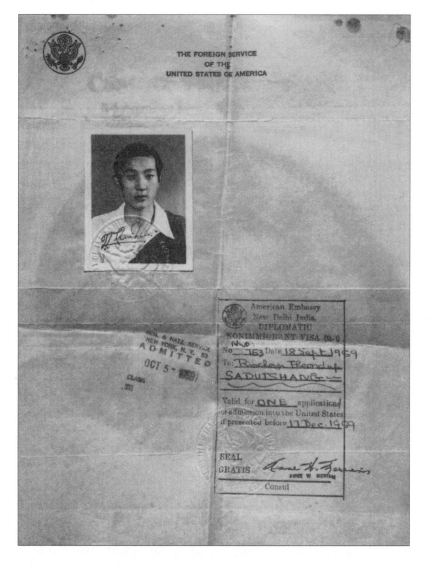

Author's identity certificate issued by the Indian government, stamped with an American diplomatic visa, 1959.

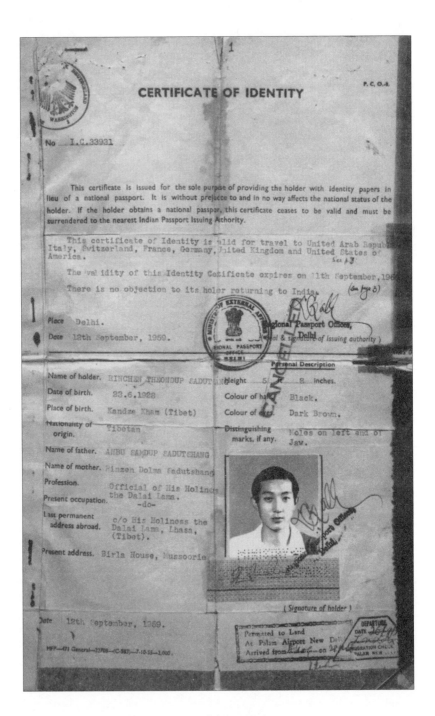

CERTIFICATE OF IDENTITY

P.C.O.4

No   I.C.33931

This certificate is issued for the sole purpose of providing the holder with identity papers in lieu of a national passport. It is without prejudice to and in no way affects the national status of the holder. If the holder obtains a national passport, this certificate ceases to be valid and must be surrendered to the nearest Indian Passport Issuing Authority.

This certificate of Identity is valid for travel to United Arab Republic, Italy, Switzerland, France, Germany, United Kingdom and United States of America. See p 3.

The validity of this Identity Certificate expires on 11th September, 1960.

There is no objection to its holder returning to India. (see page 3)

Place   Delhi.

Date   12th September, 1959.

Regional Passport Officer, Delhi.
(Seal & signature of issuing authority)

Personal Description

Name of holder.	RINCHEN THRONDUP SADUTSHANG
Date of birth.	22.6.1928
Place of birth.	Kandze Kham (Tibet)
Nationality of origin.	Tibetan
Name of father.	AHBU SAMDUP SADUTSHANG
Name of mother.	Rinzen Dolma Sadutshang
Profession.	Official of His Holiness the Dalai Lama.
Present occupation.	-do-
Last permanent address abroad.	c/o His Holiness the Dalai Lama, Lhasa, (Tibet).
Present address.	Birla House, Mussoorie

Height   5 ft. 8. inches.
Colour of hair   Black.
Colour of eyes   Dark Brown.
Distinguishing marks, if any.   Moles on left and on Jaw.

(Signature of holder)

Date   12th September, 1959.

MFP—471 General—22708—(C-583)—7-10-55—1,000.

Permitted to Land At Palam Airport New Delhi. Arrived from

The main page of the same document.

30. AN APPEAL TO THE
UNITED NATIONS

The fourteenth session of the General Assembly of the United Nations had already begun in the fall of 1959. Our delegation's first task was to call on Secretary General Dag Hammarskjöld to request his help with our appeal. He was very sympathetic and also advised us on how to proceed. Then followed many meetings with member delegates to explain our case and enlist their support. Virtually all of them knew next to nothing about Tibet, so one of the major tasks we faced was to educate the delegates about the forceful occupation of our country and to explain the current situation of our people. Such unawareness was the product of Tibet's isolation from the rest of the world for many centuries. Most of the newly independent countries in Africa, the Middle East, and South America were ignorant about Tibet's very existence. This is not a criticism, of course. After all, we ourselves were none too familiar with these countries or with international politics. We had to constantly seek advice from politicians and lawyer friends; such was the enormity of our task.

El Salvador and Malaya agreed to sponsor our case, and it was discussed in the steering committee before the fourteenth General Assembly. We had to tread carefully so as not to displease Israel and the Middle Eastern

United Nations Tibetan delegation, New York, September 1959. Author,
Shakabpa, and Gyalo Thondup.

countries, who were embroiled in their own conflict over sovereignty and
occupation. Similarly, we also had to be careful while approaching countries
that did not have good relations with India. Of course, we met the Indian
delegation several times despite the fact that their government had not formally endorsed our approaching the United Nations. Many Middle Eastern
and Southeast Asian countries advised us to get India's support, without
which they said it would be difficult for them to vote for us. As I recall,
Pakistan and Cuba were our strongest supporters. Even in their speeches at
the General Assembly regarding their stand on the question of Tibet, they
declared Tibet was an independent state now under occupation by Communist China. One of the member delegates we called on was the Pakistan
U.N. representative, Prince Aly Khan, son of the well-known Muslim leader
Aga Khan III. He was very sympathetic to our cause and assured us that his
delegation would vote for us when the question came up. We often met our
sponsors, the representatives of Malaya and El Salvador, to seek their advice
and to discuss the resolution to be presented.

During this period the United Nations had about eighty-two member nations. The CPC had still not been formally recognized, and China was still represented at the United Nations by Chang Kai-shek's Kuomintang (Republic of China) government, who were in exile in Taiwan at that time. The question of Tibet came up for discussion on the draft resolution presented by El Salvador and Malaya, and on October 21, 1959, a vote was taken on the resolution. A total of forty-five countries voted in favor, nine voted against, and twenty-six abstained. The United Kingdom and India, two of the countries most familiar with our situation, abstained. Below is a list of the countries that took part in the voting:

Yes votes: 45
Argentina, Australia, Austria, Bolivia, Brazil, Canada, Chile, Republic of China, Colombia, Cuba, Denmark, Ecuador, El Salvador, Greece, Guatemala, Haiti, Honduras, Iceland, Iran, Ireland, Israel, Italy, Japan, Jordan, Laos, Liberia, Luxembourg, Malaya, Mexico, Netherlands, New Zealand, Nicaragua, Norway, Pakistan, Panama, Paraguay, Peru, Philippines, Sweden, Thailand, Tunisia, Turkey, United States, Uruguay, and Venezuela.

No votes: 9
Albania, Bulgaria, Belorussia, Czechoslovakia, Hungary, Poland, Romania, Ukraine, and Soviet Union.

Abstained: 26
Afghanistan, Belgium, Burma, Cambodia, Ceylon, Dominican Republic, Ethiopia, Finland, France, Ghana, India, Indonesia, Iraq, Lebanon, Libya, Morocco, Nepal, Portugal, Saudi Arabia, Sudan, South Africa, United Arab Republic, United Kingdom, Yemen, and Yugoslavia.

Absent: 2
Guinea and Costa Rica.

The following is the resolution that was adopted by the General Assembly:

Resolution 1353 (XIV). Question of Tibet

The General Assembly,

Recalling the principles regarding fundamental human rights and freedoms set out in the Charter of the United Nations and in the Universal Declaration of Human Rights adopted by the General Assembly on 10 December, 1948,

Considering that the fundamental human rights and freedoms to which the Tibetan people, like all others, are entitled include the right to civil and religious liberty for all without distinction,

Mindful also of the distinctive cultural and religious heritage of the people of Tibet and of the autonomy which they have traditionally enjoyed,

Gravely concerned at reports, including the official statement of His Holiness the Dalai Lama, to the effect that the fundamental human rights and freedoms of the people of Tibet have been forcibly denied them,

Deploring the effect of these events in increasing international tension and in embittering the relations between peoples at a time when earnest and positive efforts are being made by responsible leaders to reduce tension and improve international relations,

1. *Affirms its belief* that respect for the principles of the Charter of the United Nations and of the Universal Declaration of Human Rights is essential for the evolution of a peaceful world order based on the rule of law;

2. *Calls* for respect for the fundamental human rights of the Tibetan people and for their distinctive cultural and religious life.

834 plenary meeting,
21 October 1959

We were quite satisfied with the result and thanked our sponsors for their help and keen interest. We also requested them to continue their support to us, as we planned to come back the next year to make a new appeal to the United Nations.

On our return to Mussoorie, where everyone was waiting in great anticipation, a full report was presented to His Holiness and later to the Kashag. They appreciated the fact that at least we were able to make our concern heard in the United Nations and that a human rights resolution was adopted in our favor. One other achievement that came out of this experience was that we were able to educate many countries and leaders about Tibet and its current crisis. Many of our supporters, both politicians and friends, thought it was a good achievement and said we must continue our efforts to enlist more support for our cause. Tibetans at large, however, were expecting more immediate results. Some educated officials even asked when we could return home to Tibet. It went to show how ignorant we were about the outside world. It reminded me of the well-known Tibetan tale about the frog in the well who has no idea about what lies beyond and mistakes his well for the entire world.

The author, left, with three of the Dalai Lama's brothers, New York, 1959. Thubten Jigme Norbu (a.k.a. Taktser Rinpoche), Lobsang Samten, and Gyalo Thondup.

Meanwhile, the situation in Tibet was getting worse day by day. The Chinese had by this point resorted to large-scale persecution. There were countless reports of imprisonment and torture and an alarming number of stories of Tibetans committing suicide by hanging themselves and jumping into the Kyichu River. Thousands of Tibetans trekked across the Himalayas to India and sought asylum. The number of refugees swelled at an alarming rate, and we had difficulty tackling the problem. However, the government of India was very kind and provided rations and facilities for transit camps. Many countries like the U.S.A. and the U.K. and even Thailand, Indonesia, and the Philippines provided aid. In response, the Central Relief Committee was established with an office in Delhi. All relief was routed through this office and then distributed as needed. The Tibetan refugees arriving in India suffered a great deal physically; they suffered from their arduous escape over treacherous terrain, from the sudden exposure to the heat of India, and from new diseases to which they had no immunity. But their mental hardship was far worse, as they were facing the separation from loved ones or the loss of loved ones who had been imprisoned, disappeared, or killed. The refugees were also just thoroughly bewildered. They were confronted with a totally alien environment after having left all that was familiar and dear to them behind. They all faced a future filled with uncertainty.

The next General Assembly of the United Nations was at the end of September 1960. We made preparations well in advance. The same delegation was once again sent to New York. With the experience of the previous year, we were able to lobby more ably, and at this session we found one more country, Ireland, to sponsor our case, bringing the total sponsors to three. Ireland took special interest in our case, and its foreign minister, Mr. Ericson, was tremendously helpful. This time we were able to garner more support. The General Assembly had a huge number of items on its agenda, and ours could not be taken up before the assembly adjourned at the end of December. All of the outstanding items on the agenda were postponed until the next session, in September of 1961. Once the assembly reconvened, we returned yet a third time to pursue the matter. Our appeal was finally debated in mid-December, and the following resolution adopted:

Resolution 1723 (XVI). Question of Tibet

The General Assembly,

Recalling its resolution 1353 (XIV) of 21 October 1959 on the question of Tibet,

Gravely concerned at the continuation of events in Tibet, including the violation of the fundamental human rights of the Tibetan people and the suppression of the distinctive cultural and religious life which they have traditionally enjoyed,

Noting with deep anxiety the severe hardships which these events have inflicted on the Tibetan people, as evidenced by the large-scale exodus of Tibetan refugees to the neighboring countries,

Considering that these events violate fundamental human rights and freedoms set out in the Charter of the United Nations and the Universal Declaration of Human Rights, including the principle of self-determination of peoples and nations, and have the deplorable effect of increasing international tension and embittering relations between peoples,

1. *Reaffirms its conviction* that respect for the principles of the Charter of the United Nations and of the Universal Declaration of Human Rights is essential for the evolution of a peaceful world order based on the rule of law;

2. *Solemnly renews* its call for the cessation of practices which deprive the Tibetan people of their fundamental human rights and freedoms, including their right to self-determination;

3. *Expresses the hope* that Member States will make all possible efforts, as appropriate, towards achieving the purposes of the present resolution.

1085 plenary meeting,
20 December 1961

One significant difference between the reception of this appeal versus the last was that the United Kingdom voted in support of the resolution. Its delegate made the following speech in this regard:

Mr. President,

I am making this statement in explanation of the vote.

My delegation feels the deepest indignation and distress at what has happened, and is still happening, in Tibet. We are happy that at least this brief opportunity is being afforded to us and to others who share our concern, to express in the General Assembly our sympathy for the Tibetan people in their suffering.

Since this item was discussed at the fourteenth session of the General Assembly, my delegation has read the report on the subject by the International Commission of Jurists which, as I think will be recognized by the great majority of the delegations here, is an independent, non-governmental organization comprising judges, professors and lawyers from many countries. This report contains horrifying and irrefutable evidence that China's policy in Tibet amounts to the deliberate and continuing suppression of the religious and political liberties of the Tibetan people. This has resulted in human suffering on a vast scale. Those who have spoken before me in the general debate have given the Assembly a picture of the appalling suffering inflicted on the Tibetan people. I shall not, therefore, weary or sicken the Assembly with examples or quotations from the jurists' report, which is there for all to read.

I shall confine myself to saying that Chinese policy in Tibet represents a systematic and calculated policy of oppression, continued cynically and ruthlessly despite overwhelming condemnation by the United Nations. The report of the International Commission of Jurists shows, moreover, that the actions of the Chinese Government in Tibet constitute a deliberate attempt to suppress permanently the autonomy of Tibet.

Her Majesty's Government in the United Kingdom has in the past recognized Chinese suzerainty over Tibet only on the condition that Tibet retained its autonomy. We cannot agree that any such suzerainty entitles the Chinese Government to claim immunity from the condemnation of the world and to be able freely to impose on the Tibetan people in the spurious name of progress the terrible

sufferings to which I have referred. We are convinced that these policies of the Chinese Government have indeed resulted in the conditions described in the preamble to the draft resolution which is before
us, with the effects described therein. We deplore them because they
heighten international tension, and we deplore them even more for
their inhumanity. My delegation will, therefore, vote in favour of the
draft resolution [A/L.376].

On this third trip to the United Nations, with the help of our prior
experience and more aggressive lobbying, we were able to achieve better
results. With strong support from our sponsors, especially from the Irish
delegation, we were able to get the language emphasizing "our right of self-
determination of the Tibetan people" included in the resolution. This was
indeed a satisfying achievement. Of course, from the very beginning we
wanted Tibet to be recognized as an independent country. Unfortunately,
we could not muster enough support for this recognition. However, we did
manage to take a significant step forward compared to the first resolution
of 1959. Determined to realize our goal, we immediately began planning so
that we could progress even further the next year.

In September of 1962, we once again proceeded to New York. We made
sure to arrive before the U.N. sessions began and initiated consultations
once more with our sponsors: El Salvador, Malaya, and Ireland. It had now
been almost four years since the Lhasa uprising of the Tibetan people. With
His Holiness the Dalai Lama and over a hundred thousand Tibetan refugees
in exile in India, the plight of the Tibetan people was by this time better
understood and appreciated by the world. We were finally able to get our
sponsors to present a draft resolution which strongly called for "the right to
self-determination" of the Tibetan people. As a result, the General Assembly
Resolution 2079 was passed in 1965. However, the question of how to get
any of the U.N. resolutions implemented was another matter. At this point
Communist China was still not a member of the United Nations and they
regarded the resolution as an interference in their internal affairs. However,
His Holiness and the administration of the exile government in Dharamsala
were quite pleased with our achievement.

31. A NEW DEMOCRATIC CONSTITUTION

After returning from the United States, I continued to work in His Holiness's private secretariat until May 1964. During this period, one of my main tasks was to assist in the creation of a constitution for the new exile government.

Even before the Chinese occupation of Tibet, His Holiness the Dalai Lama was eager to change and modernize the existing system of governance. He had established a reform office to redistribute land, though the completion of this task was hindered by the Chinese invasion. But the Dalai Lama's desire to change the current system of governance never waned. In February 1960, when the Dalai Lama spoke to a huge gathering of Tibetans at Bodh Gaya, he spoke of the need to have elections and to establish a democratic system of government for the Tibetans in exile. He suggested a legislative body comprising of three elected representatives from each of the three regions of Tibet and one representative from each of the four main Buddhist schools. The Tibetans in exile endorsed this proposal, and a few months later elections were held to choose representatives. On September 2, 1960, the first elected body in Tibetan history was established under the name of the Commission of Tibetan Peoples' Deputies (CTPD). My

brother Lo Nyendak was one of these first deputies. As novices, the first
deputies had to visit the various offices of the exile government in order to
familiarize themselves with the current system of administration.

An elected body having been established, His Holiness instructed the foreign minister, Liushar, to arrange a suitable draft for a new constitution. At
that time I was deputy to Liushar. Narkyi Ngawang Dhondup was secretary,
and he later went on to become the first secretary of the CTPD. Liushar
discussed the matter with the Kashag, and it was decided that a five-member
committee be appointed for this purpose. The kalons Gadrang, Shatra Surpa,
and Liushar, Secretary Phala (the former Dronyer Chenmo), and Secretary
Ta-Lama became the members of this committee. At their first meeting, the
committee decided to consult a first-class constitutional lawyer, and they
agreed to approach Purushottam Trikamdas, who had been so helpful previously through his work as a member of the International Commission of
Jurists.

I was told to speak to him, which I did, and he consented to help us.
Thereafter we held numerous meetings, and I was fully engaged in the process. We informed Mr. Trikamdas that the Tibetan system of government
was based on a dual spiritual and temporal administration. We therefore
asked that the draft constitution include three important elements.

1. The Dalai Lama should be maintained as the spiritual and temporal
   head of state.
2. The ruling body should include a representative from each of the
   four major Tibetan Buddhist sects.
3. Similarly, each of Tibet's three main regions, the so-called Bö
   Cholkha Sum, should also be represented.

Mr. Trikamdas based the draft constitution mainly on the Indian constitution, but since India was a secular nation, he had to study the constitu-
tions of Ceylon, Burma, and Thailand, which were all Buddhist countries
that gave religion a special status. He then wrote a draft that included an
independent judiciary and an independent executive and incorporated traditional Tibetan values within modern democratic norms.

To constitute the exile parliament, each of Tibet's three regions—western (Ngari), central (Ü-Tsang), and eastern (Kham-Amdo)—would elect three members. The four major Buddhist schools would nominate one member each, and in addition the Dalai Lama would directly appoint two more. Most importantly, the Dalai Lama insisted on including an article that stated that his power could be removed if a two-thirds majority of the assembly voted for it. This was fiercely objected to by the entire Tibetan population, but His Holiness insisted on it, as this constitution was going to be based on a democratic system.

We also sought the advice of the law minister of India, G. S. Pathak. In addition, I was instructed to seek advice from the former president of India, Dr. Rajendra Prasad, who had retired and was living in his home village of Zudari, in Bihar. I arrived in Bihar on February 25, 1963, and called on the former president the following day. I conveyed to him greetings from the Dalai Lama and presented to him a copy of the draft constitution and requested his valuable advice. He said he would study the paper and that I should contact him after three or four days. Most unfortunately he passed away two days later.

Despite this setback, the draft constitution was completed later that year, and Narkyi Ngawang Dhondup and I worked together to translate it into Tibetan. The exile government continued to function under the draft constitution until June 14, 1991. Thereafter it was amended and known as the Charter of Tibetans in Exile.

32. FINANCIAL
RESPONSIBILITIES IN
THE EXILE GOVERNMENT

In May 1964, I was appointed one of the managing trustees of His Holiness the Dalai Lama's Charitable Trust. Three colleagues worked with me: D. N. Tsarong, Thupten Tsepal Tekhang, and Lhundup Gyalpo Gyanatsang. This trust was established with funds from the sale of the gold and silver belonging to His Holiness's private treasury that had been sent to India in 1951 during the Chinese invasion of Kham. His Holiness had talked to Nehru about this and had been advised by him to set it up. Jayaprakash Narayan, the respected Indian leader, consented to chair the trust, which was subsequently registered in Calcutta.

Our first preliminary meeting was held in New Delhi. D. N. Tsarong had been taking responsibility for all the funds so far and he was now instructed to hand them over to the trust. Tsarong gave an account of what funds were available and how he planned to transfer these to the trust. We discovered that the total amount was only about 8.2 million rupees (US $1.7 million). Of this, a large amount, just over half, had been given out as an unsecured loan, one million rupees were in shares in Gayday Iron and Steel Company, a spun-pipe factory set up with Tibetan investments and run by Tsarong himself, and another million rupees had been invested in G. S.

Mandidip Paper Mills, a private limited company also set up with Tibetan investments. The investments in the pipe and paper factories were done with the approval of Dharamsala, but with regard to the loans and small investments, I was not happy with how Tsarong had arranged them. I suggested that Tsarong convert all of these as well as the unsecured loan worth Rs.4.5 million to cash and hand them over to the trust so that the board of trustees could select and manage future investments.

I joined my office in Calcutta in the autumn of that year. We had a staff of two: a Tibetan secretary from Dharamsala and an Indian accountant. On settling in I discovered that the decisions made in the previous meeting in Delhi had not been followed. The only cash handed over to the trust by D. N. Tsarong was some 80,000 rupees, and the rest remained loans and investments as before. As for the unsecured loan of Rs.4.5 million, the better part of the trust's funds, it had been lent by Tsarong to an Indian gentleman

The Dalai Lama at the opening of Tibet House, New Delhi, with chief guest Foreign Minister M. C. Chagla, 1965.

named Somani, brother-in-law of D. D. Sukhani and K. K. Sukhani, both directors on the board of Gayday Iron and Steel. We put a lot of pressure on Somani to return the loan, but he refused to respond.

With regard to the small investments, we sold a Rs.150,000 investment in Calcutta Electricity but decided to hold on to another Rs.200,000 investment in Hindustan Wires, which appeared to be doing all right. There was also another investment of Rs.300,000 with a gentleman in Bangalore whose name I don't recall. He refused to cooperate when asked to return the loan, so finally I went personally to Bangalore to see what I could do to recover the money. Despite further pressure, I had no option but to take him to court and attach his property, a small sawmill outside Bangalore. He had taken a loan of Rs.75,000 from a bank and mortgaged the property against the loan. It took several months, but I was finally able to take over the property. I also arranged with the bank to pay the loan we inherited as and when we were able to earn a profit from the running the mill. This property is prime land today and could be worth tens of millions of rupees. As for the remainder of the trust funds, Rs.800,000 were in debentures deposited with a bank through a broker, and we were able to convert this into cash.

Meanwhile, Gayday Iron and Steel, based in the state of Bihar, and Mandidip Paper, not far from Bhopal in Madhya Pradesh, were both struggling and running short on funds.

D. N. Tsarong approached Dharamsala for an assistant to help him in his day-to-day work. In response I received a letter from the Dalai Lama's private secretary saying that I should help Tsarong at Gayday in addition to my responsibility at the trust. I wrote back to say that I had no knowledge about industries and so wouldn't be of much help. Furthermore, this company wasn't in very good shape, and I didn't see how I could improve the situation. In response I got another letter from the private secretary saying that no matter what the situation, I should assist Tsarong. I was not happy about taking on this new responsibility and put a condition to my working at Gayday. I requested the private office to give me a letter saying that should the company go into liquidation after I joined it, I would in no way be responsible for this state of affairs. I did this because I saw the possibility of being blamed for something that I did not bring about. My request was granted, and the private office sent me an official letter stamped with the inner seal of His Holiness, dated December 8, 1970.

Traditionally, all letters and documents bore a seal of recognition. Signatures were never used. In Tibet the Dalai Lama's inner seal was locked in a special box wrapped in red silk. This box was locked by the Chikhyap Khenpo, the head of the Dalai Lama's personal staff. After locking the box he gave the key to the head of the ecclesiastical secretariat, the Ta-Lama, who would wear the key around his neck. The Chikhyap Khenpo would then put the box inside a cupboard inside the Dalai Lama's personal room. When the seal was required, the Chikhyap Khenpo would bring it before the Dalai Lama. The Ta-Lama would hand over the key to the Chikhyap Khenpo, who would then unlock the box, take out the seal, and seal the document. In this way, any document with the inner seal confers the approval of the Dalai Lama, the highest authority in Tibet.

I now spent the major part of my time at the Gayday office in Calcutta with D. N. Tsarong. As I slowly became acquainted with the working of the company, I began to grasp the full extent of its problems. The company was to have gone public in late 1961, but there were delays. Then in November 1962 the war between India and China had a devastating effect on the Indian economy, and the public were reluctant to buy stocks, resulting in further delays. Meanwhile, the Indian government had increased import duty on machinery, which affected Gayday, as all the major factory machinery had to be imported from Belgium. To add to that, the cost of U.S. dollars rose more than 50 percent between 1965 and 1967. There were substantial increases in the cost of material and the construction of the factory, and the delays drove up costs even further. A railway siding that had to be built to connect the factory to a main railway line cost Rs.1.4 million, a cost that would have been avoided had the location been better. Taken together, these circumstances led to a 100 percent increase in the cost of the project, bringing the total capital requirement to Rs.15 million.

The company managed to obtain a loan of Rs.3.9 million from the State Bank of India and another 1.9 million as working capital. It was also able

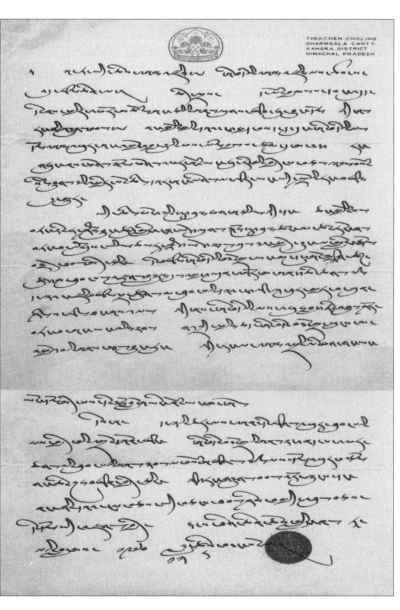

Letter from the Dalai Lama concerning Gayday Iron and Steel Company
with the inner seal.

to get some public-sector companies to buy equity shares, like the Bihar Industrial Development Bank, the Industrial Development Bank of India, the Life Insurance Corporation of India, and New India Assurance.

The company faced many growing pains in the training of workers for running the machines. As the factory was located in a remote area, ten kilometers from the closest town, facilities like markets, schools, and hospitals were not close by, and so it was difficult to get skilled staff, especially an experienced technical works manager. The original promoters of the company had been very ill advised in choosing the location. The company finally began production in October 1967. But there were continuous manufacturing problems, and finally the company had the supplier of the machinery, Deboc, come from Belgium to help eliminate the problems. He recommended several improvements, and to implement these the company would need another four million rupees. Since the assets of the company were hypothecated to the State Bank of India and the Industrial Development Bank of India, there was no option but to once again approach the Reserve Bank of India, of which the Industrial Development Bank of India was a subsidiary. They finally sanctioned the loan after several months.

However, production never reached the full capacity of 2,500 tons per month. From June 1969 to June 1970, only 4,460 tons of pipes were produced, owing not only to the lack of well-trained technical workers and shortage of funds but also to a shortage of raw materials. That year the company suffered a loss of Rs.2.2 million.

On January 16, 1971, Gyalo Thondup, chairman of the company and elder brother of H. H. the Dalai Lama, resigned. A year later in June 1972, D. N. Tsarong, the company's managing director, took medical leave for six months, and he later extended this by another six months and then resigned and settled in the United States. During his absence I was asked to temporarily take charge together with an Indian gentleman named R. G. Saraf, who had invested a substantial amount of money in the company.

In the following years there was improvement in production, but the company was plagued by a constant shortage of funds. Loans from the two banks were repeatedly delayed owing to red tape, causing huge losses. In just one example, the loan of Rs.4 million took six months to be released, and by that time the interest owed for that and previous loans amounted to 2.3 million, leaving only 1.7 million, and once more there was a shortage. This vicious cycle continued, as our only source of loans were these two financial institutions.

Since the original promoters of the company, the chairman, and the managing director had all abandoned the company, the financial institutions appointed a new managing director, one Mr. Vyas, from Bombay, but he proved unsuitable and left after just a couple of months. When the company's situation became critical, I went to Delhi to meet with George Fernandes, who was industries minister of the Janata Party government. Although Fernandes was a strong supporter of the Tibetans, he wasn't sympathetic to this business venture and would not help. Finally, a couple of months later, one of the bigger creditors took the company to court for liquidation. We informed the State Bank of India and the Industrial Development Bank of India, but they were not willing to rescue the company. Legal procedures continued, the company was eventually liquidated, and the banks took over the company's assets. Devastatingly, all the investments of the Tibetans, both of individuals as well as of the Charitable Trust of His Holiness the Dalai Lama, were wiped out.

Meanwhile, another Tibetan industrial enterprise was also struggling. The entrepreneur was my cousin Gyurme Sadutshang. He did not have a modern education, but he was resourceful and managed to set up a ten-ton paper factory at a place called Sehore in Madhya Pradesh. The entire investment for the project was put up by Tibetans, including a substantial portion by my cousin himself. The Dalai Lama's trust had a million rupees in equity shares in this company.

The company was established in 1963 and registered under the name of G. S. Mandidip Paper Mills Ltd. The G. S. stood for Gyurme Sadutshang, and Mandidip was the area where the factory was intended to be established, but later the location was changed to Sehore. The machinery was all imported from the U.K. In the initial stages there were growing pains like the lack of trained technicians and experience in running a factory. It took quite a while for the factory to become profitable. However, as the years went by, new problems arose. Pulp for making paper became more and more expensive. Water became increasingly scarce. Gradually a lack of funds, raw material, water, and decent management made the operation unviable—problems very much like those of Gayday.

In 1973 when the auditor's assessment showed that only 25 percent of the company's value was left, the Dalai Lama's trust, a major shareholder, suggested selling the company, and the management agreed. I discussed the proposal to sell the factory with Dayanand Sahay, a businessman who was on the Gayday board of directors. He knew a great number of people in the business world and agreed to help us. He was able to bring two businessmen to see the factory. The Dalai Lama's Charitable Trust initiated negotiations with one of them, B. K. Nopani, who decided to send a team of financial and technical experts for a detailed inspection.

After much bargaining we came to an agreement by which Nopani's investment company would pay a total of Rs.6.4 million, which included all the money loaned by Tibetan individuals to the company. Other secured and unsecured loans from financial institutions would be transferred to Nopani Investments. In the end the equity shareholders not only got back their money but also earned a profit of nearly 25 percent. Preference shareholders got back their investment plus 37 percent. Everybody involved in the paper factory was tremendously relieved and very happy at being able to retrieve their investments, including us at the trust. Many people came to me personally to express their appreciation and gratitude. Most people had given up hope of ever seeing their money again.

I must mention one person in particular who took part during these proceedings. Nopani appointed S. K. Dalmia to take over of the factory. He was formerly a general manager at one of the Birla textile factories. He was a kind, cooperative, and thoroughly decent person. Even much later, after the sale of the paper factory, Dalmia helped the Dalai Lama's trust obtain woolen yarn from a Birla concern, Oriental Carpet Manufacturers in Amritsar. The Tibetan government needed large quantities of woolen yarn for our carpet factories all over India in various refugee settlements. On his recommendation, we even got a special rate that benefitted us tremendously.

33. HIS HOLINESS VISITS JAPAN AND THAILAND

It seems remarkable now, with the Dalai Lama's extensive worldwide appearances, but he did not leave India for eight years after his flight from Tibet. In 1967 His Holiness visited a foreign country for the first time after going into exile. He accepted an invitation by the Society for the Promotion of Buddhism (Bukkyō Dendō Kyōkai) to visit Japan and also to hold an exhibition on Tibet. His visit was sponsored by Yomiuri Shimbun, a major Japanese media company. Tibet House, a center for Tibetan art and culture established by the Tibetan government in exile in New Delhi, prepared the exhibition. On September 25, 1967, the Dalai Lama arrived in Tokyo and was greeted by the heads of various religious organizations and a large media presence. Strict security arrangements had been made, and the Dalai Lama was immediately driven to the city. The entourage for the Dalai Lama included four people: Principal Secretary Tara-la, myself, Tenzin Gyeche, and His Holiness's personal attendant, Lobsang Gawa. We were taken to a five-star hotel called New Otami, and to our surprise, the Dalai Lama's elder brother Thubten Jigme Norbu was there to greet him, along with many members of religious organizations and a small group of Tibetans.

The Dalai Lama with Japanese board members of the Society for the Promotion of Buddhism (Bukkyō Dendō Kyōkai), 1967. The founder, Yehan Numata, is standing behind His Holiness. Back row left is the Dalai Lama's brother Thubten Jigme Norbu and the author next to him.

On the second day the Dalai Lama inaugurated the Tibetan exhibition, which featured a display of many ancient and beautiful Tibetan religious paintings, rare and sacred Buddhist statues and icons, block-printed and handwritten religious manuscripts, silver and gold handicrafts, as well as various other handicrafts. The public knew next to nothing about Tibet, but they were very appreciative of the collection. Later that day, His Holiness visited two major Buddhist temples and had a religious discussion with the heads of these.

His Holiness visited many religious and important sites in Tokyo and Kyoto. On the fifth day he gave a live television interview for the first time at Yomiuri Shimbun studio. I translated it into English, and it had to be retranslated into Japanese. Very interested in science and technology, His Holiness was especially pleased to visit an Asian country as technologically advanced as Japan.

That same year, the Dalai Lama was invited to visit Thailand by the Buddhist Association of Thailand. He left for Bangkok on November 11 with the same entourage, and again, he was greeted at the airport by a huge crowd and a large media presence. This time, His Holiness stayed at a large temple. The day after his arrival, the prime minister of Thailand called on him to welcome him and pay his respects. What impressed me very much was that an important personage like the prime minister chose to sit on the floor while His Holiness sat on a chair. I later learned that in Thailand, a devoutly Buddhist nation, no laypeople sit above or on the same level as monks.

His Holiness also called on Thailand's Supreme Patriarch Phra Ariyavangsagatayana at his temple the day after his arrival and discussed religious matters. He then visited important temples and monasteries. On the third day, he had an audience with His Majesty King Bhumibol Adulyadej at his palace. The Supreme Patriarch was also present. After half an hour of pleasant conversation, the king invited His Holiness and the Supreme Patriarch to lunch. His Holiness' three-monk retinue—Tara-la, Tenzin Gyeche, and Lobsang Gawa—were also invited. The lunch was served in a spacious hall, and there were a large number of seats for the king and the royal family in the front with the prime minister and thirty to forty senior officials behind them. However, no one except the monks took part in the lunch. His Holiness and the Supreme Patriarch sat on elevated cushions, and five servers brought their meal, approaching on their knees. As soon as the lunch was served, the king came forward and sat on a low cushion facing the Dalai Lama, whereas the prime minister did the same before the Supreme Patriarch. Three senior government officials did likewise and sat opposite His Holiness's three attendants. I was very touched and impressed by the humility and respect shown by the king, so much revered by his subjects, to His Holiness.

On the third day of his visit, His Holiness decided to participate in the monks' daily alms round. Monks collected their food for the day by going to the doors of individual families, holding their bowls in their hands and accepting whatever was offered. This is what the Buddha did in his time. For the Dalai Lama this was a most unusual departure from Tibetan tradition.

After a week's successful visit we departed. On the way to the airport His

Holiness called on the Supreme Patriarch to wish him farewell. They spoke for a few minutes, and then the Supreme Patriarch decided to accompany His Holiness to the airport and see him off. We were told this was highly unusual. It showed how greatly he esteemed the Dalai Lama.

34. THE PLIGHT OF TIBETAN REFUGEES IN BHUTAN

In 1959, after the failed uprising of the tenth of March against the Communist Chinese, Tibetans fled in large numbers to India, Nepal, and Bhutan. The majority fled to India and Nepal, but around four to five thousand entered Bhutan and were permitted to stay. King Jigme Dorji Wangchuk and Prime Minister Jigme Dorji were both sympathetic to the Tibetans and consented to rehabilitate them with government assistance. The refugees were divided into six groups. Five of the groups were allotted agricultural land close to the capital, Thimphu. The sixth group was allotted land farther north, close to the Tibetan border, at a place called Bumthang. The five settlements close to the capital were located at Karche, Bhokar, Lhuntse, Khasakha, and Jigmenang. There were also two small groups of nomads in Lingshi and Sel, both close to Paro, south of Thimphu. His majesty the king was very kind in not only providing land but also timber from nearby forests for the refugees to build their houses. Gradually the Tibetans settled down to a new life and began to support themselves. Adjusting to their new environment was far easier for them than for the Tibetan refugees who settled in India and Nepal because the Bhutanese and Tibetans are ethnically similar and share a common religious, cultural, and linguistic background.

In 1960, George Taring was officially appointed the Dalai Lama's representative in Bhutan. He was tasked with coordinating the work of the settlements and acting as liaison between the refugees and the government of Bhutan. The Tibetan government in exile thought it appropriate to appoint George Taring, as he was related to the queen, Ashi Kesang. Ashi Kesang's mother, Rani Dorji, was a sister to the Sikkimese king and to George Taring's father, who settled in Tibet.

For a couple of years the settlements progressed well, but around the end of 1962, things began to take a turn. The refugee settlements had organized a dance troupe. The king was fond of music and dance and occasionally called the troupe to perform at the palace. Among the performers was a young woman called Yangkyi who was a good dancer and sang beautifully. After some time it became evident to everyone that she had become the king's mistress. This began a series of incidents that eroded relations between the Tibetan government in exile and the government of Bhutan.

On April 5, 1964, Prime Minister Jigme Dorji was assassinated in the southern border town of Phuntsokling. At the time I was in Dharamsala working at the private secretariat of His Holiness the Dalai Lama. I was shocked and deeply saddened; not only was he a friend of my family, but he was a very close and dear friend of my brother Lo Gedun, who had been shot during the 1959 uprisings in Lhasa.

I had met the prime minister in 1961. I was in Kalimpong on a short leave from Dharamsala to be with my family. He told me how sad he felt about the death of his friend Lo Gedun and then very kindly offered me a job as a trade agent with the government of Bhutan in Calcutta. This was a potentially lucrative position. But as I felt strongly that it was my primary duty to serve the Dalai Lama at this hour of need, I declined, in all likelihood at a significant cost to the material comfort of my family. I thanked him for his generous offer and never forgot his kindness.

The assassination of Prime Minister Jigme Dorji occurred while the king of Bhutan was away in Switzerland. In the immediate aftermath of this tragedy, the prime minister's younger brother, Lhundup Dorji, took over the position of prime minister. He did so apparently without first obtaining the king's consent. The king was not pleased. When the king returned home,

Lhundup Dorji went into exile in Nepal. During this short period when Lhundup Dorji was in authority, he was not as sympathetic to the Tibetans as his brother had been. He issued an order instructing all Tibetans to cut their hair short in the manner of the Bhutanese. The Tibetans were also to wear Bhutanese dress. This, of course, created a problem, and an appeal was made through George Taring as the Dalai Lama's representative. The matter died down after the king's return.

For the next ten years everything was calm, and the settlements made good progress, becoming self-sufficient. But then Bhutan was struck with tragedy yet again. King Jigme Dorji Wangchuk died suddenly while on safari in South Africa. Crown Prince Jigme Senge Wangchuk ascended the throne the following year. The coronation took place on July 24, 1972, and my family and I were invited to attend by Ashi Kesang, who was now queen mother and who was also the sister of our friend the late prime minister.

Author and wife with King Jigme Senge Wangchuk of Bhutan at his coronation in Thimphu, 1972. On the far right is Mr. Norbu, a friend.

Now, as I mentioned above, from at least the mid-1960s it was common knowledge that Ashi Yangkyi, as she was then known, was the king's mistress. This was not just a matter of popular rumor; she even had several children by him. Far from being treated as a disreputable figure, she was given much respect wherever she traveled in Bhutan. The same is true of her reception in Darjeeling. The Tibetans in Darjeeling entertained her lavishly and gave her great respect. It was said that a local Tibetan newspaper called *Freedom*, which always covered her visits, went as far as calling her "Gyalmo," or Queen, Ashi Yangkyi. Tibetans in Bhutan sometimes tried to seek favors through her. The Bhutanese government, meanwhile, especially those close to the royal family, monitored her movements closely.

In July 1972, on the eve of the coronation of King Jigme Senge Wangchuk, the Bhutanese government gave a press conference where they made an unexpected and startling announcement. They claimed that a group of Tibetans had hatched a plot to assassinate the crown prince and also to burn down Tashichho Dzong, the royal palace in Thimphu. This revelation was so shocking that we could hardly bring ourselves to believe it. It was very awkward for George Taring's older brother, Jigme Taring, who had been deputed to attend the coronation as representative of the Dalai Lama and the Tibetan government. There was an atmosphere of general uneasiness between the Tibetans and Bhutanese attending the function.

After the coronation there was no further news about the assassination plot for quite some time. Then, on March 5, 1974, Bhutanese security personnel arrested twenty-seven Tibetans allegedly connected with the plot. One of the Tibetans arrested was a man known by his family name, Lhading, a noble family of Lhasa. Lhading was not only an official of the Tibetan government in exile and assistant to George Taring, but he was also a close relative of the Dorji family. The queen mother's own grandmother was from the Lhading family. Fortunately for George Taring, he was not in Bhutan when the arrests were made, as there is no doubt he would also have been arrested. Ashi Yangkyi, perhaps aware of potential danger, had already fled Bhutan. The Bhutanese government, it seems, believed that Ashi Yangkyi and her supporters were planning to overthrow the new king and to install her son on the throne.

The Tibetan government in exile conveyed, through the Bhutanese ambassador in New Delhi, that they were gravely concerned about the arrest of Lhading and other Tibetans. They expressed their conviction that no Tibetans would indulge in such terrible activities against the government of Bhutan and its people. They requested the immediate release of those arrested and asked for a thorough investigation to determine the truth. Dharamsala offered their full support in clearing up this matter. There was no news for quite some time, and then the Bhutanese government announced that they had sufficient evidence to prove the charges. They declared that the matter would be dealt with in a court of law.

The government of Bhutan meanwhile announced a new policy: all Tibetans who wanted to stay in Bhutan would have to take up Bhutanese citizenship. They said that this was necessary for the security of the nation. At that time, the Tibetan refugees, like Tibetan refugees elsewhere, had no desire to take up the citizenship of another country. They had high hopes of returning home to Tibet in the near future. They believed beyond a doubt that they wouldn't have to live in a foreign country forever. The refugees made a strong representation to the government of Bhutan and also asked the Tibetan government in exile to intervene. In October 1975, an emissary was sent to Bhutan by the Tibetan government in exile to ascertain the true situation, both with regard to the matter of citizenship and the arrest of twenty-seven Tibetans. The dispatching of the emissary was followed by three days of meetings, on December 4–6, between Gyaphag Dorji, the Bhutanese ambassador in New Delhi, and Thupten Nyingje, a minister in the Tibetan government in exile. At the conclusion of it all, it was mutually agreed that the matter of citizenship would not be pursued further.

A year and a half later the Bhutanese government, again citing national security reasons, announced that the Tibetan settlements were to be dispersed. They said the families living in the settlements as refugees must be integrated into Bhutanese villages. In view of this policy, and also in view of the arrested Tibetans, the Tibetan government in exile sent ministers Wangchuk Dorji and Juchen Thupten plus one assistant to Bhutan in July 1977. They were kindly received by His Majesty and given a patient hearing. At the end of the audience His Majesty said that if the Tibetan refugees were not willing to be dispersed, then they would not be forced. As for the other matters, the king said, those should be discussed with the appropriate ministers, and due consideration would be given. Consequently the Tibetan ministers met with the home and foreign affairs ministers of Bhutan. The result was a series of agreements:

1. Bhutanese citizenship would not be imposed without consent.
2. Tibetan settlements would not be dispersed.
3. Tibetans would be given freedom of movement.
4. With regard to the request for the release of Lhading and other prisoners, the matter would be looked into and given due consideration.

On the part of the Tibetans, the Bhutanese government asked for a written statement that the Tibetans in Bhutan would not undertake any activity that would jeopardize the national security of Bhutan or the interests of the country and its people.

In early 1978 the government of Bhutan, through their ambassador in New Delhi, made a strong complaint to the Tibetan government in exile. They said the Tibetan representative in New York had made a report to the U.N. Commission for Human Rights severely criticizing the Bhutanese government in regards to the Tibetan refugees. Dharamsala was alarmed by this development, and in order to clear up this most unfortunate misunderstanding and also to clear other pending matters, I was directed by the Kashag to go to Bhutan and meet the concerned authorities.

I left Calcutta on February 18 and arrived in Thimphu the very next day. On February 21, I was able to meet the home and foreign affairs ministers at the home minister's office at Tashichho Dzong. I clarified the misunderstandings, drew their attention to the other matters concerning our refugees in Bhutan, and said that I had a letter for the king and requested an audience. The ministers agreed that all the issues I had raised with them should be put before the king first.

That evening I was informed that the king would receive me the next morning. I went to Tashichho Dzong at the appointed time, presented my greeting scarf to the king, and conveyed to him His Holiness the Dalai Lama's greetings as well as those of the Kashag. I also presented a letter from the Kashag, which he read immediately. I then conveyed our sincere thanks for the recent release of six Tibetan prisoners and requested the early release of the rest of the prisoners, especially Lhading. I went on to clarify the misunderstanding caused by the letter our New York representative sent to the U.N. I handed over a copy of the original letter and explained that it was a routine annual report concerning Tibetan refugee issues all over the world. The reference to refugees in Bhutan was in relation to only certain problems refugees faced. His Majesty read the copy of the letter and did not comment. Nonetheless, I felt he was satisfied with the explanation. On the matters of compulsory citizenship and settlement dispersal, the king assured me that the whole exercise of integration was for the sake of national security and that it would not be imposed on the Tibetans. However, he hoped that overall integration would be achieved in four to five years. I was also able to take up other matters, and the king heard me out very patiently. He said that I should meet with the concerned ministers for further discussion.

The following day, I again met with the home minister and the foreign affairs minister. I briefed them about my previous day's audience. They said they were glad that I was able to have a detailed discussion with the king and that some of the issues had been resolved. They added that the rest of the issues would be dealt with in due course and that they hoped to make appropriate and favorable decisions soon.

Despite these assurances, in September 1978 the Bhutanese ambassador in New Delhi said they wished to know from Dharamsala whether the Tibetan refugees in Bhutan were willing to accept Bhutanese citizenship. Soon after, in early October, three Tibetan leaders in Bhutan were arrested for reasons unknown. This created a great deal of anxiety for the Tibetans in Bhutan. They appealed to Dharamsala for resettlement in India. The Tibetan government contacted the Bhutanese government and reminded them of the agreements arrived at in July 1977. We told the Bhutanese that we believed there must certainly have been some misunderstanding and requested the release of the three Tibetan leaders. It was also pointed out that earlier that very year, I, Rinchen Sadutshang, representing the Tibetan government, had been assured by the king that there would be no forced integration. The voluntary process of integration, I had been told, would be a patient process; more time would be given. Despite the immediate response of the Tibetan government in exile to the matter at hand in Bhutan, the situation remained unresolved for some time, and the Tibetan refugees in Bhutan continued to press for resettlement in India. The Tibetan government approached New Delhi about this possibility, but the Indian government was reluctant to bring such a large number of refugees into India and advised further negotiations with Bhutan.

After several more months with no resolution, we enlisted the help of Kusho Bakula, a member of the Indian parliament from Ladakh who was not only an incarnate lama but a devotee of the Dalai Lama. Kusho Bakula sought an appointment for the Tibetan representative in Delhi with Prime Minister Moraji Desai, and meanwhile I was once again sent to Bhutan.

I requested an appointment with the Bhutanese foreign affairs minister, and it was granted for December 4. I waited a few days in Delhi for the Indian government's decision, but my wait was in vain. Kusho Bakula and Kalon Thupten Nyingje received an appointment with the Indian prime minister only when I had already left Delhi and had stopped overnight in Calcutta. On the evening of December 2, Thupten Nyingje called me in Calcutta and told me that the Indian government had agreed to allow the immigration of the refugees from Bhutan, so I told Thupten Nyingje that I would conduct my discussions in Bhutan accordingly.

I left for Thimphu the following day and kept my appointment with Lonpo Dawa, the minister for foreign affairs, for the morning of December 4. I met him at his office in Tashichho Dzong, and once again I explained our position. I told him that if no reconsideration could by given by the Bhutanese government on the question of forced citizenship, then our only option was to move the refugees to India. He asked me if the Indian government had approved of such a move. I told him that we had approached the Indian government and had every hope of obtaining their approval. However, I did not reveal to him that Thupten Nyingje had conveyed to me that we already had approval. The foreign minister said the government of Bhutan would not change their decision. I informed him that, upon obtaining formal approval from the government of India, we would send two officials to Bhutan to establish who among the Tibetan refugees wanted to come to

India versus who opted to stay behind in Bhutan. At that time, I told him, all of the details with respect to both groups of refugees could be settled. The next morning as I was leaving Thimphu, I was asked to come over to the foreign ministry. I went at once and met Lonpo Dawa at the door of his office, where he handed me a letter. I accepted the letter and then left for India.

When I reached Delhi the next day, I was told by Thupten Nyingje that the Indian foreign secretary wished to see me immediately. So the following day I went to meet Foreign Secretary Jagat Mehta. He asked me about my trip to Bhutan before eventually revealing that he had already been informed of my trip by the Bhutanese authorities. The Bhutanese had said that I claimed to have the approval of the government of India for the immigration of Tibetan refugees from Bhutan. He questioned me about when and how this alleged approval was obtained. I told him that the report from the Bhutanese authorities was not entirely true. I told him that I had said we were very *hopeful* of obtaining such an approval. I expressed to him that I felt there had been some serious misunderstanding and that I was very upset.

On my return to the Bureau of His Holiness the Dalai Lama in Delhi, I confronted Thupten Nyingje, who was staying there, and related to him what the foreign secretary had said. I questioned him as to why he had misled me by telling me on the telephone that during his meeting with the prime minister, the Indian government had agreed to our request for relocating the refugees. Strangely, he had no answer but just stood there silently. I told him it was irresponsible for a man in his position to give me misinformation and that I would have to report everything to the Kashag when I reached Dharamsala the next day.

After my arrival in Dharamsala a full Kashag meeting was held where Thupten Nyingje was also present. I briefed the Kashag on my mission to Thimphu. Then I described my meeting with the Indian foreign secretary, which entailed proffering a detailed explanation of how Thupten Nyingje had misled me. Everyone looked at Thupten Nyingje for an explanation, but he again kept quiet. Later that afternoon the whole Kashag had an audience with His Holiness the Dalai Lama. Once again I had no option but to inform His Holiness about the embarrassing situation. His Holiness too was upset and questioned Thupten Nyingje, but again he said absolutely nothing and merely bent his head. To this day I am unable to understand why he did what he did.

Thupten Nyingje's inexplicable behavior aside, there was still the perplexing question of the Bhutanese minister of foreign affair's behavior. The letter Lonpo Dawa had given me on the day of my departure from Bhutan contained an account of what had transpired at our meeting. What I had actually said during our meeting was abundantly clear from this letter, which was signed by Lonpo Dawa and dated December 6, 1978. The letter reads: "…the question of the above Tibetan refugees has been moved by the Dalai Lama with the government of India, and that you felt there would be no problem in obtaining the requisite approval…" Though it was clear, even to the Bhutanese minister himself, that I did not claim that we had already obtained approval from the Indian government, it appears that the minister had immediately informed the Indian ministry of external affairs otherwise. This was most regrettable and caused a great deal of embarrassment to us.

At the end of it all, Dharamsala chose to write to Bhutan and once more request the implementation of policies to which they had committed in agreements previously reached with the Tibetan exile government at various meetings. The matter continued to go unresolved. However, in view of the large number of refugees repeatedly asking to be relocated to India, stronger efforts were made to persuade the Indian government to approve their immigration. Finally a total of one thousand refugees were brought to India between January 1982 and March 1983. Of these, seven hundred were resettled in the Dehradun area, and the remaining three hundred were sent to the Tibetan refugee settlement in Mungod in South India. Beyond the one thousand refugees resettled during that year, the rest of the Tibetan refugees in Bhutan remained there and agreed to take up Bhutanese citizenship. They were not dispersed, however, and remained in their original settlements.

As for the twenty-odd Tibetan prisoners, it was claimed that they were tried in a court of law and convicted of their crimes. A request was made to the Bhutanese government for permission to send a defense lawyer from India, but it was denied. Tragically, all the prisoners, including Lhading, eventually died in prison.

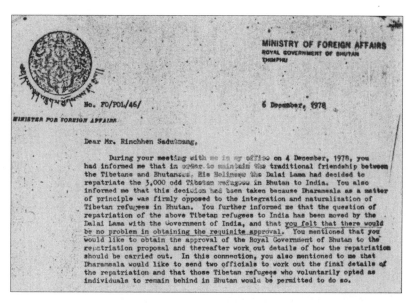

Letter from the Bhutanese foreign ministry, December 6, 1978, during the time of trouble for the Tibetan refugees settled there.

35. PROMOTION AND
A NEW PORTFOLIO

I n June 1978 I was designated to the post of kalon, or minister. Soon after, there was a Kashag meeting, and in the course of some portfolio changes, I was assigned to be His Holiness's representative in New Delhi. Wangchuk Dorji preceded me in this position. He had been posted to this position temporarily and had expressed his desire to continue. The Kashag, however, decided that this post should be occupied by someone who was not only capable of handling the responsibility but who had the advantage of an English education. As such, I was told to take charge of the bureau as soon as possible.

I took charge of the bureau on September 15, 1978. My appointment was for two years. The Bureau of the Dalai Lama in New Delhi was the most important office of the exile government outside of Dharamsala. It was the base for coordinating all Tibetan activities across India with Dharamsala. The bureau's primary task was to deal with four Indian ministries—external affairs, home, education, and rehabilitation—with regard to Tibetan refugees. It also had to deal with matters directly related to His Holiness. The external affairs ministry had a permanent liaison officer wherever His Holiness resided, which was in Mussoorie between 1959 and 1961 and thereafter

Author greeting newly elected Prime Minister Moraji Desai of the Janata Party,
New Delhi, 1978.

in Dharamsala. The liaison officer's status was that of a junior deputy secretary, and he or she dealt directly with the Dalai Lama's private secretariat.
In matters relating to security, education, or rehabilitation, the bureau had
to deal directly with the ministries concerned. All other matters were taken
up with the external affairs ministry. Our dealings and cooperation with the
external affairs ministry was therefore extensive. The Tibetan desk at this
ministry was under the charge of a joint secretary who handled the northeastern region of India. Under him was a deputy secretary who handled the
day-to-day affairs.

Soon after His Holiness took refuge in India, his topmost priority was
the education of the Tibetan refugee children, who were entering India in
large numbers. His Holiness visited Delhi and took up the matter with the
Indian government. Nehru himself had emphasized the importance of education for the refugee children, and His Holiness's feelings were completely
in accord with the prime minister's. Nehru asked the ministry of education

to do whatever was necessary, and gradually four boarding schools were set up in the hill stations of Mussoorie, Simla, Dalhousie, and Darjeeling, all in northern India. These were collectively called the Central School for Tibetans and were under the Indian ministry of education. Each school was to take up to five hundred students. The Tibetan government in exile was allowed to provide Tibetan teachers to teach Tibetan and religion so that young Tibetans would not forget their language, culture, and religion. Several years after the schools were established, our own education ministry came to the conclusion that the schools were far from satisfactory. In 1981 we appealed to the Indian ministry of education and asked that the schools be allowed to run independently. Although the minister of education, Vasant Sathe, was sympathetic to our appeal, it was not successful owing largely to objections from the teachers' union.

One important function of the bureau was to maintain a close relationship with the various foreign embassies in New Delhi. Periodically we informed them about the latest news on Tibet and tried to garner support

During the birthday celebrations of the Dalai Lama in New Delhi, July 6, 1980. Author, far right, is introducing guests to His Holiness.

The author and his wife with the ambassador of Greece at the Dalai Lama's
birthday reception in New Delhi, 1980.

for our cause. Each year, on the sixth of July, we held a reception to celebrate His Holiness's birthday. This reception was usually attended by many
embassy personnel as well as officials of the government of India, especially
from the ministries we dealt with. The following year, in 1980, I was most
fortunate when the celebration of His Holiness's birthday coincided with his
visit to Delhi. I requested His Holiness's presence at the annual reception,
and the request was granted. We prepared a grand celebration and invited
many guests. Since His Holiness was going to be present, some officials even
approached us to make sure they would receive invitations. Many ambassa-
dors, senior officials of the government of India, and intellectuals attended
this particular reception.

36. CHANGES IN CHINESE GOVERNMENT POLICY

In early 1978 Chinese policies in Tibet were becoming more liberal, even if only slightly so. Dharamsala was able to get in touch with the Chinese government and asked for permission to send a delegation to visit central Tibet, which had become known as the Tibetan Autonomous Region. Meanwhile, taking advantage of the more liberal political situation, many Tibetan individuals from across the Tibetan diaspora were applying for visas to visit the relatives they had left behind in Tibet.

The first Tibetan to obtain a Chinese visa to enter Tibet was Tsultrim Tersey, who had settled in Switzerland in the early 1960s along with a thousand or so other Tibetans. He was originally from Bathang and had relatives living there under Chinese rule. When he arrived in Nepal en route to Tibet, I sent him a message asking him to stop in Delhi for a day or two on his way back to Switzerland. On his return to Nepal he sent a message saying that the situation in Tibet was rather fluid and that he would not advise the visit to Tibet that had been planned by our Tibetan Youth Congress. He did not come to see me at the bureau even though he had a layover in Delhi en route to Switzerland. I later surmised that he may have had an ulterior motive. Perhaps he wanted to delay visits to Tibet by Tibetans because he wanted to report his firsthand information to some person, persons, or organization before anyone else.

The Tibetan Youth Congress negotiated with the Chinese embassy in Delhi, and it was agreed that a group of ten youths would be granted visas to travel to Tibet. I was asked to talk to the Chinese officials at the embassy to finalize details regarding foreign exchange, transportation from the Nepal border onward, and so on. I explained to the Chinese that the youths would be using travel documents issued by the Indian government that were known as identity certificates (IC's), and they had no objection to this. However, when the group arrived in Delhi and we sent the travel documents for visas, the Chinese would only issue visas on a separate piece of paper that designated the bearer as an "overseas Chinese." We refused to accept this and tried to convince them to issue regular visas, but they would not agree. Finally the trip was canceled, and the entire episode was explained to the press at a press conference.

Meanwhile Dharamsala was negotiating with the Chinese to send small delegations to visit various parts of Tibet. Eventually the Chinese approved three delegations. The first consisted of senior Dharamsala officials Kalon Juchen Thupten, the home minister; Kalon Lobsang Dargye, the finance minister; Kalon Phuntsok Tashi Taklha, brother-in-law of the Dalai Lama and security minister; and Lobsang Samten Taklha, director of the Tibetan Medical and Astrological Institute as well as His Holiness's elder brother. The delegation left Delhi on August 2, 1979, and spent about four months in Tibet. Their first stop was Lhasa and the surrounding areas. On their return journey they spent some time at Chamdo and Karzé in Kham. The visit was an enormous success, despite the fact that the Chinese programmed the whole tour. Everywhere they went they were mobbed by the Tibetans, elated to see the Dalai Lama's representatives after so many years.

The Chinese did not allow the delegation to visit places not already on the schedule; nor did they allow the delegation to meet with individuals without special permission. Lobsang Samten Taklha and Kalon Phuntsok Tashi Taklha managed to obtain special permission to visit Dapon Sampho, a *rimshi* in the previous regime and an old friend. Dapon Sampho was incarcerated in one of the largest prisons in China. Back in the days of free Tibet, Dapon Sampho had been one of the two commanders-in-chief of Drapchi Magar, the largest army unit in Lhasa. Ironically, what had previously been his own army headquarters was now his prison. After the delegation returned from Tibet, I saw a photograph of Dapon Sampho and did not recognize him at all. I saw a frail old man in shabby prison clothing; he had aged incredibly, and I felt very sorry for him. Kalon Phuntsok Tashi Taklha also kindly brought me a photo of my sister Pema Chöden Goshampa and my cousin Sochö. Whereas I was able to recognize my sister, I found it hard to believe that the old man in the photo was my cousin. He was dressed in worn-out clothes with patches. It was heartbreaking to think that the eldest son of Sadutshang was reduced to this sad figure toward the end of his life.

The delegation had also visited Beijing on their return journey, and there they met the Panchen Lama, Ngabo Ngawang Jigme, and Baba Phuntsok Wangyal. The Panchen Lama and Phuntsok Wangyal had been reinstated after prolonged imprisonment. The delegation also called on senior Communist Party members and discussed the situation in Tibet. They tried their best to try and lay the foundation for future negotiations.

The delegation returned to Delhi on December 24, 1979, and I received them at the airport. They had thirteen boxes of unaccompanied baggage. Indian customs would not clear these without checking them first, though we explained that the boxes contained nothing but requests for prayers and donations to the Dalai Lama. The next day customs officials went through the boxes. There were hundreds and hundreds of letters requesting His Holiness the Dalai Lama to pray for the deceased as well as for the living. These letters were accompanied by the customary *khatak*, white silk ceremonial scarves, and offerings of money in the form of Chinese silver coins and notes. There were also other gifts of small images of the Buddha, small jewelry items of gold, and similar such things. The silver items could not have weighed more than a few kilos and the gold perhaps a few hundred grams. It took a long time to process the tax exemption formalities from the concerned department. Eventually, however, the boxes were released.

Group photo of the Tibetan government in exile, Dharamsala, early 1980s.

37. OVER THE YEARS

By the early 1980s, I had given the prime years of my life to the service of the Dalai Lama and my government. When I first started to work in Dharamsala, my salary was seventy-five rupees a month, barely enough to meet my own personal needs, let alone the needs of my family. Although my salary gradually increased, if I hadn't had some money of my own, my family would have suffered. I had a wife and six children, but I put the needs of the exile government before theirs. As I mentioned, the government of Bhutan had offered me a potentially lucrative position, and the Indian Central Bureau of Investigation also offered me a good job. But I declined both opportunities because of my loyalty to my country and the Tibetan government in exile, which was sorely in need of officials who were familiar with India and who could communicate in English.

My obligation to my family was of great concern to me, and despite my service to the government, I was still able to provide each of my six children with a good education. My eldest daughter, Sonam Deki, graduated from Loreto College in Calcutta. My second daughter, Yangchen Dolkar, went to England for her higher studies. My eldest son, Tsetan Dorji, studied at one of India's premier medical colleges, Jawaharlal Institute of Postgraduate

Author, his wife, and children, January 1968. Sonam Deki, Namgyal Phuntsok, Sonam Lhamo, author's wife Tseyang, author, Kelsang Nordon, Yangchen Dolkar, and Tsetan Dorji.

Author's six children during his eldest daughter's wedding, 1975. Sonam Deki, Yangchen Dolkar, Tsetan Dorji, Namgyal Phuntsok, and twins Sonam Lhamo and Kelsang Nordon.

Medical Education and Research (JIPMER). My younger son, Namgyal Phuntsok, joined the Indian Institute of Technology in Delhi but changed his mind midway and became a full-fledged chartered accountant instead. Both of my boys attended St. Joseph's College, my old school in Darjeeling. My youngest children, twin daughters Sonam Lhamo and Kelsang Nordon, also completed their higher education in India. Sonam graduated from Lady Brabourne College in Calcutta, and Kelsang graduated from Lady Shriram College in Delhi.

I had spent virtually all of my money in providing the best education I could for my children. As the years passed, I realized that I had neglected to give sufficient attention to the financial condition of my family. Since many young Tibetans had become well educated, and quite a number of them had joined the staff of the Tibetan government in exile, I felt that it was high time I gave some thought to the long-term welfare of my family and to give my family some well-deserved attention. As my two-year appointment as His Holiness's representative in Delhi wound down to its final months, I decided it was time to leave. I submitted my resignation to His Holiness the Dalai Lama with my deep regrets, first recounting the various stages of my service to his government. It seems that His Holiness was not very happy with my letter because it took several months for me to get a reply. Meanwhile, when it became known that I had submitted my resignation, the secretary of information Namgyal Dorji, the secretary of religious affairs Ngawang Chösang, and the secretary of finance Gedun Gelek all came to Delhi and asked me to withdraw my resignation. I reiterated the circumstances of my family obligations and my observation that many young and talented people were now in government service.

I had served His Holiness the Dalai Lama and the Tibetan government for over thirty years and had the satisfaction of knowing that I was able to help to the best of my ability in an hour of dire need. Apart from myself, other members of my family had also contributed selflessly to the Tibetan cause. My brothers Lo Gedun and Wangdor fought the Chinese in 1959 when they attacked the Norbulingka palace. Many years before his death in that defense, Lo Gedun had also led a group of Khampas in escorting the Dalai Lama to safety in Yatung in 1951 when the Chinese first invaded

With the author's two brothers and their wives, 1975. Lo Nyendak and his wife
Tsewang Chodon, Wangchuk Dorji and wife Pema Chodon, author
with wife Tseyang.

Kham. My brother Lo Nyendak, after being a leader in the Chushi Gangdruk resistance movement, went on to be among the very first members of
the Tibetan parliament in exile, serving three successive terms in the 1960s.

I am proud to say that two of my own children have kept up the family
tradition of serving the Tibetan people. As soon as she graduated from college, my eldest daughter, Sonam Deki, joined the Tibetan Homes Foundation in Mussoorie, which serves to educate Tibetan children. She worked
for many years as assistant to the head of that institution, Mrs. Mary Taring. Later, Sonam Deki was in charge of the Tibetan Industrial Rehabilitation Society (TIRS), an organization that sets up economically viable small
industries for Tibetans in order to help them become self-sufficient.

After graduating from medical school, my eldest son, Tsetan Dorji, left
for the U.K. in order to specialize in chest medicine, for he saw the heavy

toll that tuberculosis was taking on the refugee community. I persuaded him to move to the United States, because I believed that his career would best flourish there, little realizing how deep-seated his thirst was to serve our people in exile. Tsetan Dorji returned to India in 1983 and began working at the Tibetan Delek Hospital in Dharamsala, and he was promoted to chief medical officer five years later. In 1988 he was appointed personal physician to His Holiness the Dalai Lama. In 1990 he received a Fulbright scholarship to do a masters degree in public health at Harvard University, and for twelve years beginning in 1995, he served as director of Delek Hospital. Of the several awards he has received in his career, the most outstanding honor came when he was awarded the Unsung Hero of Compassion, an honor that he received personally from the Dalai Lama in the United States. Our entire family is extremely proud that he has been able to serve both His Holiness and the Tibetan people during such time of need.

After I retired from government service I tried my hand at a few minor business ventures in order to provide an easier life for my family. After several years I was also able to sell a few items of my wife's traditional jewelry, which gave my wife and I much needed financial security, so that I have never had to depend on any of my children for financial support. Although as a kalon I was entitled to a pension and medical benefits from the Tibetan government in exile, I never took them, not wanting to put any extra financial burden on my government.

The highlight of my retired life was a trip my wife and I made to Tibet in August 2006 accompanied by our daughter Yangchen Dolkar. We stayed with my nephew Sonam Topgyal Goshampa, who owned a travel agency. We found we had to be very careful making international calls from his house. We suspected his phone was bugged, as he had constant contact with people outside of Tibet.

The main reason for our trip was to make a pilgrimage to as many of the holy sites in central Tibet as possible. The first thing we did after our arrival in Lhasa was to visit the Tsuklakhang temple and pray to the holy Shakyamuni statue, held so precious by millions of Tibetans. We visited the Potala, the Norbulingka, and many temples in Lhasa. Then we drove outside Lhasa and visited the great temple of Sakya and, in Shigatse, Tashi

Lhunpo Monastery, seat of the Panchen Lama. Everywhere we went Tibetans guessed immediately that we came from outside of Tibet. Some asked us for mani pills blessed by the Dalai Lama, which we had taken care to bring. We had also brought along plenty of *sungdu*, or protection cords, which had also been blessed by the Dalai Lama.

It was very sad for me to see the Potala, once the home of the Dalai Lama and the center of our government, turned into a museum. The same went for the Norbulingka, well tended in some areas and completely neglected in others. I even recognized one of His Holiness's cars abandoned in an open shed. Such indifference would have been unheard of in the old days.

As we went around Lhasa we found the only area that was still recognizable was the Barkhor, the inner circle of town, and we saw several of our friends' homes. However, we couldn't even find the area where our old home stood, as there were so many new houses built after pulling down old ones. Moving around Lhasa by ourselves proved harder than we thought. Everything had changed drastically. And all the taxi drivers were Han Chinese who, though they lived in Lhasa, couldn't speak a word of Tibetan. The Chinese were now a majority in the very heart of Tibet.

My other reason for visiting Tibet was to see my older sister, Pema Chöden Goshampa. She was old and very bent but in good spirits, despite the terrible upheavals she had been through. She spent all of her time in prayer in the shrine room where she also slept. Fortunately all of her children were doing well, and materially she was comfortable enough.

At the end of September we returned to India on the last flight available, as there were no flights in the winter months back then. It was good to be back home, free to speak and do as one wished, after the strain of being under constant surveillance. Lhasa was not the town we knew. It had lost its uniqueness and most of it now looked like any other Chinese town. However, we saw that the Tibetans there had not lost their hopes and dreams for Tibet at all, or their spirit. This was touching and inspiring. I sincerely hope the time will come when Tibet will belong to the Tibetan people again. Nothing is impossible. After all, the Jews returned to their homeland after many hundreds of years.

Now, as I sit in the peace and quiet of the evenings in the veranda of my bungalow in the small town of Rajpur, I look across to the forested hills opposite and watch the flowering bougainvillea and the many parrots and squirrels that come to feed on the rice my wife gives them, and I feel blessed. I have a very caring family, I am independent monetarily, and I have freedom of thought, speech, and religion, unlike my fellow Tibetans in Tibet.

Receiving His Holiness the Dalai Lama at Dehradun airport, 2012, with D. N. Tsarong on the left of His Holiness and the author on the right.

A private audience with the Dalai Lama in Dehradun, 2012. Author, the Dalai Lama, author's wife Tseyang, and daughter Yangchen Dolkar.

Most of all, I and all Tibetans have a magnificent spiritual teacher in the Dalai Lama, from whom I have had the fortune to receive many a teaching. My wife and I spend as much time in prayer as we can in the twilight of our lives, but we also stay in touch with current Tibetan affairs. Often we look back and relive the days gone by in the country we love so dearly, the country of our birth we were forced to leave and to which we had long hoped to return. When I left my mother's arms and the green hillsides of Kham as a five-year-old boy, I could never have foreseen where my journey would lead.

INDEX

Page numbers followed by "ph" indicate photos.

ABOUT THE AUTHOR

Rinchen Sadutshang was born in 1928 near the Tibet-China border to a well-off trading family, educated in a Jesuit school in the Himalayan foothills of British India, and served in the Dalai Lama's government both before and after the 1959 Communist takeover of Lhasa. A refugee alongside tens of thousands of his countrymen, he played a crucial role in bringing the plight of the Tibetan people to the world's attention. He passed away in 2015.

ALSO AVAILABLE FROM WISDOM PUBLICATIONS

Like a Waking Dream
The Autobiography of Geshé Lhundub Sopa
Geshé Lhundub Sopa
Paul Donnelly
Foreword by His Holiness the Dalai Lama

"Geshé Sopa is one of the greatest living Buddhist masters of his generation. This marvelous life story, rich in detail and told in his own words, will captivate the hearts and minds of anyone who reads it."
—José Ignacio Cabezón, Dalai Lama Professor and Chair of the Religious Studies Department, UC Santa Barbara

A Hundred Thousand White Stones
An Ordinary Tibetan's Extraordinary Journey
Kunsang Dolma

"Refreshingly honest and brave, this book leaves us looking at our lives with completely new eyes."—Jaimal Yogis, author of *Saltwater Buddha*

The Voice that Remembers
One Woman's Historic Fight to Free Tibet
Ama Adhe
Joy Blakeslee

"A riveting account of the desecration of a culture, a religion, a family, and a landscape."—Mickey Spiegel, Human Rights Watch

The Lawudo Lama
Stories of Reincarnation from the Mount Everest Region
Jamyang Wangmo
Foreword by His Holiness the Dalai Lama

"It will stretch your mind and move your heart."
—Lorne Ladner, editor of *The Easy Path*

Mission to Tibet
The Extraordinary Eighteenth-Century Account of Father Ippolito Desideri, S.J.
Translated by Michael J. Sweet
Edited by Leonard Zwilling

"Everyone with an interest in Tibet, Tibetan Buddhism, world history, and world religion will enjoy this wonder-filled account of Desideri's pioneering adventure, intimately detailed from Rome to Lhasa and back."
—Jeffrey Hopkins, author of *Meditation on Emptiness*

A Saint in Seattle
The Life of the Tibetan Mystic Dezhung Rinpoche
David P. Jackson

"A fine addition to the library of anyone who wants to understand the modern history of Tibet and of Buddhism in the West."—*Buddhadharma*

About Wisdom Publications

Wisdom Publications is the leading publisher of classic and contemporary Buddhist books and practical works on mindfulness. To learn more about us or to explore our other books, please visit our website at wisdompubs.org or contact us at the address below.

Wisdom Publications
199 Elm Street
Somerville, MA 02144 USA

We are a 501(c)(3) organization, and donations in support of our mission are tax deductible.

Wisdom Publications is affiliated with the Foundation for the Preservation of the Mahayana Tradition (FPMT).